A Guide to
the Indian Wars
of the West

John D. McDermott

UNIVERSITY OF NEBRASKA PRESS

LINCOLN AND LONDON

To Elizabeth, John, and Jimmy

Contents

x   *Contents*

Illustrations

Introduction

The English adventurer Sir Richard Burton referred to the U.S. Army in 1860 as "escorts for squatters, a police of the highway."[1] But it was much more than that. At the peak of the nineteenth-century Indian wars, the army had an effective strength of something less than fifteen thousand men, yet its soldiers manned one hundred thirty-six forts, posts, camps, and cantonments; sixteen arsenals and armories; and three recruiting and one engineer depot. The troops guarded some three thousand miles of frontier and an equal length of seacoast. They scouted thousands of weary miles in uncharted territory. Besides its role as the agent of empire, the army physically attacked the wilderness, building forts, roads, and bridges, at times conducting extensive farming operations and gathering some of the first scientific data on the great hinterland. Troops watched over railroads and telegraph lines and escorted paymasters' and quartermasters' trains. They guarded parties surveying railway territories, boundary lines, and public lands. In later stages of frontier occupancy, the army was a source of jobs for pioneers, and its supply requirements fostered settlements near its garrisons. After discharge, some soldiers stayed to live in the places that they had defended.[2] But the frontier army is most remembered for its campaigns against the many tribes of the West: the Sioux, Cheyennes, Apaches, Comanches, Kiowas, Bannocks, Nez Percés, Arapahos, and many others. The soldiers were the government's agents for subduing those groups who resisted the Euro-American juggernaut, and they have borne the brunt of criticism for conquering and suppressing those diverse and rich cultures. Yet most denigrators forget that as the nation's police force, the same troops often protected the rights and lands of Indians against white encroachment.

Those who served in the army sacrificed a great deal. One of the army's most efficient leaders, Nelson A. Miles, wrote in the *North American Review*, "No one who has not experienced it can comprehend or appreciate the fortitude, hardships, and sacrifices displayed and endured by our Army in its years of experience in Indian warfare; frequently in the wildest and most rugged sections of the country, amid canyons, mountains, and lava-beds, under the tropical heats of the South or in the Arctic blizzards of the extreme North. Yet year after year it discharges whatever services is required of it with most commendable fidelity."[3] General Miles concluded that "this nation of 50,000,000 people calls upon its Army for more than double the labor required of any other troops in the world."[4] In return for this service, the frontier army received little reward or praise, partly because the general public rarely saw the frontier soldier who performed in remote places; therefore, few took interest in his fate. Furthermore, the Indian-fighting army labored in a no-win situation. General William Tecumseh Sherman succinctly expressed the dilemma when he wrote, "There are two classes of people, one demanding the utter extinction of the Indians, and the other full of love for their conversion to civilization and Christianity. Unfortunately the army stands between them and gets the cuff from both sides."[5]

In the case of the Indians who inhabited the prairies, plains, and mountains of the West, the engagements with the army were battles for survival. They fought to keep their homeland and their way of life. Indians realized very early that if whites came and settled near them game would be killed or driven away. This meant that Indian families would have no means of livelihood. At a council held at Fort Phil Kearny in April 1868, a Sioux warrior explained why he had been fighting: "The white men drove our deer and buffalo away and we had to fight each other and the white man for the possession of the land to hunt upon or starve."[6] And fight they did, caught as it were in a total war, where their women and children became combatants. Two Moon remembered the sacrifices that were necessary, when he spoke about the attack on his village by U.S. Troops on March 17, 1876: "The soldiers burned all our teepees, food, robes, and everything they could find. They fired on all they saw, wounding many and killing some. And our hearts were bad when our babies and children cried from the cold."[7]

The army officers who were their opponents did not mince words. The soldier-novelist Charles King labeled them "foemen far more to be dreaded than any European cavalry." Frederick Benteen declared: "[They were] good shots, good riders, and the best fighters the sun ever shone on." Anson Mills concluded that "they were the best cavalry on earth," and Wesley Merritt defined them as "the finest light troops the world has ever known."[8]

We must not forget that conflict had its dark side. Because the Indian wars were between people who did not understand one another, they were excessively cruel. Perhaps the only thing to compare with the heinous massacre of friendly Indians at Sand Creek would be the equally terrible treatment of white settlers caught by raiding Indians at midcentury. No side had a monopoly on virtue. These circumstances might be best understood as human nature run amok.

This book tells something of that tragic drama played out in the great panorama of the West. It is written with the hope of providing basic knowledge about the Indian wars, why they occurred, who were their participants, what were the results, and how the interested student or traveler can learn more about them. It is also written to foster tolerance and compassion for the warriors on both sides, the ones fighting for their homeland, the others for their country. Let the blame fall where it may, but remember that those who plan wars rarely fight in them.

Many have contributed to this volume in one way or another by providing documents or insights or by sharing their knowledge of the land. For their assistance, I wish to express my gratitude to the National Archives, especially to Michael P. Musick, Michael Meier, Michael E. Pilgrim, Todd Butler, and Robert Kvasnicka; the Library of Congress, especially to Marilyn Ibach; the National Anthropological Archives of the Smithsonian Institution; the Department of the Interior Library; the Military Service Institute, Carlisle, Pennsylvania; the National Park Service, especially to Mardell Plainfeather, John Dorner, Kitty Deernose, John James, and William Gwaltney; the Nebraska Historical Society, especially to James Potter and Tom Buecker; Ramon Powers and the staff of the Kansas Historical Society; the staff of the South Dakota Historical Society, especially Nancy Tystad Koupal; the North Dakota Historical Society, especially Janet Daley Lysengen; the Montana Historical Society, especially Charles E. Rankin; the Colorado Historical Society, especially David Halaas and Andrew Masich; the Iowa Historical Society; the Ohio Historical Society; and the Missouri Historical Society. Special thanks to the staffs of Fort Laramie National Historic Site, the History Research Division, Department of Commerce, Cheyenne, Wyoming, especially Ann Nelson and Jean Brainerd; the American Heritage Center, Laramie, Wyoming, especially Rick Ewig; the Denver Public Library, especially Lisa Backman; and the Buffalo Bill Historical Center, especially Paul Fees and Emma Hansen.

Other special collections used included those of the American Antiquarian Society, Worcester, Massachusetts; the Bieneicke Library, Yale

University; the Bancroft Library, Berkeley, California; the Fort Caspar Archives, Casper, Wyoming; the Casper College Library, Casper, Wyoming; the Sheridan County Fulmer Library, Sheridan, Wyoming; the Pioneer Museum, Douglas, Wyoming; the University of Nebraska, Lincoln, Nebraska; the St. Charles Historical Society, St. Charles, Missouri; the University of Colorado Library, Boulder, Colorado; and the Colorado State University Library, Fort Collins, Colorado.

Many thanks are owed to my friends and companions on the trail over the years: Peter Brown, president, History America Tours, Dallas, Texas; Jerry Russell, president, Order of the Indian Wars, Little Rock, Arkansas; Don Rickey Jr., Evergreen, Colorado; Jerome A. Greene and Paul L. Hedren of the National Park Service; Mike Koury, president, Old Army Press, Fort Collins, Colorado; Jerry Keenan and Erwin N. Thompson, Boulder, Colorado; Robert M. Utley, Georgetown, Texas; Rick Young, Fort Caspar Museum, Casper, Wyoming; Susan Badger Doyle, Pendleton, Oregon; Jim and Sara Mundie, Dallas, Texas; Rubie Sooktis and the Charles Sooktis family, Lame Deer, Montana; Stuart Conner and Ken Feyl, Billings, Montana; Richard Allan Fox, Vermillion, South Dakota; Craig Bromley and Todd Guenther, Lander, Wyoming; and Sterling Fenn, Redding, California.

Finally, special thanks go to John Aduddell, Sleepy Creek, West Virginia, who provided assistance with historic transportation; and to Douglas C. McChristian, National Park Service, who reviewed the chapter on equipment. Special thanks go to R. Eli Paul, Nebraska Historical Society; David Dixon, Slippery Rock University, Pennsylvania; Colby Stong, Mifflin, Pennsylvania; and Margot Liberty, Sheridan, Wyoming, all of whom read the whole manuscript and made many valuable suggestions.

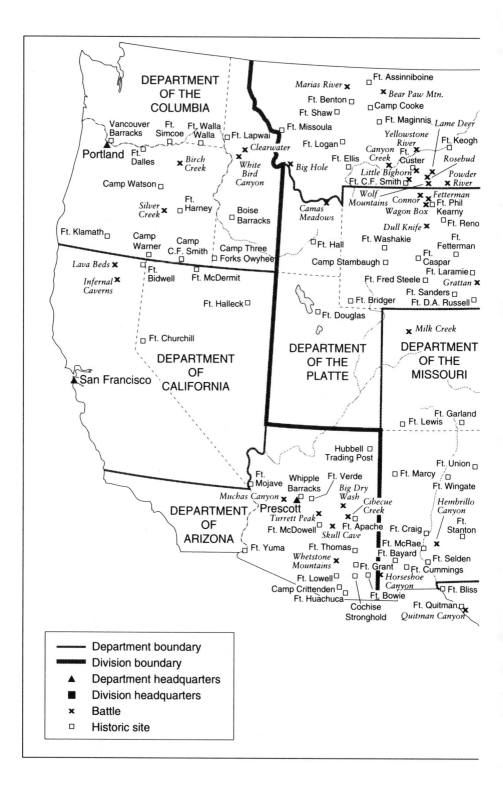

DEPARTMENT
OF THE
COLUMBIA

Marias River ✕

✕ Ft. Assinniboine

Ft. Benton ☐

✕ Bear Paw Mtn.

Ft. Shaw ☐

☐ Camp Cooke

☐ Ft. Maginnis

Lame Deer

Vancouver
Barracks

Ft.
Simcoe

Ft. Walla
Walla

☐ Ft. Lapwai

Ft. Missoula

Yellowstone
River

Ft. Keogh

Portland

Ft.
Dalles

✕ Clearwater

Ft. Logan ☐

Canyon
Creek

Ft.
Custer

Rosebud

✕ Birch
Creek

White
Bird
Canyon

Ft. Ellis ☐

✕ Little Bighorn ✕

✕ Powder
✕ River

Camp Watson ☐

✕ Big Hole

Ft. C.F. Smith ☐

Wolf
Mountains

✕ Fetterman

Silver
Creek ✕

Ft.
Harney

Boise
Barracks

Camas
Meadows

Connor ✕☐ Ft. Phil
Kearny

Wagon Box

Ft. Klamath ☐

Camp
Warner

Camp
C.F. Smith

Camp Three
Forks Owyhee

☐ Ft. Hall

Dull Knife ✕

Ft. Washakie

☐ Ft. Reno

Ft.
Fetterman

Lava Beds ✕

Ft.
Bidwell

Ft. McDermit

Camp Stambaugh ☐

Ft.
Caspar ☐

Infernal ✕
Caverns

Ft. Laramie ☐

Ft. Halleck ☐

Ft. Fred Steele ☐

Grattan ✕

☐ Ft. Bridger

Ft. Sanders ☐
Ft. D.A. Russell ☐

☐ Ft. Churchill

☐ Ft. Douglas

✕ Milk Creek

San Francisco

DEPARTMENT
OF
CALIFORNIA

DEPARTMENT
OF THE
PLATTE

DEPARTMENT
OF THE
MISSOURI

Ft. Garland ☐

☐ Ft. Lewis ☐

Hubbell ☐
Trading Post

Ft. Union ☐

Ft.
Mojave ☐

Whipple
Barracks

Ft. Verde

☐ Ft. Marcy ☐

Ft. Wingate

Muchas Canyon ✕

▲ ☐

Prescott

Big Dry
Wash ✕

Cibecue
Creek

Hembrillo
Canyon

DEPARTMENT
OF
ARIZONA

Turrett Peak ✕

Ft. McDowell

✕☐

Ft. Apache

Ft. Craig ☐

Ft.
Stanton ☐

Skull Cave

Ft. McRae ☐

✕

Ft. Yuma ☐

Ft. Thomas ☐

Ft. Bayard

Whetstone
Mountains ✕

☐ Ft. Selden

Ft. Grant ☐ ☐

Horseshoe
Canyon ✕

☐ Ft. Cummings

Ft. Lowell ☐

Camp Crittenden ☐ ☐

Ft. Huachuca ☐

Ft. Bowie

Cochise
Stronghold

☐ Ft. Bliss

Ft. Quitman ☐

Quitman Canyon ✕

	Department boundary
▬▬▬	Division boundary
▲	Department headquarters
■	Division headquarters
✕	Battle
☐	Historic site

Ft. Pembina

DEPARTMENT OF DAKOTA

Ft. Union
Ft. Totten
Ft. Buford
Ft. Stevenson
Killdeer Mountains ✕
✕ *Big Mound*
Ft. Abraham Lincoln
Ft. Rice
Ft. Abercrombie
Ft. Yates
✕
Ft. Sisseton
Whitestone Hill
✕ *Slim Buttes*
Ft. Snelling ▲ St. Paul
Wood Lake ✕
✕ *Birch Coulee*
Ft. Bennett
Ft. Ridgely
Bear Butte
Ft. Sully
Ft. Meade
Pipestone
War Bonnet Battlefield
Wounded Knee ✕

Chicago ■

✕
Ft. Robinson
Ft. Hartsuff
Mud Springs ✕
Ft. Sidney
Ft. Atkinson
Omaha ▲
✕ *Blue Water*
Ft. Omaha
Ft. Sedwick
Ft. McPherson
Massacre Canyon ✕
Ft. Kearny
✕ *Summit Springs*

Ft.
Morgan ✕
✕ *Beaver Creek*
Ft. Leavenworth ▲
Beecher's Island
Sappa Creek
Ft.
Ft. Hays
Ft. Riley
Jefferson Barracks
Wallace
Ft. Harker
Sand Creek ✕
✕ *Punished Woman*
Ft. Larned
Ft. Scott
Ft. Lyon
Ft. Dodge
Bent's Old Fort

Ft. Supply
Ft. Gibson
Adobe Walls ✕
Washita Battlefield
Ft. Reno
McClellan Creek ✕
Soldier Springs
Anadarko Affair
Ft. Bascom
Ft. Cobb
Palo Duro Canyon ✕
✕ *Mulberry Creek*
Ft. Sill
Ft. Sumner

Ft. Richardson
Ft. Griffin

DEPARTMENT OF TEXAS

Ft. Concho
Rattlesnake Springs ✕
Ft. Stockton
Ft. McKavitt
Ft. Davis
Horse Head Hills ✕
San Antonio ▲ Ft. Sam Houston
Ft. Clark
Ft. Duncan
Ft. McIntosh

0	100	200	300 mi
0	100	200	300	400 km

Ft. Ringgold
Ft. Brown

The American West has not given us, so far, sufficient men to match our mountains. Or not since the death of Crazy Horse, Sitting Bull, Dull Knife, Red Cloud, Chief Joseph, Little Wolf, Red Shirt, Gall, Geronimo, Cochise . . . (to name but a few), and their comrades. With their defeat died a bold, brave, heroic way of life, one as fine as anything recorded history has to show us. Speaking for myself, I'd sooner have been a liver-eating, savage horseman, riding with Red Cloud, than a slave-owning sophist sipping tempered wine in Periclian Athens.

Edward Abbey, "Down the River with Henry Thoreau," in *Word from the Land.*

The Common Soldier
Shout long and loud
for victory won,
By chief and leader
staunch and true;
But don't forget the
boys that fought
Shout for the common
soldier too.

Anonymous,
Cincinnati Daily Gazette,
July 7, 1865

It is bad to live and to be old,
Better to die young
Fighting bravely in battle.

Song of the Blackfoot Crazy Dogs

1. The Context

1. Causes and Limiting Factors

Nothing occurs in a vacuum: Every happening has its origin, every circumstance its cause. What follows is a discussion of the reasons for the Indian wars in the West and why they developed as they did. Placing these events in their context permits perspective and brings understanding. Some causal factors are beyond the control of any individual or group, and knowledge of them decreases possibilities for snap judgments and hasty condemnation. Miscalculations, ineptitude, misunderstandings, stupidities, misalignments, inherent defects, bureaucratic bungling, and chicaneries of one kind or another that fostered, precipitated, or perpetuated conflict and impeded solutions are also dealt with in this chapter.

Differing Ideas of Land Use

The Indian wars were the logical outcome of nineteenth-century attitudes. Principal among them were differing ideas of land use.[1] Plains Indians had what anthropologists call "a carelessness as to land." In their scheme of things, little pieces of land were unimportant. As nomads, they roamed over large areas, believing in the right of occupancy of a region rather than a parcel. Among the Plains Indians, the land was less important than the animals that occupied it. Buffalo herds could be anywhere, and where you found them you found their hunters. Iron Nation nicely summarized this concept at a council in 1865, when a peace commissioner asked him where the Sioux warrior Frog lived. Iron Nation responded, "Everywhere; where he is."[2] When it came to negotiate for land by treaty, the first Euro-Americans thought that they were purchasing a title in fee simple. The Indians just as certainly believed that they were sharing hospitality with a stranger. They were giving him permission to live in that area and roam over it as they did, seeking its bounties wherever they might find them.

At the same time, the first Americans had a personal affinity with the land. Among those nineteenth-century observers who commented on this relationship was George Armstrong Custer. Writing in the *New York Herald* in 1875, he explained that Indians had a strong attachment for the ground that contained the bones of their ancestors. "Love of country is almost a religion with them," he wrote. "It is not the value of the land that they consider," he noted, "but rather [it] is a strong local attachment that the white man does not feel, and consequently does not respect."[3] Custer's former scout, Curly, explained this when he spoke at a council held in October 1907, concerning opening some of the Crow Reservation for public sale: "The soil you see is not ordinary soil," he declared. "It is the dust of the blood of the flesh and bones of our ancestors. We fought and bled and died to keep other Indians from taking it and fought and bled and died, helping the whites. You will have to dig through the surface before you can find the earth, as the upper portion is Crow. The land as it is, is my blood, and my dead; it is consecrated, and I don't want to give up any portion of it."[4] The Indian method of burial exemplified this belief. Placed in trees or on scaffolds to decompose, the remains eventually rested on the earth's surface, worked by the rain and scattered by the wind. Whites, on the other hand, buried their dead in the earth and marked the spot for eternity.

Europeans brought the concept of private ownership of real estate with them to the New World. They believed that each man had the right to control a piece of land and do with it whatever he desired. This belief was evident in the pattern of white settlement in the United States. European countries vied with one another in claiming land for their empires. They held "sovereignty of the soil" by right of discovery. As it worked out, the Spanish settled the Southwest, the English occupied the Northeast, and the French inhabited Canada. In this game of conquest, European countries did not dispute one another's claims so long as the rights of sovereignty were vested in a Christian nation. As far as native peoples were concerned, they recognized that Indians had what they termed the "right of occupancy," a right that could only be taken away by purchase or conquest. However, it was not a right superior to that of a European power whose representatives had taken possession of lands in America. In 1828 President John Quincy Adams described U.S. policy toward Indians at the time: "At the establishment of the Federal Government the principle was adopted of considering them as foreign and independent powers, and also as proprietors of land. As independent powers, we negotiated with them by treaties; as proprietors, we purchased of them all the land which we could prevail on them to sell." He added that "as brethren of the human race, rude and ignorant, we endeavored to bring them to the knowledge of religion and letters."[5]

Thus, while Euro-Americans believed in ownership in fee simple, American Indians held that the land belonged to those who had cherished it from time's memory. The first conflicts between the races in the Rocky Mountain West came as the result of interference with the Indian pattern of land use. Emigrants on their way to Oregon, California, and Utah in the mid- and late-1840s traveled through prime hunting grounds of the Sioux and Cheyenne, scaring away game and creating resentment. Indians realized very well that if whites, or even another Indian tribe, came and settled near them the game would be killed and their families would starve. This was the one reason for warfare cited over and over again by Indians in contemporary interviews and in the minutes of treaty councils of the period. When technology in the form of the deep breaking plow extended possibilities for intensive agriculture and white occupation to the prairies and plains, severe confrontation over land was inevitable.

Treaties

The vehicle for transferring land from Indians to whites was the treaty. On the surface it appeared to be an appropriate means of divestiture, but it was inherently flawed because it rested on false assumptions. First, tribes settled things by consensus, by talking things out until all agreed by not objecting. In their deliberations, no voting took place; consequently, for Indian participants, the discussions of the treaty council were the agreement. Further complicating the matter was the lack of debate that occurred during these sessions. Both parties delivered speeches composed in advance. Commissioners rarely responded to specific objections or to questions raised by Indians, and if they did so, it was at another time in the course of another speech. When Indians voiced their grievances and received no response from the commissioners, they assumed that these matters had been recognized. They did not understand that when they signed the treaty they were agreeing only to those statements written within.

The second major flaw in the treaty process was the means of enforcement. Under federal law, the agreement had no relevance until ratified by the Senate, and, occasionally, the Senate did not act. Furthermore, if it did, it sometimes changed the document's provisions. Explaining this to Indian participants was difficult at best. On the other hand, Indians lacked an organization strong enough to compel its own members to keep peace. The practice of giving presents during treaty negotiations appeared to many Indians as a sign of weakness, as if whites were paying tribute.

Failure to understand the dynamics of interaction and decision making in Indian society led whites to compound the situation by requiring one person to act for all others. At the Fort Laramie Treaty of 1851, peace commissioners insisted that the Sioux appoint a leader to be responsible for all attending bands. When they refused, the commissioners appointed one anyway, the Brulé Conquering Bear who, of course, could not fulfill the requirements forced on him. In 1871, in recognition of past failures, Congress passed legislation stating that in the future Indian tribes would no longer be treated as foreign nations with whom treaties should be enacted. However, neither the executive nor legislative branches paid any attention to the new statute and continued to do business as usual well into the twentieth century.

The Indian Ring

A common belief held by Indians in the West in the mid–nineteenth century was that whites could not be trusted, that they often acted in bad faith. In this they had a great deal of justification. However, this was not a new perception. As early as December 3, 1793, the president of the United States asked for legislation to prevent fraud in the Indian trade. Seventy-six years later, the same subject received attention in the report of a presidential commission looking into the Indian problem. The investigators declared that in addition to the class of robbers and outlaws who conducted their nefarious pursuits on the frontier, a large class of professedly reputable men had emerged who used every means in their power to bring about Indian wars. Their motive was profit, which they gained from the presence of troops and the expenditure of government funds. This system of fraud was so widespread that the press of the day called it the "Indian Ring."

Politicians were at the top of the pyramid of corruption. Members of Congress and officials in the executive branch of the federal government used their powers to secure selection of their friends as Indian agents, traders, and contractors. At various times the president, the secretary of the interior, and the Indian commissioner were involved in the appointment of agents, who, in turn, had to be approved by the Senate. Any of these officials or politicians or members of their staff were likely targets for bribes or other favors. Even relatives of these powerful men in Washington used their connections to line their pockets. In 1876 the brother of President Ulysses S. Grant, Orville Grant, admitted before a congressional investigative committee that he had accepted $1,000 to withdraw from the competition for a tradership at Fort Berthold, North Dakota.

The second partner in the Indian Ring was the agent. He had many ways of acquiring wealth at the expense of his charges. For instance, he could withhold annuities (the food and other goods sent to the agencies each year for the subsistence and benefit of the tribes) and sell them to someone else. In 1867 Chief Spotted Tail of the Brulés told peace commissioners his belief about the way the distribution of annuities operated: "My Great Grandfather," he said, "pays us a heap of goods and presents. . . . He sends these presents by men who swindle us out of it. He sends a man here whom they call agent, who I think when he starts from the states, puts a portion of the money sent in his pocket. When he comes out here, he has two hearts and puts another portion in his pocket and gives us the balance. Hence our poverty."[6] At least one agent sold part of the annuity goods entrusted to him to merchants in a nearby town. In 1875 Major A. K. Long found Indian Bureau flour on sale in grocery stores in Sidney, Nebraska.

The agent could also inflate the number of tribal members at his agency to get surplus annuities for sale to others. In 1871 C. A. Howard of Spotted Tail Agency sent in requisitions for supplies for 9,170 Brulés, but an investigator later found there were only 4,775 Sioux actually living there. A corrupt agent could also put his relatives on the payroll. In 1866 government inspectors charged Walter A. Burleigh at the Yankton Agency with having hired and paid his daughter and another woman to teach school, when in fact there was not, nor had there ever been, a school there. Another get-rich method was to falsify payment records. When agent Burleigh hired workmen at Yankton Agency, he charged the government twice what he actually paid them. After learning about all the agents' opportunities for fraud, it is not surprising to read that an Episcopal bishop from Minnesota wrote the president in 1862 that it was common knowledge that an agent with a salary of only $1,500 a year could retire with an ample fortune in four years.

The agent often worked in collusion with the third member of the Indian Ring, the trader. In 1866 the senior inspector general of the army, General Randolph Marcy, wrote to a joint committee of the Congress investigating Indian affairs: "I am of the opinion, from all I have learned of men who have had good opportunities of judging and from my own observations, that a great portion of the money which has been sent out for payment to the northwestern Indians during the past ten years has never reached them. I would therefore discontinue all money annuities, as they only serve to fill the pockets of agents and traders."[7]

In a letter to the editor of the *Army and Navy Journal*, October 26, 1867, a man who reported that he had spent a year among the Sioux stated, "It is a notorious fact that but a portion of the annuity goods sent to the Indians in the vicinity of Fort Laramie during many years was given to them. The remainder were placed in charge of dishonest traders, who traded them to the very Indians to whom they belonged as a right."[8] In an article in *The Nation* in 1891, a former employee of the post sutler at Fort Laramie remembered a Sioux man telling him that the agent gave them only one-tenth of the annuities due them and gave the other nine-tenths to traders, who forced the Indians to barter pelts for them.

The fourth member of the Indian Ring was the contractor, the person who actually supplied the foodstuff and goods that the tribes received. In some cases, contractors provided inferior goods. For example, J. J. Dobson of Philadelphia in 1875 was accused of furnishing the Sioux with undersized and faulty blankets. In other instances, contractors provided inappropriate or useless goods. Indians interviewed at Fort Laramie in 1866 were dissatisfied with their annuities. According to the testimony of Todd Randall on April 16, 1867, "A great many articles are issued of no use or value to them such as mosquito nets, umbrellas, shot guns, and smoking tobacco, salt pork, children's shawls and other small items. They neither need or [sic] desire any of these things."[9] In some cases, the contractor received payment for products that greatly exceeded market prices. For instance, in 1871 Grenville Dodge received a contract for corn at $2.26 a hundred weight, while the prevailing cost was $1.50. Some contractors were in effect middlemen who sublet their orders to others who provided the goods at lower costs. J. W. Bosler of Carlisle, Pennsylvania, received a contract in 1871 for $756,700 worth of goods, mostly beef. While he was paid to provide live beef at six and one-half cents a pound, he found another contractor who provided him with the cattle at four and one-half cents a pound.

Finally, whites living near reservations found many different ways to take advantage of the tribes and the federal government. E. L. Godkin, writing in *The Nation* in December 1869, noted that white populations that came in contact with Indians on the frontier were more or less lawless in their habits, quick with their weapons, and unscrupulous in their dealings. In his view these roughnecks were one of the leading reasons for Indian hostility. In 1867 Captain Robert S. La Motte at Fort Ellis, Montana, wrote his mother that most of the Indian stories of recent vintage were invented by parties who were interested in keeping troops in the field, such as provisioners and transportation contractors. He also accused Wells, Fargo

& Company, the mail contractor, of staking out its broken-down horses where Indians might easily steal them, the government having agreed to pay for such losses.

Manifest Destiny and Nationalism

Whites justified their treatment of American Indians on grounds of "Manifest Destiny." Indian Commissioner Lewis V. Bogy expressed the typical sentiment of the period in a letter to the secretary of the interior on January 23, 1867. In agreeing that Indians should be put on permanent reservations, he declared, "The spread of our white settlement throughout this vast section of country . . . should not be checked, as it cannot be prevented."[10] In an 1875 address Colonel Henry B. Carrington voiced the same belief of inevitability: "The present generation is in the iron grip of the advancing empire and will be hurled aside in its progress; for their [*sic*] is no amalgamation of the Indian with any other race. . . . The tidal wave must sweep on."[11] In 1900 the hero of Beecher Island, George Forsyth, voiced the still common belief with a Darwinian twist when he declared, "It was the advance of civilization against barbarism, with the assurance in the end of the 'survival of the fittest,' a harsh, cruel, but seeming inexorable law, that has obtained since the dawn of creation."[12]

From the perspective of more than a century, we can see that white America's belief in Manifest Destiny was but an example of the nationalism sweeping the western world. Historian Crane Brinton has called it the most noticeable political development in the nineteenth century, with each country seeking to excel over its neighbors and accumulate more power and goods. In Brinton's words, "The nation-state came to be a church, or organized group of true believers, which developed rituals to give the faithful a sense of belonging to a high place in the pecking order." In Brinton's view, as it developed, nationalism became "a denial of the Christian equality of all souls before God" and refutation of the Enlightenment's positing of "the equality of all men before a righteous Nature."[13] In this context, the attacks on the basic nature and abilities of the American Indian are more readily understood.

Underestimating the Adversary

Another important determinant in the Indian wars was the lack of respect the U.S. Government held for its adversaries' fighting skills. Recent warfare studies have concluded that the most important single factor in precipitating armed conflict is misperception, especially in a leader's view of his opponent's capabilities and power. The strategy adopted by army commanders in the 1876 Sioux Campaign was evidence of this view. Rather than sending one overwhelmingly large force to accomplish its mission, it sent three supposedly self-sufficient columns led by George Crook, Alfred Terry, and John Gibbon. Custer's division of his command reflected the same belief. At least Custer based his actions on the valid principle that Indians fled when attacked in their villages.

Disrespect lay in views concerning the Indian's nature and abilities. One method of denigrating your opponent is to treat him as something different and apart. The Alternity Theory teaches that one common way to confirm your opponent as "The Other" is to feminize him, make him into a woman or a child. Lieutenant Eugene F. Ware in his book *The Indian War of 1864* did this in describing some of the first Indians he met when traveling west in Nebraska. Of the Omaha males he encountered, he wrote: "It seemed to me that . . . the men were about fifty-five percent feminine. I think that some of the contempt which the early settlers had for the Indian was due to his effeminate actions and appearance. In addition to this, the Indian grew no whiskers and had a general inefficient manner, and was not in stature and build the equal of the white boys that were in our company."[14]

Ware's pronouncement was preceded by centuries of misinformation about and depreciation of Native Americans, from the castigation of Cotton Mather, the seventeenth-century New England divine who believed that they were active disciples of Satan, to the eighteenth-century French biologist Comte De Buffon, who saw them as an underdeveloped species or race, to a contemporary of Custer who wrote in a frontier newspaper: "In peace they are rough and brutal . . . showing no affection whatever for their families. In war cruelty and torture are their chief study . . . they fight like demons and show no mercy."[15] Such views did not engender patience or compassion in Indian wars, and military leaders in the heat of battle occasionally expressed radical views. For example, after Modocs killed peace commissioners under a flag of truce in 1873, General William Tecumseh Sherman telegraphed his commander of troops in California, "You will be fully justified in their utter extermination."[16]

As might be expected, whites praised and condemned Indian practices in terms of their closeness to or deviation from Anglo-European standards. Among the observers were army officers and their wives, who had the chance to see Indian peoples in a variety of settings. Although officers and their mates viewed Indian warfare as inevitable, they did not delight in the prospect, often expressing compassion for those whose cultures they believed doomed, as well as acknowledging their courage and fighting prowess. Most officers concluded that the blame for warfare rested on both sides.

Distrust of a Large Standing Army

An attitude contributing to the length of the Indian wars was the ingrained distrust of a new democratic republic for a large standing army. Signer of the Constitution Elbridge Gerry succinctly stated this belief in 1783 when he wrote, "Standing armies in time of peace are inconsistent with principles of Republican Government, dangerous to the liberties of a free people, and generally converted into destructive engines for establishing despotism."[17] Thus, following the Revolutionary War, the U.S. Army consisted of one company of artillery, retained to guard West Point, Pittsburgh, and a few other posts. By 1790 the force had grown to 1,216 men. In 1849 the number had increased to 10,320, and just before the Civil War, the army consisted of 13,024 men. At the end of the conflict in 1865, there were 1,034,064 volunteer troops serving in the U.S. Army, but by November most of them had been paid, mustered out, and sent home. A year later there were only 11,043 left, most of whom were U.S. Colored Troops. These were almost all discharged by late October 1867.

Following the Civil War, in 1866 the number of regular army troops was 43,059. General Grant wanted to increase the force to eighty thousand but Secretary William Stanton and Congress did not. On July 28 Congress voted to establish an army of 54,302 officers and men. Actual strength reached about 57,000 on September 30, 1867, the peak for the period until 1898, but by 1870, it had fallen back to 37,313, and by 1875, the force had been reduced to 27,525. Just before the Custer fight, the U.S. Army's strength stood at 25,331, and on June 19 the Democratic House voted to reduce the number further to a new postwar low of 22,000 officers and men. Compared to other countries during this period, the U.S. military forces were infinitesimal. According to one estimate, the population of the United States on June 1, 1876, was 46,284,344. This meant that .05 percent of the population was in the army. In England troops represented .51 percent of its population, in Prussia 1.26 percent, in Russia 1.82 percent, and in France 1.9 percent. To put it another way, the army in England was ten times the size per capita of American forces, Prussia twenty-five times, Russia thirty-six times, and France thirty-eight times.

What were the consequences of this predisposition against large standing armies? It meant that only in time of crisis did the country marshal its great human resources for combat. In the case of the Indian wars, the conflict was not considered a threat to the Republic, and so military forces remained the same. If the U.S. government had wished to conquer all Indians by feat of arms, and had the full support of American voters, it could have done so with great rapidity. Instead, it relied on small numbers of soldiers on the frontier to enforce its policy, which vacillated between rewards and punishments. At the same time the government used troops from this small pool to defend its coastlines and borders and impose Reconstruction on the South. In reviewing the experience of the Indian wars in 1878, General Philip Sheridan declared: "No other nation in the world would have attempted reduction of these wild tribes and occupation of their country with less than 60,000 to 70,000 men, while the whole force employed and scattered over the enormous region . . . never numbered more than 14,000 men. The consequence was that every engagement was a forlorn hope."[18] While Sheridan might bemoan the fact of insufficient troops to do the job, he was responsible in part for their sometimes inadequate performance. The general and other military leaders of the day had not developed a coherent military policy or strategy regarding Indians. There were no manuals on tactics for conducting Indian campaigns, and the army remained more interested in fighting wars against future conventional enemies than in developing an effective system to handle the guerrilla warfare of the Plains tribes.

Division of Authority

This distrust of the military is also seen in the bifurcation of authority in Indian policy. Congress removed Indian affairs from the War Department in 1849, and in 1876 when the House voted to return the bureau to its original home, the Hon. John A. Logan of Illinois rose in opposition when the bill reached the Senate floor. Speaking on June 24, just one day before the Battle of the Little Bighorn, Senator Logan declared:

> I have learned from history, by my reading from my childhood, that the downfall of governments was by putting power in military hands. I have learned that the republics must and can only be maintained by civil authority, not by military. Put the Indian Department under the War Department, the Pension Bureau next, then the Land Office next, then abolish the Interior Department next, and then you

have got one fourth of the government under the charge of the military, and thus a long step toward the resumption of military authority in this country. Remember the voices of Clay and Webster, of the great statesmen in this land, against the usurpation and inroads of military authority.[19]

Senator Logan's viewpoint prevailed, and the transfer did not take place.

The results of the division of responsibility for Indian affairs are well known. Marcus A. Reno summarized the problem in the concluding paragraph of his July 15 report on the Battle of the Little Bighorn, "The harrowing sight of the dead bodies crowning the height on which Custer fell . . . is too recent for me not to ask the good people of this country whether a policy that sends opposing parties in the field armed, clothed, and equipped by one and the same Government, should not be abolished."[20] Recommending a novel approach to the matter of equipping the Indians with good firearms was Department of Dakota commander Winfield Hancock, who suggested that the weapons sold to them should be of inferior quality, suitable for hunting only. Although many correctly point to federal programmatic schizophrenia as a major difficulty in conducting nineteenth-century Indian affairs, many detractors forget that structural divisiveness probably prevented a stronger military effort that would have resulted in the loss of many more lives on both sides.

Not only was Indian policy inherently divisive, it was criminally inefficient. For example, records show that no supplies worth mentioning had been issued at Red Cloud and Spotted Tail agencies since April 10, 1876, and that the Sioux were on the verge of starvation due to Congress's failure to vote an appropriation and the Indian Bureau's inability to forward the supplies needed. This was a situation repeated before and after in many parts of the West. Certainly inefficiency, indifference, and graft were factors in forcing the showdown on Custer Ridge and elsewhere.

Immigration Policy

Perhaps as much to blame for the conflict was U.S. immigration policy. The great numbers of land-hungry newcomers from the Old World in the nineteenth century created pressure for expansion to which the president and Congress responded. By 1860 there were four million foreign-born settlers in the United States. During the 1870s the peak year of immigration was 1873 when 459,803 persons landed on American shores. Compare these numbers with the population figures of native peoples, and the inevitability becomes clear. Estimates are that American Indians totaled about 1,850,000 at the time of Columbus and declined to 248,253 by 1890. During their peak in the 1870s, the Teton Sioux numbered about 31,650, the Northern and Southern Cheyennes about 4,000, and the Arapahos even fewer.

Railroads

An important tool of migration on the Great Plains was the railroad. Here again, Euro-American technology in the form of the steam engine had made rapid expansion possible, and development of the high-speed printing press had increased the ability to disseminate settlement propaganda, encouraging migration and creating new pressures. In 1883 General Sherman stated that the completion of the transcontinental railroad was the most important factor in bringing "peace" to the West. In stimulating urbanization, railroads helped to bring together diverse resources, concentrating the nation's power in more easily and quickly accessible centers. This not only permitted the rapid transport of the few troops available to hot spots but allowed the amassing of supplies and equipment in a more timely fashion. In the case of the Great Plains, the railroads were the technology that provided access to what had been for years an impassable barrier of distance and aridity. Unlike those in the East, railroads in the West preceded populations, uniting isolated areas, fostering end-of-the-tracks settlements, and creating new pressures on native groups and their subsistence.

General Sherman probably summarized the causes of the Indian wars as well as anyone, when he wrote: "We took away their country and their means of support, broke up their mode of living, their habits of life, introduced disease and decay among them and it was for this and against this they made war. Could anyone expect less?"[21] But also underlying the conflict were assumptions held by Euro-Americans and their leaders about land, the country's destiny, the nature of native peoples, and large standing armies. Contributing factors were demographics, new technology, bifurcation of authority, bureaucratic ineptitude, and the power of other national priorities.

2. Opponents

Indians of the West

Only a few of the many Indian tribes west of the Mississippi River were large enough, strong enough, or skilled enough in warfare to fight back against white intrusion and face the U.S. Army in combat. This chapter discusses who they were along with their backgrounds, numbers, and involvement in the Indian wars.[1] Tribes are described within six recognized regional groupings for Indians of the western United States, namely, by Plains, Plateau, Great Basin, Southwest, Northwest Coast, and California culture areas. The latest estimate is that at the time of Columbus these tribes numbered 1.85 million persons. By far most of the engagements between Indians and soldiers occurred on the Great Plains and in the Southwest, for the tribes who lived there had the most highly developed horse culture, giving them the ability to strike and run.

THE PLAINS

Prominent in the Indian wars were the native peoples of the Great Plains, the land of short grass and climatic extremes extending from Mexico to Canada, encompassing all or parts of Texas, Oklahoma, Colorado, Kansas, Nebraska, Wyoming, the Dakotas, and Montana. In terms of Indian cultural areas, the Great Plains is the largest. When Francisco de Coronado arrived on the southern Great Plains in 1541, he met nomadic bison hunters whose dogs were their only pack animals. Escaped Spanish horses soon gave these tribes the ability to move quickly over great distances to find buffalo, making the kill a great deal easier. This left more time for other activities, such as making clothing and accouterments and raiding other groups. Horses were crucial to the new existence, and tribes warred with one another over them.

The Comanches were among the first bands to acquire horses, which gave them early dominance in intertribal warfare. Horse stealing became a

TABLE 1: ESTIMATED POPULATIONS OF RELEVANT PLAINS TRIBES

Arapaho	3,000 (1780)	Omaha	3,000 (1802)
Arikara	2,600 (1804)	Osage	6,200 (1780)
Assiniboin	8,000 (1829)	Oto-Missouri	931 (1843)
Blackfeet	7,600 (1855)	Oto	500 (1895)
Cheyenne	4,000 (1875)	Pawnee	1,440 (1879)
Comanche	6,000 (1816)	Plains Cree	1,000 (1858)
Crow	4,000 (1780)	Ponca	800 (1780)
Gros Ventre	3,000 (1780)	Shoshoni (Snakes)	1,500 (1820)
Hidatsa	2,100 (1804)	Sioux	40,000 (1870)
Kansa	866 (1861)	Utes	4,500 (1845)
Kiowa	2,000 (1780)	Wichita	3,200 (1780)
Mandan	252 (1855)		

principal way of gaining honors and winning a mate, because horses were important gifts required at marriage. As the animals became available to other tribes in the North, new tribes began to roam the plains, freed of living in villages along the rivers of the West. Agricultural peoples who lived along the Missouri—the Pawnees, Arikaras, Wichitas, Mandans, and Hidatsas—were probably the first to settle on the plains. Later many tribes migrated there, including the Arapahos, Comanches, Cheyennes, Plains Crees, Plains Ojibwas, Kiowas, Crows, and Sioux. The Plains tribes lived dangerously, depending on large game for their subsistence and war for their status.

The people of the plains spoke thirty or more distinct languages. Because of this diversity, tribes developed a universal way of communicating by signs. The Indian practice involved expansive use of the arms and body for visibility at a distance, making it different from sign language later developed for the deaf, which relies primarily on finger signs for face-to-face communication. Often the motions imitated life. For instance, the sign for the Crow was to place downward palms at the level of the shoulders and make a flapping motion. Some were more subtle: To show anger, the practitioner placed a clenched fist on his forehead and made a boring-in motion. In the last quarter of the nineteenth century whites began to record the motions in books. Army officer William Clark authored one of the first primers, entitled *The Indian Sign Language*, in 1885. Most agree that the volume by William Tomkin appearing in 1927, *Universal Sign Language of the Plains Indians of North America*, remains the best compilation.

Plains tribes varied in size, with some, such as the Cheyennes, being few in number but making up for it in fighting skills. Population estimates vary, and more recent scholarship tends to increase the nineteenth-century numbers. The figures are included here to help define the tribes in proportion to one another, as well as show odds in the fight against the army on the plains. However, specific tribal compilations sometimes do not exist for the nineteenth century, so approximate numbers have been provided.

The tribes most involved in wars on the Southern Plains were the Kiowas and Comanches. Living in present-day western Kansas, Oklahoma, and eastern Texas, the Kiowas occupied territory along the Arkansas River and its tributaries, while the Comanches controlled land along the Canadian River. In 1790 the two tribes made peace, and, for the next hundred years, they raided into New Mexico and Texas, moving as far south as Chihuahua, Mexico. Leading the Kiowas at mid–nineteenth century were Satank and Satanta, while Quanah Parker was the chief of the Comanches most known to whites.

On the northern plains, the principal tribes fighting the army were the Sioux, Cheyennes, and Arapahos. The Sioux were a large tribe consisting of seven divisions: the Sissetons, Wahpetons, Wahpekutes, Mdewakantons, Yanktons, Yanktonais, and Tetons. The first four groups, sometimes referred to as the Santees, called themselves the Dakotas. Because of dialectical differences, the Yanktons and Yanktonais were Nakotas, and the Tetons became the Lakotas, who were the ones that swept onto the Northern Plains. This last group had seven subdivisions, several of which became famous in the Indian wars of the 1860s and 1870s. They were the Oglalas, Brulés, Unkpapas, Miniconjous, Sans Arcs, Two Kettles, and Blackfoot. From the Oglalas came Red Cloud, Man-Afraid-of-His-Horses, Little Big Man, and Crazy Horse. Sitting Bull, Gall, and Rain-in-the-Face were Unkpapas, while Spotted Tail was a Brulé and Big Foot a Miniconjou. Lakota territory stretched from the Missouri River in South Dakota on the east to the Big Horn Mountains of Wyoming on the west. The North Platte River marked its boundary in the south and the Canadian border in the north, encompassing the lands drained by the Yellowstone River in Montana. Leaders among the Santees who achieved notoriety were Inkapaduta and Little Crow, the former the principal in the Spirit Lake, Iowa, raid in 1857, and the latter the leader of the so-called Minnesota Uprising of 1862.

The Cheyennes and Arapahos were allied with the Lakotas. Both were smaller tribes that broke into southern and northern branches after the establishment of Bent's Fort in 1832. North of the North Platte in Nebraska, in Wyoming, and in southern Montana were the Northern Cheyennes, among whose chiefs in later years were Dull Knife, Little Wolf, and Two

TABLE 2: ESTIMATED POPULATIONS OF RELEVANT GREAT BASIN TRIBES

Paiute	7,500 (1845)
Western Shoshoni	2,500 (1845)

Moon. The Southern Cheyennes in Kansas and Colorado looked to Black Kettle, Tall Bull, and Roman Nose for their leadership. Left Hand was important among the Southern Arapahos, while Black Bear was a well-known chief of the northern branch.

Enemies of these tribes were the Crows of Central Montana, the Shoshonis of western Wyoming, the Pawnees and Omahas of Nebraska, and the Arikaras of North Dakota. All smaller tribes, they allied themselves with the whites, serving as scouts and auxiliaries for the army, notably in the Powder River expeditions of 1865 and 1876–1877. The Pawnee Scouts under Luther and Frank North compiled a particularly enviable record. Chief Washakie of the Shoshonis was especially well known for his fighting skills and later leadership. Chief Plenty Coups of the Crows led his people into the twentieth century. In northern Colorado the Utes under Ouray, gave the army trouble in the late 1870s.

THE GREAT BASIN

The Rocky Mountains and the Sierra Nevada flank this vast, bowl-shaped arid region, located between the Mojave Desert on the south, southern Oregon and Idaho on the north, central Wyoming on the east, and the eastern boundary of California on the west. Only low grasses, sagebrush, juniper trees, and other plants could adapt to the dry climate. Antelope, jackrabbits, mice, rats, gophers, snakes, lizards, birds, and even grasshoppers provided food. Inhabitants used nets to trap birds, ducks, geese, and rabbits. Indians traveled in small bands, roaming the desert in search of the scarce food and living in temporary cone-shaped dwellings fashioned from brush-covered poles. The Shoshonis, Paiutes, and some Utes shared this foraging lifestyle. Because they had little time for introspection, these tribes had the simplest religion. Medicine men acted as healers and composed songs to befuddle game for trapping. These groups also changed with the coming of the horse. The Western Shoshoni raided in Nevada during the early years of the Civil War, but lost power when General Patrick Connor defeated them at Bear River in 1863. Wovoka, the originator of the Ghost Dance, was a Paiute. Surprisingly, it was not the Plains Indians who killed the most whites along the Oregon-California Trail, but instead warriors of the Great Basin and those farther west. Ninety percent of the

TABLE 3: ESTIMATED POPULATIONS OF RELEVANT PLATEAU TRIBES

Kutenai	1,200 (1780)	Wallawalla-Umatilla	1,500 (1780)
Spokan	2,000 (1780)	Kalispell	1,200 (1780)
Atsina	3,000 (1780)	Cayuse	500 (1780)
Nez Percé	3,000 (1849)	Bannock	1,000 (1845)
Blackfeet	5,000 (1780)	Northern Shoshoni	3,000 (1845)
Palouse	5,000 (1780)	Yakima	3,000 (1780)
Flatheads	3,000 (1800)	Colville	2,500 (1800)

nearly four hundred overland trail emigrants killed along the trail died west of South Pass, Wyoming.

THE PLATEAU

These tribes lived between the Bitterroot and Cascade mountain ranges on the east and west and between central British Columbia and central Oregon and Idaho. The region consisted of tree-covered mountains, quick flowing streams, valleys, canyons, and desolate volcanic wastelands. Those in a river environment developed water craft and an elaborate fishing technology. Fish provided about half the food base, the rest coming from large game and tuberous roots. These included the Klamaths, Salish, Cayuses, Colvilles, Coeur d'Alenes, Kalispels, Palouses, Umatillas, and Walla Wallas. Periodically invading the Northern Plains to hunt were the Flatheads, Nez Percés, Yakimas, and Spokans. They borrowed their dress and certain decorative art designs from the Plains Indians but little else. Two other tribes, the Bannocks and the Northern Shoshonis of Idaho, showed the plains influence.

In 1847 Cayuses murdered Marcus Whitman and his wife and many others living at the mission at Waiilatpu. Perpetrated in response to a measles epidemic, the bloody episode marked the beginning of the Indian wars in the Northwest. All the conflicts that followed were reactions to the intrusion of white miners or settlers, notably the Rogue River Indian War of 1855–1856, the Yakima War of 1855–1856, and the Coeur d'Alene or Spokan War of 1858.

Most remembered in the history of the Indian wars are the Nez Percés. Occupying eastern Oregon and most of Idaho, the Nez Percés had separated into Christian and non-Christian groups by the 1860s. It was the latter, led by diplomat Chief Joseph and the war chiefs, including White Bird, Looking Glass, and Rainbow, that attempted to find refuge in Canada after fighting U.S. troops at White Bird Canyon on June 17, 1877. Many books have been written about their flight to freedom, which for most fell a few miles short of Canada in northern Montana. Problems in Idaho in 1878 and 1879 led to campaigns against the Bannocks and Sheepeaters. The first resulted from white intrusion on the Camas Prairie, where camas roots were a prime source of food for the Indians. The Sheepeater War began when whites accused the Sheepeaters of several murders that they probably did not commit.

THE NORTHWEST COAST

Occupying a narrow strip along the Pacific Coast from southeast Alaska to Oregon were the Northwest tribes. With perhaps the most distinctive Indian culture yet developed, these native peoples subsisted easily on fish, other foods found in the ocean, and plants and berries. Because the coastline was not particularly attractive to whites, the Indians of the Northwest Coast did not have the violent conflicts that other native cultures did. In the early days, they were relatively free to pursue the arts, of which wood carving, manifested in totem poles, was one. Eventually, white culture impacted them as well, but it was not through warfare with the U.S. Army that swift and dramatic change occurred.

CALIFORNIA

At the time of white penetration, perhaps as many as 250,000 Indians lived in California, speaking 120 distinct languages. They lived in 500 small villages. Because of the region's bounty, they were able to subsist by hunting, fishing, and gathering, fixed agriculture not being necessary. Beginning in the 1700s, they interacted first with the Spanish and then with Mexicans and Americans, the result being that by the mid–nineteenth century only 85,000 remained. The number continued to decline in the next several decades, so that by 1890 only about 18,000 were left. The mission system, the use of the land for ranching, the influx of white settlement due to gold strikes and its incumbent destruction of the Indians' supportive environment, and periodic mass killings were responsible.

The only California Indians to mount an effective resistance to whites were the Yumas and Mojaves in the early 1850s and the Modocs, led by Captain Jack, who fled their reservation in 1872 to return to their homeland in the Lost River Valley. Ensconced in the Lava Beds of northern California, the Modocs held off U.S. troops for six months.

TABLE 4: ESTIMATED POPULATIONS OF RELEVANT SOUTHWEST TRIBES

Apache	5,000 (1680)	Tiwa Pueblo	12,200 (1680)
Navajo	12,000 (1864)	Pecos	2,500 (1680)
Hopi	2,800 (1680)	Yuma	3,000 (1776)
Papago	6,000 (1680)	Jemez	2,500 (1680)
Pima	4,000 (1680)	Keresan Pueblo	4,000 (1760)
Majave	3,000 (1680)	Tewa Pueblo	6,000 (1680)
Piro Pueblo	9,000 (1500's)	Zuñi	2,500 (1680)

THE SOUTHWEST

The main tribes in the Southwest were the Apaches, Navajos, Pueblos, Hopis, Hopi-Tiwas, Zuñis, Acomas, Lagunas, Pais, Pimas, Papagos, Mojaves, Chemeheuvis, Cuchans, and Yaquis. Only the Apaches and the Navajos were important in the nineteenth-century Indian wars, the former remembered for their ferocity and resolve, and the latter for their crushing defeat and trek into exile.

The Apaches and Navajos arrived in the Southwest much later than other Indians, perhaps as recently as one thousand years ago, apparently having migrated from northwest Canada. Unlike the Hopis, Zuñis, and the others, who were desert farmers, the Apaches were hunter-gatherers and the Navajos hunter-herders. The most common Apache dwelling was the wickiup, a domed or cone-shaped frame covered with grass or brush. Navajos lived in hogans, cone-shaped frameworks covered with bark and earth.

Some of the most warlike of all the North American Indians, the Apaches earned the title of "tiger of the species" from General George Crook, who defeated them on more than one occasion. Although they often utilized horses for transportation, they viewed the animals principally as a meat source, fighting mostly on foot. The most aggressive Apaches were the three bands of Chiricahuas, who launched raids from their mountain strongholds into New Mexico, Arizona, and northern Mexico. Led by Mangus Coloradus, Victorio, Nana, and Loco, the eastern Chiricahuas ranged through much of western New Mexico from the Rio Grande to the Arizona border, from the Datil Mountains to the Mexican boundary. Chato and Geronimo were the famous chiefs of the southern Chiricahuas, who often raided into northern Sonora and Cichuahua, Mexico. The third and central band, under Cochise, occupied southwestern Arizona and southwestern New Mexico.

Other major groups were the Jicarilla Apaches, who roamed northeastern New Mexico, parts of the Oklahoma panhandle, southeastern Colorado, and some of southwestern Kansas; the Western Apaches, who occupied virtually the whole mountainous portion of the eastern half of Arizona; and the Mescalero Apache, who were located in south central New Mexico. All the Apaches fought the U.S. Army at one time or another, the trouble beginning in the mid-1860s and lasting until Geronimo's last surrender in 1886.

Numbering from eight to nine thousand in the mid–nineteenth century, the Navajos raised corn and herded sheep and horses. After 1864 when Kit Carson's troops soundly defeated them, they were forced to walk eight hundred miles from Arizona to Fort Sumner, New Mexico, to a new reservation. After four years the government sent them back to their homeland, where they remain to this day.

The Army

Facing the Indians on the western landscape in the nineteenth century were the troops of the U.S. Army, mostly whites of European ancestry, many new to the continent.[2] The army had grown out of the needs of the frontier. Except for the War of 1812, the Mexican War, and the Civil War, U.S. troops were primarily concerned with the frontier as explorers, policemen, builders, and buyers, and in the beginning their role was crucial to the success of settlement. However, it took time for the military to develop into a meaningful force. The army disbanded at the end of the Revolutionary War, and for a short time America's military might consisted of but one company of artillery retained to guard West Point, Pittsburgh, and a few other posts. Had it not been for the Indian wars that soon broke out, the United States may never have developed a standing army. The formation of the First Regiment of Infantry in 1784 was in response to Indian trouble in the Old Northwest. By 1808 the number of infantry regiments had grown to seven. During the War of 1812, which was largely an Indian war, the government authorized forty-eight infantry regiments (a number not equaled until 1917), but after peace was restored Congress reduced and reorganized the force into eight infantry and four artillery units.

Modern cavalry in the United States traces it origins to the Regiment of Mounted Rangers organized during the Black Hawk War of 1832, another frontier fight. Long commanded by Stephen Watts Kearny, this regiment made several treks across the plains, including one along the Santa Fe Trail during the Mexican War that led to the acquisition of New Mexico, Arizona, and California. The Second Regiment of Dragoons came into existence in 1838, and with Kearny's troops later became the First and Second Regiments of Cavalry. Guarding the Oregon Trail in 1846 necessitated formation of a third unit, the Regiment of Mounted Riflemen, which garrisoned Fort Kearny in 1848 and Fort Laramie and Fort Hall in 1849.

During the Mexican War of 1847 Congress authorized volunteer troops to supplement the regular army, establishing a precedent that prevailed in three wars. In 1848 the army reverted to its previous complement of eight regiments of infantry and four of artillery but was able to retain the three units of mounted troops. In 1855 the army expanded to include two more regiments of infantry and two of cavalry, the latter the first actually to be called by that name. The Dragoons, Mounted Riflemen, and Cavalry remained separate branches of mounted service until the Civil War, when the name "cavalry" became inclusive, with the First and Second Regiments of 1855 renumbered in 1861 as the Fourth and Fifth.

The popularity of volunteer service as a means of meeting a crisis reached its zenith during the Civil War, when various states provided a million men for the war effort. These regiments freed regular army troops from duty in the West. Cavalry regiments serving in the West were the First and Second California; the Second and Third Colorado; the Seventeenth Illinois; the Seventh Iowa; the Fifth, Sixth, Ninth, Eleventh, Fifteenth, and Sixteenth Kansas; the Third Massachusetts; the First Michigan; the Twelfth, Thirteenth, and Fourteenth Missouri; the First and Second Nebraska; the First Nevada; the Twenty-first New York; the Eleventh Ohio; the Sixth West Virginia; and the Third Wisconsin. When the war began, Congress expanded the regular army to nineteen regiments of infantry, six of cavalry, and five of artillery, which meant an increase of about thirty thousand men. Nine new infantry units contained three battalions of eight companies each, or twenty-four companies in all. Before that time, the normal number for the entire regiment had been ten companies.

When the war ended these larger regiments were separated and renumbered so that in 1866 the regiments of infantry totaled forty-five. In the case of the infantry, the number of companies returned to ten, which remained constant until 1898. The first battalions of regiments eleven through nineteen retained their numerical identity, while the second battalions became regiments twenty through twenty-eight, and the third became regiments twenty-nine through thirty-seven. New additions were four regiments of African-American troops (thirty-eight through forty-one) and three regiments of the Veterans Reserve Corps (forty-two through forty-five), special units that provided employment to wounded soldiers who had served two years and were able to perform partial duty. Congress increased the cavalry by four regiments, numbers seven through ten, with the last two being for black soldiers. Called "buffalo soldiers" by their Indian adversaries, they compiled an exemplary record. The men who served in them had lower percentages of desertion and higher reenlistment rates. Most officers were white, but in 1877 Henry O. Flipper of Thomasville, Georgia, the first black to graduate from West Point, began service in the Tenth Cavalry. Significant reorganization of the army occurred in 1869, when the army bill reduced the number of infantry units to twenty-five, with the four black regiments consolidated to form the Twenty-fourth and Twenty-fifth. The cavalry remained at ten and artillery at five. Congress reduced the authorized strength to forty-five thousand officers and men.

ARTILLERY

After the Mexican War the artillery consisted of five regiments of twelve companies each, the numbers remaining constant throughout the Indian wars period. After 1866 the army called an artillery company a "battery." Each company or battery commonly manned four to six guns, occasionally eight or more. In 1871 the army refined its terminology, designating mounted batteries as "light batteries." A section manned one gun and two sections formed a platoon, except with light batteries, where three were required.

HIGH COMMAND

During the Indian wars the generals of the army were Major General Winfield Scott (July 5, 1841, to March 11, 1861), Major General George B. McClellan (November 1, 1861, to March 11, 1862), Major General H. W. Halleck (July 23, 1862, to March 9, 1864), General Ulysses S. Grant (March 9, 1864, to March 4, 1869), General William T. Sherman (March 8, 1869, to November 1, 1883), General Philip H. Sheridan (November 1, 1883, to August 5, 1888), and Lieutenant General John McAllister Schofield (August 14, 1888, to September 29, 1895). In the post–Civil War period, there were also five major generals and usually sixteen brigadier generals. The general commanding the army had authority for discipline and military activities, while the secretary of war handled fiscal affairs. The Office of the Adjutant General in Washington was the administrative office of the army. Below it in descending order were divisions, departments, districts, and posts, created, reconstituted, or disbanded to best carry out the army's mission. Also at the Washington level were the Offices of the Quartermaster General, the Commissary General, the Paymaster General, the Judge Advocate General, the Inspector General, the Surgeon General, the Chief of Ordnance, the Chief of Engineers, the Chief of the Signal Corps, and the Provost Marshall. Although the titles of these units are for the most part self-explanatory, the Quartermaster Department probably had the most varied duties, because it handled contracts for all the army's outside services, from the hiring of masons, to the purchase of livestock, to the employment of civilian couriers. Most of these offices had regional counterparts in the divisions and departments, and each garrison had its own post quartermaster and commissary of subsistence.

REGIMENTAL ORGANIZATION

During the height of the Indian wars, infantry regiments had ten companies each and the cavalry twelve. The army identified these units by consecutive letters of the alphabet, except for "J," to avoid confusion with "I" in orders written in longhand. Those in the guardhouse were jokingly referred to as the men of Company Q. Cavalry companies were not officially called "troops" until 1883. Each regiment of infantry had one colonel, one lieutenant colonel, and one major. Each cavalry company had one colonel, one lieutenant colonel, and three majors. However, a full complement of officers on a campaign was a rarity, many being on detached service of one kind or another, including duty as recruiting officers or members of courts-martial. The term "battalion" often appears in the literature of the Indian wars, but it was an imprecise term for the most part. Battalion meant at least two but not more than seven companies, with four being the usual number.

COMPANY OFFICERS

Infantry and cavalry companies had one captain, one first lieutenant, and one second lieutenant. Additional lieutenants served as the regimental adjutant and quartermaster. Although the law permitted one brevet second lieutenant per regiment to reward outstanding noncommissioned officers, regimental commanders rarely filled this position. Officers earned brevet rank, that is, a rank higher than the one they enjoyed, for "exceptional gallantry and meritorious service." This often meant that the individual had

TABLE 5: BIRTHPLACES OF OFFICERS, 1888

Alabama	25	Vermont	50
Arkansas	8	Virginia	97
California	13	Washington	4
District of Columbia	68	West Virginia	3
Florida	11	Wisconsin	31
Georgia	27	At sea	1
Illinois	89	Austria	1
Indiana	76	Belgium	1
Iowa	15	Canada	17
Kansas	7	Chnta Napoor	1
Kentucky	80	Corfu	1
Louisiana	11	East Indies	1
Maine	82	England	28
Maryland	81	France	9
Massachusetts	147	Germany	32
Michigan	67	Hungary	1
Minnesota	13	Ireland	83
Mississippi	19	Italy	3
Missouri	55	Malta	1
Nevada	1	Netherlands	1
New Hampshire	47	New Brunswick	2
New Jersey	51	Nova Scotia	3
New Mexico	2	Poland	1
New York	447	Prince Edward Island	1
North Carolina	23	Prussia	15
Ohio	202	Sandwich Islands	1
Oregon	9	Saxony	2
Pennsylvania	370	Scotland	15
Rhode Island	32	South America	3
South Carolina	19	Sweden	3
Tennessee	28	Switzerland	3
Texas	19	Wales	1
Utah	3		

participated in a battle and done his duty. Those who earned brevet rank had the right to be addressed by the title, and, in the unlikely case in which two officers had the same date of commission, the man with the brevet assumed command. Otherwise, it meant nothing. At the end of the Civil War the army used the brevet to acknowledge the rank held by officers who had served in volunteer units. The particular officer usually received a brevet of the rank he had achieved during this period or sometimes the next higher designation. George Armstrong Custer is a good example. His regular army rank before becoming a commander of volunteer units was captain, but he advanced in the volunteer ranks to major general in 1864. When the nation returned to peacetime Custer was able to obtain the rank lieutenant colonel in the regular army, but he forever had the right to be addressed as General Custer because of his Civil War experience.

Officers tended to be educated, and most of them, before and after the Civil War, had graduated from the U.S. Military Academy at West Point. Those who came into the service through the volunteer ranks could be from any profession, and because of the great number of casualties during the Civil War, a significant number of officers who survived had risen from the ranks, having been commissioned on the battlefield. James Powell, the hero of the Wagon Box Fight in 1867, was one of these.

Table 5, published in 1888, shows the states and countries of origin for officers who fought in the Indian wars.

Because of the slow rate of turnover in the post–Civil War army, this 1888 tabulation probably presents an accurate picture of those who had been fighting in the West for decades. According to the table, a little over eleven percent were born in foreign countries, which included some exotic locations for the time, such as Chnta Napoor, Corfu, the East Indies, and Malta. Prior to the Civil War, many more men from the South served as officers, and when they left to fight with the Confederacy, the Union lost a number of its finest soldiers. Of the 1,080 officers in the army in April 1861, 313 chose to fight with the South. Among those who had fought in the Indian wars were Albert Sidney Johnston and JEB Stuart.

NONCOMMISSIONED STAFF

Noncommissioned officers provided both leadership and training. As one veteran put it, "as the noncoms are, so will the company be,"[3] and more than one observer has noted this group of soldiers had a very high casualty rate in the Indian wars. Army regulations proscribed a full complement of noncommissioned officers. Highest ranking in the company were a first sergeant and a quartermaster sergeant. The infantry company had four additional sergeants and the cavalry five, and each had eight corporals. There were two artificers in the infantry and two farriers and blacksmiths in the cavalry. The infantry had two musicians and the cavalry two trumpeters. Other special positions included one saddler for the cavalry and one wagoner for each of the companies in both branches of service. In addition to these was the regimental noncommissioned staff, consisting of a sergeant major, a quartermaster sergeant, a commissary sergeant, a chief musician, and a hospital steward. Each cavalry regiment also had a saddler sergeant and a chief trumpeter and each infantry regiment two principal musicians.

ENLISTED MEN

Much has been written about the heritage, social standing, and skills of enlisted men during the Indian wars. The consensus is that they were a mixed lot, some who were hard cases and ne'er-do-wells, fleeing from responsibility and the law. Some were desperate urbanites enlisting for the pay, and some were simply looking for adventure. But there were some surprises. An enlisted man of the Seventh Cavalry remembered that among his acquaintances in the ranks were the former business manager of the *Brooklyn Eagle*, a bookkeeper recently employed by a fire insurance company, a well-to-do coupon clipper, a physician given to drink, a preacher, an English earl, a Hungarian count, and an Austrian army officer. William Hynes reported that the men in Company E of the Second Cavalry in 1866 represented nearly every state in the Union and almost every country in Europe. According to Hynes, as for personal beliefs, whether religious, political, or otherwise, not a variation had been omitted or even slighted. As he put it, "The democracy of the school of Athens was re-established."[4] About half the men who joined the army from 1865 to 1874 were born in other countries, twenty percent of them coming from Ireland and twelve percent from Germany. As the years passed, the number of men who possessed prior familiarity with firearms and horses diminished as the East industrialized. Also, farming families provided fewer recruits because of the manpower needed at home. The result was that the army had to put more emphasis on training if it was to remain effective.

Legislation in 1869 provided that a cavalry company must have between 60 and 78 privates. For the infantry the limits were 50 and 100. Only in the engineers and ordnance branches were there privates first and second class. For a number of reasons, including congressional parsimony, cavalry and infantry companies never reached upper limits. By 1876 the number authorized for a cavalry company had declined to 54 privates and the infantry to only 34. By the regulations an infantry regiment in 1866 had an aggregate personnel of 732, cavalry 1,239.

TABLE 6: ARMY STRENGTH, 1849–1890

1849	10,320	1870	37,313
1850	10,315	1871	35,353
1851	10,334	1872	35,512
1852	10,299	1873	32,554
1853	10,248	1874	32,602
1854	10,329	1875	27,525
1855	12,729	1876	27,489
1856	12,698	1877	27,472
1857	12,688	1878	27,746
1858	12,923	1879	27,924
1859	12,943	1880	27,926
1860	12,931	1881	27,976
1861	13,024	1882	28,002
1862	43,332	1883	27,995
1863	43,562	1884	28,028
1864	43,562	1885	27,996
1865	43,246	1886	27,996
1866	43,059	1887	28,167
1867	54,641	1888	28,795
1868	52,922	1889	28,764
1869	52,935	1890	28,792

THE STRENGTH OF THE ARMY

In view of the army's mission the number of men available was never great. Table 6 shows the actual size of the army from 1849 to 1891.

Decline in the army's strength after the Civil War resulted from several circumstances. First, as lines of communication and transportation expanded, the ability to react more quickly increased. Railroads made it possible to rush troops to different parts of the country, lessening the necessity for so many permanent posts in the West. A backlash against Reconstruction in the South caused reduction in the size of the army, and eastern humanitarians exercised their influence to decrease the army's presence in Indian country. Finally, the Panic of 1873 forced Congress to make further cuts in military appropriations. Perhaps the act that most undermined army morale occurred in 1877 when U.S. troops were still fighting the Northern Sioux in Wyoming and Montana and were just beginning the conflict with the Nez Percés in Idaho. When the army appropriation act expired on June 30, Congress was in no mood to pass another. Consequently, for over four months, until mid-November, officers and men did not receive a cent of pay, many having to borrow from sutlers and other lenders to survive.

These then were the opponents who fought each other on the prairies, on the plains, and in the mountains, beginning in the early 1850s and ending, for the most part, in 1891. During the twenty-five-year period that followed the Civil War, 923 officers and enlisted men died, and 1,061 suffered wounds. Army records estimate 5,519 Indians killed and wounded. Also engaged were white civilians, 461 of whom died in these battles and 116 of whom were wounded. General Sheridan reported that the proportions of casualties to troops engaged on the Great Plains in 1876–1877 were greater than those of the Civil War or the Russo-Turkish war then being fought. It was an intense, dramatic confrontation, played out in a great, varied landscape. No wonder the Indian wars remain America's Trojan War.

3. Material Culture

Indians of the West

When one thinks of the Indian warrior in the wars of the West, the first image that comes to mind is often that of the mounted Plains Indian, headdress streaming, painted horse in full gallop. This has become the American Indian of Wild West shows, pageants, movies, and television.[1] The practice of wearing elaborate dress in battle was due in part to the belief that if a man died in conflict he wanted to meet the Great Spirit looking his best. Consequently, a similar show of apparel was common when a man was ill or seriously injured.

PLAINS INDIAN CLOTHING

Plains Indian women made clothing almost exclusively from animal skins and parts and decorated them with the feathers of birds, porcupine quills, glass beads, animal teeth, and shells. The most elaborate and important headgear for men was the war bonnet. It reached its full development only after the acquisition of the horse around 1800. With few exceptions, only high-placed leaders wore the headdress, and only on important occasions of war or peace. They often wore the headdress as a mark of courage and for protection by magic as much as for adornment. Some women might wear the war bonnet under certain ceremonial conditions, but children never did. Not all tribes wore it with equal frequency, and some not at all. Feathers arranged in other ways were also widely used as head decorations.

Among the Plains Indians there were two types of war bonnets. Most tribes arranged the feathers so that they sloped back, but the Blackfeet and others in the far north fixed theirs to stand straight up. Some tribes in the central and northern plains trimmed the caps of some bonnets with white fur and a pair of horns instead of eagle feathers. Medicine men seemed to have been the principal if not exclusive users of this type of headgear, which became known as "doctors' bonnets." In winter the northern tribes wore animal skin caps. Some central groups, especially the Arapaho, wore rawhide eye shades, and for dress occasions some southern groups wore straight-sided fur caps with open crowns. Ceremonial participants used many kinds of decorations on the head, usually of feathers, fur, hair, quills, or beads.

The principal body covering in cooler weather was a robe made of a whole buffalo skin, in most cases dressed with the hair on. The user wore the hair side out in temperate times and next to the body in winter. The wearer put the robe on in any way that suited his or her convenience, but the tail was customarily on the right. Women frequently decorated robes on the flesh side with painted designs, narrow rows of quill or bead work, or broad quilled or beaded bands often set with discs. After the introduction of machine-made cloth by the traders, buffalo robes were replaced by woolen blankets, which women also frequently decorated with broad quilled or beaded bands.

Rarely worn at first, shirts became increasingly popular. They ranged from those with a simple poncho-like pattern made of one skin, to complex garments made of two or three skins cut into sections and sewn together. Tanned skin of the deer family was the material used on the plains and most other areas for all garments. In the extreme north, tailoring of the upper part of the garment developed at an early date. Initially, the legs of the skins were left dangling at the bottom, and the sides and sleeve seams were left open. At the front and back of the neck hung a flap, usually triangular in shape but frequently squared among northern tribes. The first northern shirts were extremely long with painted decorations, stripes, or life forms, usually in black. Northern and central shirts were identified by the use of quilled or beaded bands over the shoulders and down the sleeves. Indians of the southern plains preferred long fringes from the shoulders and a small section of fringe at the elbow.

A famous special shirt was that worn for the Ghost Dance in 1890 by the Sioux. Made of cotton cloth, the garment hung loose and featured painted circles, crescents, and crosses. Also adorned with representations of eagles, magpies, crows, sage hens, and other birds and animals having special significance in Sioux mythology, many were fringed and decorated with feathers. Medicine men preached that the Ghost Shirt rejected bullets.

The men normally wore breechcloths. Originally made of soft tanned skin, cloth ones later came into use. About four to six feet long and about a foot wide, the breechcloth passed between the legs and tucked under the belt in front and back. The ends hung down from the belt like narrow aprons. Breechcloths worn during ceremonies often reached to the ankle or ground and were decorated. Made of a narrow strip of skin worn around the waist, the belt supported the breechcloth and the tops of the thigh-length leggings when these were worn. Usually undecorated, the belt also supported pouches, knife sheaths, and the like.

Worn in colder weather, leggings were made from a single deer or antelope skin. Usually finished with fringe on the outer side, they reached from the ankle to the thigh. Held in place by thongs tied to the belt, they were decorated by painting or by attaching long strips of beaded or quilled skin or cloth. When given army trousers as treaty goods, wearers made them into leggings by removing the seat. In the last quarter of the nineteenth century, blue or red flannel replaced skin in most cases.

The moccasin was the footwear of the plains. The common type was ankle high and made of soft leather with a tongue and a hard sole. In contrast many northern and Mississippi Valley tribes wore soft-soled moccasins. There were a number of patterns involving different numbers of skin pieces, each tribe having, to some extent, cuts peculiar to itself. For winter use some tribes used moccasins of buffalo skin with the hair inside. Moccasins were cut in lefts and rights and often had skin fringes trailing from the heels. Women usually decorated moccasins by painting them or by attaching quills or beads, although some remained plain. Solidly beaded moccasins and quilled uppers were mostly restricted to the central plains tribes, though these also used less decorated footwear.

Hair was important to the warrior. Different tribes adopted different styles, the Omahas braiding their hair with feathers, the Pawnees shaving their heads but leaving a strip of hair running from brow to nape of neck, and the Crows gathering their hair into a tall greased pompadour. Men carefully plucked facial hair with tweezers made from bone or metal.

A woman's dress reached from the shoulders to between the calf and ankle. Two types were prevalent. In one the maker joined two animal skins together up the sides and across the top, leaving arm and neck openings. The other was a bodice-sleeve unit made from one or more skins, sewn or tied about waist high to a skirt cut from two or more skins. Central and northern plains tribes used the first type, and the second was common among all tribes in the cultural area except for the Crows. In later years the sleeves of Crow dresses were cape-like, cut to varying lengths and widths. They were either open at the bottom or tied with thongs. The shape of the sleeves and the cut of the dress bottom varied from tribe to tribe.

Decorations of the bodice and sleeves were the most easily recognizable regional variations. In the South, decoration was absent or limited to narrow painted or beaded edging. Central tribes favored covering the bodice and very large cape-sleeves with solid or almost solid beading. The northern tribes used a broad band that usually contained parallel stripes in two or more colors and followed the curves on the bottom of the bodice and sometimes ran out on the cape-sleeves. Fringes in the various regional styles were cut into or sewn around the edges of the garment. Sewn on shirts or dresses according to tribal custom or the whim of the owner were beads, quills, rows of pendant thongs, elk teeth, shells, and tin jinglers. After the introduction of commercial cloth by traders, some changes were made in the cut of the dresses, but in general they followed the old styles.

Women also wore the buffalo robe, but it was usually smaller and lighter than that of the men. Each gender used different designs in painting robes. Men preferred sunburst patterns or representations of war or hunting scenes, while women favored a more or less elaborate oblong design across the shoulders and a broad stripe around the edge. Women's leggings reached from ankle to knee, kept in place by a garter tied around the leg above the calf. Some tribes tucked the ankle flap of moccasins up under the legging, while others, especially in the South, made the moccasin and legging in one piece. Some of these southern boot-moccasins had a long flap that hung from the knee to the middle of the calf. Cloth leggings became common in later years. Decorations included quills, beads, fringes, and paint, following the regional styles. Women's moccasins were similar to those of the men except when they were combined with the leggings.

Women wore belts around the waist over the dress. They were wider than those worn by the men and featured beads, brass nails, and discs. Pouches, bags, and other items hung from the belt. Children wore little or nothing in their early years and later dressed in small replicas of their parents' garments.

In the North, Indians sometimes wore fur mittens. Famous warriors wore feathers and other objects as indications of their brave deeds. Men wore breastplates of long slim bone beads strung horizontally in parallel rows, while women strung the same type of bead in vertical parallel rows reaching from the neck to below the waist. Other decorative items included earrings, necklaces, bracelets, and armlets of brass, beads, bear claws, silver, or beautiful combinations of shells from the Pacific. Each ceremony had special costumes. Membership in various societies meant wearing distinctive regalia.

OTHER TRIBES

Many Indian groups in the West wore similar attire. In the South, tribes needed fewer clothes, and the poorer ones wore little except the breechcloth. In the Southwest, Pueblo men wore blanket, rabbit, or feather robes and shirts with sleeves. Their breeches were short and partly open on the outer sides. Breechcloth, leggings to the knee, moccasins, hair tape, and headband completed their dress. Women wore a blanket that extended to the knees fastened over one shoulder and a small calico shawl thrown over the blanket and the shoulders. Completing the costume were belt and legging-moccasins. The Apache men dressed similar to Indians of the plains, as did their women, except for legging-moccasins with a shield toe. The Navajos were originally garbed like Plains Indians but in later years dressed similar to the Pueblos. The tribes of the Great Basin wore little clothing, except for the breechcloth. On the North Pacific Coast, men wore blanket or mat robes, legging-moccasins, and basket hats. Women added leather aprons to their repertoire. Among California Indian men total undress was not uncommon. Women wore a waist garment and narrow aprons, occasionally a robe-cape over the shoulders or under the arms, and basket cap. As the tribes interacted with whites their clothing began to reflect European styles, and women began to use silks, ribbons, sateens, and velveteens to modify native dress.

BOW AND ARROW

The traditional weapon of the American Indian was the bow and arrow, and an adept practitioner could discharge six shafts a minute and twenty in succession with great accuracy. With the coming of horses the longbow gave way to a shorter version, usually about three feet in length. By 1865 most warriors made their arrows from sheet or scrap iron. Writing in the *National Tribune* in 1921, one 1860s soldier remembered the advantages and limitations of the weapon: "They could discharge their arrows much faster than we could fire our Springfield breechloaders," he declared, "but they could not shoot any closer than a good ball player could throw a baseball."[2] Combatants also used their strung bows as weapons to unseat enemy riders, much as one draws something in with a crooked cane.

Some warriors carried lances into battle along with shields to protect them from those similarly armed. Usually from twelve to fifteen feet in length, lances were effective weapons against cavalry in close quarters, except when troopers had sabers, which neutralized them. Made from the thick skin of the neck of the bull buffalo, shields were often painted and decorated with bits of fur or hair attached around their sides. Most men carried tomahawks. Warriors made them by inserting long knives into shafts or handles of wood and horn or bought steel ones from traders. Sometimes they carried axes made of shaped stone bound to a shaft with rawhide. Knives also were trade items, although some Indians did fashion their own from other metal objects. Plains Indians carried a coup or touching stick into battle. Some used quirts or ornamented rods, while others carried sticks large enough to serve as clubs. Sometimes warriors added large triangular metal points or other blades to these bigger sticks, so that they became lethal weapons if desired.

FIREARMS

By the late 1860s many warriors had firearms of one kind or another, either obtained in trade or captured. By the time of the Custer fight, about two-thirds were armed with pistols or rifles. Archaeological investigations at Little Bighorn Battlefield in 1984 and 1985 yielded bullets, balls, and shot and cartridge cases for twenty-nine types of weapons, everything from obsolete muzzle loaders to modern repeating weapons, such as Winchesters and the Henry rifle.

Although federal policy restricted the sales of arms to Indians, the tribes found willing sellers among Indian traders and mixed-blood gun runners from Canada. They too traded with emigrants along the major travel routes, acquiring not only weapons but powder, lead, primers, and equipment for reloading cartridges that they carried with them as prized possessions. In time the Indians became experts at remolding miniballs and reloading shells. Sources disagree concerning the ability of various tribes with firearms. Most, however, agree that the Nez Percés were good shots. Perhaps the truth lies in the statement made by "F" in the *Army and Navy Journal* in 1882. In describing Apaches, the anonymous veteran said, "The Indians are inferior marksmen to the whites, but are more certain shots, since they will not fire until almost upon the object."[3]

The Army

CLOTHING

In trying to determine what troops might be wearing at any particular time during the Indian wars in the West from 1849–1890, two key points to remember are: first, for economic reasons, the army expected men to wear their uniforms until they wore out; and second, the leadership did not demand strict uniformity but allowed troops to use clothing and accouterments that kept them functioning at an acceptable level.[4] Occasionally, officers and men modified army issue or discarded it to find more workable substitutes and use their own resources, which reflected American character traits of individuality and practicality.

The traditional color for the regular U.S. Army was blue, dark blue and sky blue being used. Corps or branches of the service were recognized by separate facing colors, such as those for side seams on trousers, cuff edging, sleeve stripes, hat cords, and braiding around caps. The corps colors were:

TABLE 7: CORPS COLORS

Early Dragoon Light	Orange-yellow
Infantry	Sky blue
Cavalry	Yellow
Artillery	Scarlet
Ordnance	Dark red
Medical	Emerald green
Quartermaster	Buff with white piping
Commissary	Gray and white piping
Engineers	Red with white piping
Signal Corps	Orange

Beginning in 1833 mounted troops wore a twelve-buttoned, high-collared waist-length jacket of dark blue wool. Popularly called the "shell" jacket, it was actually longer than the European prototype, extending slightly beyond the waist to fit over the hips in front and in back. In 1858 the army issued a four-button fatigue blouse or sack coat that served both infantry and cavalry. Extremely popular, as it was more comfortable than other outerwear, it was difficult to keep clean, and repeated washings shortened its life. Both the jacket and the fatigue blouse continued as regular issue until 1872. From 1857 to 1872, those in the cavalry and light artillery wore only the jacket, while all other enlisted men wore a long nine-buttoned frock coat, usually as part of the dress uniform. Officers, who had to purchase their clothing from private sources, wore a coat similar in pattern but usually made of fine quality broadcloth. The army issued white summer uniforms between 1832 and 1851, but few officers wore them in later years.

Late in the 1850s, brass scales replaced worsted epaulettes, and the pompom-topped shako gave way to the wide-brimmed "Jeff Davis" hat, rumored to have been designed by the then secretary of war. Reminiscent of the hat worn by the Pilgrims, it became the headgear in 1855 for the two newly created cavalry regiments. The army adopted it for all troops in 1858. A stiff, flat-topped, black felt hat, it sported ostrich feathers and a tasseled hat cord, with staff or regimental insignia on the front. One side of the hat brim (left for infantry, right for cavalry) folded up and hooked to a brass eagle on the side of the crown. All grew to hate it. One officer called it "the most ugly, uncomfortable, and unsoldierly covering that a malignant spirit could have devised for the heads of suffering humanity."[5] After 1859 the men wore the forage cap or kepi for casual wear. A slightly modified version came out in 1862.

The field uniform showed more variation, as experience caused adaptation. For example, a soldier in the Sixth Infantry serving in Kansas in 1857 reported that, "Every man is wearing a broad-brimmed hat, each of a different color; white trousers of rough material; a woolen shirt of red, green, blue, or brown . . . usually open in the front and worn like a coat."[6]

During the Civil War, soldiers generally wore the same weight uniform winter and summer, which was unhealthy as well as uncomfortable much of the time. In 1868 the Surgeon General's office issued a report in which its author went so far as to declare the uniform, "a serious hygienic defeat."[7] However, at that point the army was not about to change because of the huge surpluses left over from the late conflict. The excess was staggering. On June 30, 1865, the Quartermaster Department reported that it had on hand 1.5 million brogans or bootees, over a million general-purpose sack coats, 890,249 forage caps, 435,000 pairs of boots, 361,509 pairs of trousers for mounted troops, and 297,089 cavalry jackets, as well as many other items in huge quantities, all for an army that had been reduced from well over a million men to about thirty-five thousand.

Perhaps the saving grace for the post–Civil War soldier was that the remaining uniforms were of very poor quality, often the product of entrepreneurial greed and inattentive workmanship. Consequently, they did not last as long as they might have. To save money on cloth, contractors sometimes cheated by making uniforms smaller than ordered. This meant that some of the surplus turned out to be unserviceable, fit only for the smallest minority. At the same time, commanders were quick to point out uniform defects and in some cases rejected them outright.

To adapt to the situation, troops began to improvise even more. None of the commanding generals of the main Indian wars' period—Grant, Sherman, and Sheridan—were not particular about the uniform, and their subordinates took the lead from them. Two examples were George Custer, who wore buckskins in the field, and George Crook, who often wore civilian garb and rode a mule. Crook's subordinate Charles King reported that he never saw Crook in correct uniform until he was in his coffin. Writing at the end of the period in 1883, Colonel Albert Brackett reported that the dress code remained very flexible: "While scouting, the men wear almost every conceivable article of dress, and it has sometimes appeared to me that they try to make themselves as outlandish as possible. Broad-brimmed white hats are both becoming and serviceable, and so is a good hunting-shirt, and it would seem as if there is no harm in permitting the men to wear them."[8] Thus, tolerance for improvisation, coupled with the fact that men wore their uniforms until they disintegrated, meant that in the field almost anything was possible, from midcentury obsolete issue, to clothes purchased from domestic sources, to the latest innovation from the Quartermaster Department. By the time that new uniforms of good quality began to appear in 1873, the habit of adaptation had already become ingrained.

The basic field uniform for the enlisted man on campaign in the 1870s was the navy blue rolled-collar blouse, with light blue trousers, and a campaign hat or forage cap. From 1872 to 1874 those needing new clothing received a plaited fatigue blouse, which was replaced in 1874 by a dark blue flannel coat. Also used was the cavalry shell jacket that became obsolete along with the frock coat in 1872. For wear under the blouse the enlisted man wore a coarse, pullover shirt of flannel or knit. In warm weather soldiers discarded the blouse and wore the gray (some of the later ones were blue) flannel undershirt as the outer garment. Some of the men substituted shirts purchased privately, such as the black-and-white checkered "hickory" shirt or the double-breasted fireman's shirt. In cold weather the enlisted man wore a heavy overcoat, a double-breasted affair of sky blue kersey (a lightweight woolen cloth) with a long cape.

Trousers were made of sky blue kersey. Those worn by noncommissioned officers had a cloth stripe running down the outside seam of each leg. Those for sergeants were one inch wide and those for corporals half that width. For undergarments the men wore white drawers, probably of cotton or flannel. An 1862 manual for infantry suggested that soldiers wash their underclothing once a week. In the winter the men sometimes improvised by making heavy drawers out of their old wool blankets. In the summer they often dispensed with them altogether, prompting one enlisted man to propose that their undershirts be equipped with tails to cover the evening "spectacle" when the men disrobed for bed.[9]

During the 1860s infantrymen and some artillerymen usually wore ankle-high shoes or "bootees," while most artillerymen and cavalrymen wore calf-high boots. The men hated issue bootees the most, which were made of coarse, heavy leather and colored black. Manufacturers fastened the soles by means of pegs, hand-stitching, or brass screws. Some rights were almost indistinguishable from lefts, and about the only way to make them fit was to wear them wet so that the drying leather would conform to the shape of the foot. While marching, infantrymen frequently wore their trousers tucked into their socks to keep dust from getting down into their feet. Soldiers rubbed their feet and socks with soap or tallow to prevent blisters when wearing new footwear. After 1874 inmates at the newly established Fort Leavenworth military prison made the shoes for the army, ensuring better quality control. Mounted troops wore their trousers either outside their boots or stuffed into them. The 1872 model boot was an improvement, using oak-tanned Spanish leather with wider and slightly higher tops, but many in the ranks continued to buy their own footgear or wear moccasins and leggings on campaign. In 1876 the army approved a new boot with a higher leg, giving the rider more protection, and in 1884 authorized an even higher cut. In 1888 the army issued the first canvas leggings to the infantry.

After the Civil War, while the army was on campaign, the broad-brimmed hat replaced the jaunty little forage cap in common use, reflecting the need to protect the face when chasing Apaches in the sun-scorched desert and the Sioux on the sun-drenched plains. Most wore hats similar to those worn by civilians on the plains, or, in a few cases, the army campaign hat of 1872. Poorly made of black felt, this headgear quickly lost its shape. The hat featured hooks and eyelets so that it could be worn with the sides up. To prevent sunstroke men were advised to put a silk handkerchief in the crown of the hat, or a wet cloth, or moistened green leaves or grass. Initial broad-brimmed hats were black, being replaced by gray in the mid-1880s. Officers and men also wore broad-brimmed straw hats in later years. In 1880 General Orders No. 72 authorized the use of cork summer helmets for rank and file in hot climates. Patterned after the British helmet used in India, the officers' version featured a spike on top. The modified kepi remained in use, mostly for fatigue, stable, and guard duty until 1898.

Informality was the keynote among officers on campaign. Some wore the undress uniform, and in later years, others wore only buckskins with a blue fireman's shirt. Embroidered insignia on cloth shoulder straps sewn on the uniform coat noted the officer's rank. Officers' trousers were of the same color as those of enlisted men, distinguished with a stripe one and one-half inches wide, yellow for cavalry and sky blue for infantry. Many officers disliked their heavy overcoats, one man complaining that they had been mistaken for coachmen.

Just as troops found ways of dealing with blistering summers in the West, they also found ways of blunting its frigid winters. For example, the winter clothing was described by a member of the Sixth West Virginia Volunteer Cavalry serving at Platte Bridge Station (Wyoming) in 1865: "We had been providing ourselves with the customary winter outfit of clothing, which consisted of a wolf skin, or buffalo cap, buffalo skin overshoes with leggings attached which reached to the knees and then fastened by long buckskin strings was allowed to hang down the side of the legs. Buffalo mittens, and the customary cavalry uniform, completed the costume. These 'extras' had to be furnished by ourselves, and cost considerable."[10] After the Civil War, the army did issue a buffalo-hide moccasin or overshoe, and after 1874 some troops had part-rubber footwear called the "snow excluder." In 1876 the army adopted a single buckle "arctic" overshoe, with the upper part made of cloth. In 1889 the two-buckle arctic overshoe became the standard issue, resembling modern-day winter footwear. In 1876 the army issued buffalo-hide overcoats and Canadian-made felt boots for use on the plains. After experimenting with sealskin caps and gauntlets for several years, the Quartermaster Department in 1881 settled on muskrat skin as the most serviceable fur.

FIREARMS AND ACCOUTERMENTS

In 1849 the principal heavy arms for dragoons was the musketoon, made with a barrel about two-thirds the length of a musket.[11] It used the same cartridge as the musket but had a mule's kick. Because of its lack of range and accuracy, the army began experimenting with rifled carbines, such as the Merrill, Perry, Burnside, and Sharps, the first breech-loading weapon. By 1858 the latter was the weapon of the First and Second Dragoons and eight companies of the First Cavalry and two of the Second. By the early 1850s, the mounted regiments carried the Colt cap and ball six-shooter, which replaced the single-shot muzzle-loading horse pistol. Although issued to all regiments, the saber was rarely used. After 1841 mounted riflemen carried the .54 caliber U.S. Percussion Rifle, known as the Mississippi or Yager Rifle, and after 1842 infantrymen carried the .69 caliber percussion smoothbore musket. In 1855 the army began to manufacture the .58 caliber U.S. Rifle and U.S. Rifle Musket, calling in the old weapons for alteration.

The .58 caliber rifle-musket was the principal arm used by the infantry during the Civil War. However, during that conflict many other weapons came into use, including Henry and Spencer breech-loading repeating rifles using rim-fire cartridges. After the Civil War the army was slow in adopting new weapons, because the Ordnance Department grappled with a shortage of funds. Congress did not act because of the great surplus of arms and the quantities of muzzle-loading .58-caliber ammunition left over. The solution was to convert thousands of muzzle loaders to breechloaders using brass or copper cartridges. One of the most prevalent was the 1866 model, known as the Allin alteration, named for E. S. Allin, the master armourer at the Springfield Armory. From 1867 to 1869 many troops carried muzzle-loading rifle muskets. Finally in 1869 Congress authorized the adoption of the Springfield single-shot breechloader. In 1872 the army convened a board to examine and test existing weapons, and, after examining over a hundred types, it adopted the single-shot model 1873 Springfield breechloader, having a bullet velocity of 1,350 feet per second and an effective range of one thousand yards. This shot a center-fire, .45-caliber cartridge, the caliber that the Ordnance Department selected as most desirable for all rifles, carbines, and pistols.

Paper cartridges for the old muskets had been packed in tin-lined leather boxes that fit into tin containers, but the new metal cartridges bounced freely about, making enough noise to render surprise attacks difficult at best. The troops solved the problem by devising looped belts to hold their ammunition. However, they soon discovered that the tannic acid in leather corroded the casing, which made the cartridges tend to stick in the belt and then in the weapon's breech. To avoid these possibilities, soldiers scrubbed their cartridges daily or made belts from heavy canvas. In 1866 Captain Anson Mills had his saddler make leather looped belts for his men, taking out a patent. The new belt also had the advantage of distributing the weight more evenly. In late 1876 the Ordnance Department finally bowed to popular demand and had thirty thousand canvas and leather belts made at Watervliet Arsenal.

The Model 1888 Springfield was the last of the army's single-shot, large-caliber, black-powder rifles and the principal shoulder arm of the National Guard as late as 1898. When smokeless powder became available in the United States, a board in 1890 recommended adoption of the Danish .30-

caliber, bolt-action Krag-Jorgensen rifle, which fired smokeless cartridges and had a box magazine. Having a range of four thousand yards, it could fire forty shots per minute. This was adopted in 1892.

The cavalry used a number of different carbines during the Civil War, including Burnsides, Gallaghers, Sharps, Smiths, and Spencers, mostly .52 caliber. All except Spencers, which had copper shells stored in magazines, used paper or linen cartridges and copper caps. By the end of the Civil War the Spencer had become the standard weapon, but it lacked the power and range for western conditions. In 1867 the Ordnance Department began to convert Sharps carbines to the .50/70 cartridge. In the late 1860s the army switched to breechloaders, and by 1873 the Springfield .45/70 had become the standard weapon. However, it did not reach all regiments immediately; the Seventh Cavalry, for example, only acquired it in 1875. Officers frequently used nonissue weapons. Crook carried a shotgun, while Custer had two British-made pistols and a Remington sporting rifle.

Cavalrymen carried a brass-hilted saber that hung from a black leather waist belt. Most men left them behind on campaign, because they proved to be an unwieldy, heavy, noisy nuisance. Some, however, did make use of them: Lieutenant George Washington Grummond was armed only with a saber in a fight with the Sioux on December 12, 1866, near Fort Phil Kearny, and Italian revolutionary Lieutenant Charles DeRudio carried one at the Little Bighorn. Balancing the saber, which hung from the left side, was a revolver positioned on the right, worn butt to the front, encased in a black leather holster. Cavalrymen also generally carried a "butcher knife" in their belts. In the early years of the Plains Indian wars, the cavalry carried Colt and Remington revolvers. In 1873 the army issued the Colt .45, the famed "Peacemaker," which used a self-contained metallic cartridge.

In 1844 the army adopted a new saddle for dragoons and field artillery, designed by Major Samuel Ringgold.[12] Three years later came the Grimsley dragoon saddle, the first to be covered with wet rawhide, making it less susceptible to damage and lighter than the iron-reinforced Ringgold. From 1855 to 1859 the army experimented with the Campbell, Hope, and Jones saddles, assigning them to various mounted units. At the end of the testing period, the army chose the McClellan, a black leather-covered beechwood contrivance with a blue webbing girth and hickory wood stirrups. It remained the U.S. Army saddle, virtually unchanged, for nearly a century.

Although George B. McClellan declared that his saddle was the result of intensive study of European makes, Randy Steffen has pointed out that it incorporated major features of the Grimsley, the Campbell, and the Hope. One of the improvements of the McClellan was an extra strap for a horse-holder to control the animal while its owner moved forward to fight on foot. The strap had a snap hook at the loose end, enabling the men to link their horses together by their rein rings or halter rings as they dismounted. In 1879 General Sherman approved the adoption of the Whitman saddle for testing and for general use when the supply of McClellan saddles fell below twenty thousand. However, enthusiasm for the Whitman dissipated over time, and in 1885 the improvements planned for the Whitman were incorporated into the new McClellan.

Army saddle blankets were blue, with a yellow border and a large yellow U.S. monogram. When ready for duty in the field, the typical cavalry-man of the 1870s carried a folded overcoat strapped to the pommel, a coiled lariat, a fourteen-inch picket-pin, a nose bag containing curry comb and brush, a small canvas sack filled with oats, a tin cup, a covered tin canteen, and a haversack containing rations suspended in a cloth pocket. In his saddlebags were extra ammunition, some spare clothing, and a few personal items. On his person the cavalry trooper wore a carbine sling, a black leather belt two and one-half inches wide that went over his left shoulder and crossed his body to the right hip; on the end was an iron swivel in which the ring at the base of the carbine snapped, so that the weapon dangled behind the right leg. On the right side of the saddle was a small leather socket attached to the girth ring into which the barrel of the carbine could fit to steady the weapon while riding. However, most men preferred to carry the carbine across the pommel of the saddle, usually secured by a loop.

Cavalry horses were often smaller and hardier than those found in European regiments, usually standing fifteen to sixteen hands. The army bought those that were between five and nine years old, well broken and sound in all particulars. A few regiments, such as the Seventh Cavalry, as-signed horses to companies by color, but the practice was not common. In the Seventh those of Company A were coal blacks, C were light sorrels, E were grays, G and K were sorrels, H were blood bays, Company M were mixed, and Companies B, D, I, and L were bays. Regulations required the branding of all horses on the left shoulder with the letters *U.S.*, and in the cavalry the practice was to place the brand of the regiment and sometimes the number of the company on the left thigh. Undoubtedly the most famous horse in the cavalry in the late nineteenth century was Comanche, the light bay or buckskin ridden by Captain Miles Keogh in the Battle of the Little Bighorn. Found wounded on the battlefield, Comanche survived to live until 1891. Stuffed, he can be seen at the Dyche Museum of the University of Kansas in Lawrence.

The army used mules, especially for pack animals, although General Crook used them for mounting his infantry in June 1876 in the Sioux Campaign. The packsaddle used was the aparejo, consisting of a strong leather sack, about two feet wide and from fifty to sixty inches long.

ARTILLERY

The bronze, smooth-bore, twelve pounder Napoleon was the cannon commonly used at posts during the Indian wars. More effective and popular than the limber-drawn Napoleon was the model 1841 mountain howitzer, designed to operate in a country destitute of roads. Carried in parts on pack mules, it could be quickly assembled to fire a shell some nine hundred yards to a mile away. Mystified by the weapons, the Indians called them "shooting wagons" and Big Spirit Irons. Cannons that shot exploding shells were particularly fearsome. Arapaho Chief Black Bear surmised that while the white chief fired the first shot, the white chief's Great Spirit had fired the second for his white children. One of the first uses of cannon in battle on the plains occurred during the Grattan fight near Fort Laramie on August 19, 1854. In this instance, troops fired two improperly sighted howitzers once before being wiped out by the Sioux. Cannons were used more effectively at Apache Pass in 1862, at Adobe Walls in 1864, in the Rush Creek, Nebraska, fight in 1865, at Fort Phil Kearny in 1866–1867, in the Modoc War of 1872, and at the Battle of the Big Hole in 1877. The army acquired Gatling guns in 1866. Invented in 1862, the six- to eight-barreled weapons were the forerunners of the machine gun. A hand-turned crank fired the barrels in succession. By 1871 R. J. Gatling had perfected a ten-barrel version of the weapon to the point at which it could fire one thousand shots per minute with killing force in a mile's range. Originally .58 caliber, later models were .50 and .45 caliber. Sometimes infantry troops were detailed to handle them. This was the case with the Great Sioux Expedition of 1876–1877, when Twentieth Infantry troops were the gunners. Because of the problem of moving quickly with these weapons over rough terrain, Custer left his with General Terry before riding on to the Little Bighorn. The army used the rapid-fire hotchkiss gun in some campaigns, including the Nez Percé Indian War. They were also prominent at Wounded Knee.

MEDICAL NEEDS

Those going on campaign without a doctor were instructed to carry basic medicines and appliances. Recommended were the following: a few dozen pills of opium and of quinine, some cathartic pills, an ounce or two of tincture of opium, a few doses of salts, a bottle of volatile liniment, a pocket-case, a set of splints, a few roller bandages, a fine sponge, some patent lint, a few square inches of oiled silk, a yard of adhesive plaster, a package tow, and a few bottles of whiskey or brandy. Just as Indians used the travois to carry burdens over the rough terrain of the American West, so soldiers on campaign used litters to transport their wounded. Henry Blanchard Freeman described in his diary on June 29, 1876, the litter fashioned to carry troops wounded at the Little Bighorn to the steamboat Far West. The men used poles sixteen feet long, with a crossbar four feet from either end, secured with rawhide strings.

WOMEN

During the Victorian era, most Euro-American women wore at minimum a dress, hoopskirt, and head covering. The hoop was worn by almost all women, from those working in fields to domestic servants, to factory workers, to society matrons. A complete wardrobe included the dress, ranging from the washable cotton frock to the unwashable formal dress in dark colors; the hoopskirt, called the crinoline; a petticoat worn over the hoop; a chemise; a corset; underwear, usually of linen or cotton, with silk becoming popular in later years; stockings held up by garters; shoes or laced boots; a head covering, including a bonnet made of felt or straw, a wide-brimmed straw hat tying under the chin, or hair ornaments, such as combs, flowers, or bows; a handbag, reticule, or small purse; gloves or mitts (fingerless gloves); a parasol for daytime; and an outer garment, such as a shawl, mantle, cape, or jacket, worn for comfort or fashion. Being far from dress shops, many frontier army wives had to make their own clothes from patterns. Margaret Carrington remembered that "Frank Leslie's and Madame Demerests's magazines became each a desideratum, and linsey-woolsey, delaines, and calico nowhere else underwent such endowment with fashioned shapes as in Absaraka."[13]

Women living at army posts also adapted to winter climates. Frances Carrington remembered that the women at Fort Phil Kearny had buffalo boots. Made by company shoemakers of harness leather, the boots had buffalo skin leggings attached, with the hair turned in. They reached almost to the knee and fastened on the outside with leather straps and brass buttons. The women also used mink, otter, and beaver skins to supplement their regular clothing.

CIVILIAN MEN

Civilian men in the West during the Indian wars period were generally dressed in working men's clothes, with a full shirt tucked into heavy trousers held up by suspenders. Exceptions were sutlers and a few other businessmen who made their appearance at army posts. They might wear a white shirt with cravat or necktie, peg-top trousers without front or back crease, and a frock coat, either single- or double-breasted. Men parted their long hair in the center and brushed it to the sides. Long, bushy sideburns and a drooping mustache were the fashion. According to the *Army and Navy Journal* in 1868, "The habit of wearing the beard is a manly and noble one."[14] Especially noticed among those garbed in civilian clothes were army scouts. An interesting and colorful lot, some, including Jim Bridger, wore "store clothes" and a low-crowned felt hat, while others, such as Buffalo Bill Cody, dressed in buckskins, high-crowned Stetsons, and jack-boots.

In reviewing the experience in clothing and accessories for domestic and military use, the Indians of the West emerge the winner. Having lived on the plains and the mountain plateaus for many decades, they knew how to adapt to their environment. In the summer they wore little; in the winter they donned skin and fur raiments and heavy buffalo robes. Because they made their own clothes, they made them to fit. On the other hand, the U.S. soldier struggled with mostly the same kinds of things in all seasons, and although the army continually modified or changed its set items of clothing, equipment, and accouterments, it never did get it just right. Part of the problem was that the goods were mass produced and the producers perhaps were more interested in making a profit than providing quality. Only the willingness on the part of the military to permit innovation for functionalism saved the day. By the end of the century, forever utilitarian, the Euro-American soldier learned to adjust to the new land.

4. Warfare

Indians of the West

Most of the tribes in the West emphasized achievement in warfare. Killing was not the primary objective; more important were bravery demonstrated and honors won. Among the Plains tribes in particular, war was absolutely necessary for the men.[1] Without recognized competence in it, a man could not expect to gain prestige or a mate. Historians generally group Indian reasons for going to war into four categories: to acquire horses, to protect themselves and their territory from intruders, to exact revenge, and to gain respect.

All except the California tribes and the Paiutes had warrior organizations that promoted, participated in, or planned military activities. Each tribe had from four to twelve war societies of varying organization and stature, including those of boys interested in learning and old men who confined themselves to supervision. Usually named for an animal protector or some duty, function, or costume, each military society had its own obligations, special taboos, dance, songs, costume, and insignia. The societies acted as tribal police at assemblies and ceremonies and controlled hunts and raids. They sometimes fought together in battles. Especially known for their bravery and fighting prowess were the Cheyenne Dog Soldiers, who at times lived together as a separate group.

Warriors made elaborate preparations before going on a raid or into battle. These included rituals to satisfy spiritual helpers and to seek spiritual guidance. Some fasted to have visions. Probably best known is the vision Sitting Bull experienced after offering one hundred pieces of flesh during a sun dance several weeks before the Battle of the Little Bighorn. Seeing soldiers falling upside down in the Indian camp, he predicted a great victory soon to come. When on the warpath, Sioux would sometimes attempt to view the future. One method was to kill a badger and remove its entrails. In the red mirror of blood that formed in the animal's stomach cavity, warriors sought evidence of triumph or disaster. If a man observed a gray hair, he was assured long life. If he saw himself bloody without hair, he would lose his scalp. Seeing a long black face foretold death from disease. For those who saw demise in the bloody mirror, turning back was acceptable. However, the man so informed expected to die within a year.

War parties were composed of volunteers. The leader or leaders assigned men to various duties until fighting began, then each fought in his own way, friend often fighting with friend. Occasionally warriors made pacts to stand or die in battle, immobilizing themselves by attaching a rope around the waist, driven into the ground with a pin. Sometimes women went with war parties, usually as servers, but occasionally as combatants. Accepting responsibility for the success or failure of an expedition, the leader usually had the power to divide plunder.

CODE OF COURAGE

Plains Indians' emphasis on personal courage manifested itself in the practice of counting coup. Coup is a French word meaning blow or punch, and counting coup was the ritual means of showing bravery in battle. In most tribes the warrior counted coup by being the first to touch a live adversary, scalp a foe, or strike a dead enemy. Usually three different men, sometimes four, might count coup on the same opponent. Sir Richard Burton, who interviewed a number of Plains Indians in 1860, reported other variations. According to Burton, the highest honor was to ride single-handedly into the enemy camp and touch a lodge with lance or bow. The second was to take a warrior prisoner, and the third was to strike a dead or fallen man. Least important was to slay an enemy in hand-to-hand fighting. Coups had to be verified by others, and the warrior had the right to recount his exploits publicly at appropriate times. As might be expected, Plains Indian leaders had amazing numbers of coups. For example, in 1891 the Oglala Chief Red Cloud stated that he had counted coup eighty times. In some tribes feathers were tallies of a man's prowess in war. Among the Sioux the number of eagle feathers worn denoted the number of enemies killed, the wing feathers of the bald eagle indicting a male and black eagle feathers representing a woman. If they had shot an enemy, warriors put a round red spot on the feather. A broad red streak across meant that the opponent had been scalped.

SCALPING AND MUTILATION

The taking of whole body parts or scalping has been practiced in many cultures from earliest times to the present. Many tribes in the West were participants, as were many white frontiersmen. Unlike the simple cut and jerk method portrayed in films, scalping was not a simple feat. In 1860 Sir Richard Burton had the nerve to query a Sioux about his methodology and received a remarkable description of how it was done. When reaching a downed enemy, a warrior draws his knife and grasps the hair, twisting it to draw it tight on the head. Next he makes two semicircular incisions about the part to be removed, then loosens the skin with the knife point. Sitting on the ground, he places his feet against the subject's shoulders for leverage and holding the twisted hair with both hands applies force. If he is successful, he will soon disengage the scalp with a sound something like "flop." In some cases warriors took the whole scalp with eyebrows and ears. After being stretched and dried on hoops, such scalps often became a warrior's canvas for retelling the story of its taking. Many tribes believed that scalping killed the soul.

Most Indians in the West believed that the body eventually followed the soul into the afterlife; consequently, disfigurement at the time of death or soon thereafter was thought to be eternal. Thus, the motive for disfigurement was an enemy's perpetual suffering and unrest. Not understanding the reason, whites assumed that all victims had been tortured before being killed, and the saying, "keep that last bullet for yourself," was oft-repeated in the rank and file. Some tribes, including the Comanches and Apaches, did torture their prisoners. The Sioux, Cheyennes, and Arapahos, who figured so prominently in the wars on the Northern Plains, did not. Generally, captors adopted women and children but did not take male prisoners. Perhaps the most publicized incident of soldier mutilation was that attendant to the Fetterman fight of December 21, 1866. In this case, the victors smashed the skulls of their opponents, cut off ears and noses, took out eyes, disemboweled some, pincushioned others with arrows, burned a few corpses, and otherwise severely mutilated the bodies.

THE WARRIOR

There is no doubt that the Plains Indian warrior was a formidable opponent. In the early days of intertribal warfare, no other fighting force in the West could match him. Equipped with a long lance and a bison-hide shield and carrying a quiver filled with as many as one hundred arrows, he fought from horseback or on foot. In the beginning the superior firepower of the U.S. soldier offset the skills of the Indian. However, as the years passed, and as firearms became more available, the warrior began to regain his early dominance. In 1883 General George Crook stated that the ability of the tribes to obtain the breech-loading rifle and the metallic cartridge had revolutionized Indian warfare. No longer equipped with inferior arms, warriors were truly formidable adversaries. In 1880 Captain Charles King pointed out that the Indians' system of warfare was the essence of lifelong experiences of men who had done nothing for generations but fight over broad western lands. When it came to maneuvering on horseback, King declared, "We are but babes in arms."[2] As horsemen, warriors performed feats that amazed American cavalrymen. Riding at full speed, they could sling themselves alongside their horses for protection and suddenly rise and fire arrows with deadly accuracy.

Warriors also had special skills in gathering intelligence. They were marvelous trackers and sign readers. George Custer wrote of them, "They can count an army within a score of its number by the depth that a trail is worn; they can give within a dozen the number of horses in a column by the amount of turf nibble at the last feeding place. They can tell the speed, the direction, and the strength of armies far as the dust that rides from its [*sic*] feet is perceptible."[3] They also knew the land. The Indians knew the whole country and took any route they pleased. They traveled by landmarks from one stream to the next. Because they did not travel in "Indian file," as the whites seemed to suppose, they did not leave a deep-marked path, and, after the village had moved on, the trail soon disappeared and left no mark in the grass.

LEADERSHIP

In battle every man followed his instincts. A respected war chief might lead his tribesmen to the attack, but from there on it was every man for himself. "We paid no attention to the chiefs," said a Santee Sioux, Lightning Blanket, in 1862. "Everyone did as he pleased."[4] The Nez Percé warrior Weyehwahtsiskan agreed. "Unlike the trained white soldier," he declared, "the Indian goes into battle on his mind's own guidance."[5] This concept, though easy to state, is probably the most difficult to remember in trying to understand the outcome of specific battles in the Indian wars.

INDIAN STRATEGY

The Indian warrior was essentially a raider. He did not like pitched battles because there was very little to be gained from them. Nomads did not defend any particular place at any given time; they sought only to control a region. As George Forsyth put it, they were "always seeking the maximum of gain at the minimum of risk."[6] Because each fought as an individual, every man tried to leave plenty of room about him. This made it difficult for U.S. soldiers who fought as a group, with four members being the smallest unit in the cavalry.

LIVING OFF THE LAND

Indians in the West had a great advantage over the troops who pursued them, because they were able to live off the land. This was all the more remarkable because to whites the land often seemed incapable of supporting life. In 1858 "a late captain of infantry" eloquently summarized this ability when he wrote, "When they get short of provisions, [they] separate and look for something to eat, and find it in the water, in the ground, or on the surface; whose bill of fare ranges from grass-seed, nuts, roots, grasshoppers, lizards, and rattlesnakes, up to the antelope, deer, elk, bear, and buffalo, and who having a continent to roam over, will neither be surprised, caught, conquered, overawed, or reduced to famine by a rumbling, bugleblowing drum beating town passing through their country on wheels, at the speed of a loaded wagon."[7] Indian historian Stanley Vestal stated that the Plains Indians could travel this way with their families and cover fifty miles a day.

One Plains Indian secret in being able to travel light was a special, prepared, long-lasting food called "pemmican." Made from the flesh of buffalo, deer, or other wild meat, it was cut in long thin strips and dried in the sun. When cured or "jerked," women pounded the meat into shreds and stuffed it into skin bags. The bones were pounded and the marrow extracted, melted, and poured while hot into the sacks with the shredded meat. According to one observer, when properly made it was not unlike pâté de foie gras. Enlisted man William Seeger, who served with General Sully in the 1864 Sioux Campaign, reported that a man could travel farther and last longer on pemmican than any other food of the same bulk and weight. However, he did not recommend the taste, which reminded him of candles. Some added ground chokecherries or other fruits, pits and all, which made it tastier and even more nutritious, if somewhat hard on the teeth.

Another practice increased warriors' ability to sustain long journeys. Scout Jim Bridger identified the means of sustenance in a particularly telling description of tribal mobility recorded by Lieutenant Eugene F. Ware at Fort Laramie in August 1864:

> Now, here is a band of Injuns that want to go off on a horse-stealing
> expedition, each one of them riding a spare pony. They whistle up

their dogs, and start off. The dogs can keep up with the horses, and when they camp, the horses can eat grass, and the Injuns eat the dogs. That is the reason they don't have to have any commissary wagons. They don't have to have any corn for their horses, nor any bacon and hard-tack, and that is the reason that they can always run away from our people, and we never can chase them down on one of these raids, and catch them unless we travel like they do.[8]

Without their horses the Indians of the West would have been unable to compete with U.S. troops. Although they may not have had the weaponry in the early years, they had superior equestrian skills, having acquired them from childhood. Soldiers quickly found that Indian ponies when in good shape were better suited to travel on the plains than their grain-fed American horses. Private George Saunders of the Eleventh Kansas Cavalry noted in his diary in June 1865 that cavalry horses could not sustain a march of fifteen miles a day, while the poorest of their appropriated Indian ponies had little difficulty maintaining the pace. One of the reasons that tribes could travel faster than troops was that their members had multiple mounts and rode a second horse when the first tired. Finally, the pony was the ultimate helpmate, because he sheltered his master in battle. Major Martin Anderson of the Eleventh Kansas described it: "They rode in a circle and when they came round in range they lay close down on the sides of their horses, nothing visible but a foot above each horse's back, and they did their firing under the necks of their horses. We could not get at them much that way, but could only kill the ponies."[9]

TACTICS AND METHODS

Offensive tactics were quite simple: They consisted of concealment and surprise. Warriors of many tribes had an uncanny ability to hide themselves from enemy eyes. Jim Bridger commented more than once that, "Where they ain't no Injuns, you'll find 'em thickest."[10] The Apaches were especially noted for their ability to blend into the landscape and appear anywhere. John Bourke remembered that, rubbing their bodies with clay or sand and covering their heads with yucca shoots or "sacaton" grass, these warriors knew how to disguise themselves so thoroughly that a man might almost step on one before detecting his presence. Another officer serving in Arizona agreed. "Chase them," he declared, "and they sink into the ground or somehow vanish; look behind and they are peeping over a hill at you."[11]

Because an Indian's hair was so black, veterans advised newcomers to look for that color in the landscape. At the same time, infiltrating warriors always attempted to hide their hair with a piece of buckskin or some sagebrush or greasewood. Indians were also adept at making use of any bit of cover. Cavalry commander A. G. Brackett commented on this trait: "In Indian fighting," he wrote, "the savages have a way of hiding behind rocks, bushes, and trees, where our cavalry men cannot get at them when mounted."[12]

Ambush was also in the Indians' book of tactics. The goal was to entice a few soldiers to pursue them into a place where greater numbers could surround and dispatch them. The Fetterman Disaster on December 21, 1866, was probably the most successful implementation of the tactic. In this case young Crazy Horse and a half-dozen others lured William Judd Fetterman and his command of eighty men into following them over Lodge Trail Ridge where as many as fifteen hundred Sioux and Northern Cheyennes waited, concealed in gullies and ravines. Employed again and again in the Indian wars, the decoy was a strategy that took advantage of the desire of novices for honors and a means of compensating for disparity in horses. According to Stanley Vestal, older, less daring, and less well-mounted warriors invented the ploy. They purposely sent rash youths forward to attack. Being few, the youngsters were necessarily driven back, drawing the pursuing enemy with them. This arrangement gave the older, slower warriors a chance to take part in the battle and get their share of the honors and spoils of war.

DEFENSE

In defensive warfare the Indians of the West had two dicta: flee and disperse. Those who had attacked Indians in their villages knew that the first act was to cover the retreat of women and children, and the second was to break into small groups to make pursuit more difficult. To counteract this strategy, army commanders tried to attack Indian villages from several directions. Thus, George Armstrong Custer split his forces before the Battle of the Washita in which he was successful and at the Battle of the Little Bighorn in which he was not. His first concern was not numbers but the hope of getting some of the warriors to stand and fight.

Indians had several interesting methods of gaining the advantage in warfare. They burned buffalo hair upwind to stampede cattle. In fighting in the 1850s and 1860s, when Indians saw the gleam of the soldier's ramrod, they knew that the men were in the process of reloading and came in close for the attack. At Julesburg on February 2, 1865, the Cheyennes put sand on the frozen South Platte so that their heavily laden ponies could cross without falling. Attackers used arrows like mortars, discharging them at an angle of about forty-five degrees so that they descended in an arc, finding targets among men and horses ensconced behind barriers or sheltered in depressions.

Occasionally, Plains Indians used poisoned arrows. W. J. Hoffman witnessed the preparation of poisoned arrows by the Unkpapa Sioux in 1873 near Grand River Agency:

> The arrow-maker and the owner of the weapons went to the prairie dog town, a short distance from camp where they soon found a rattlesnake—*Crotalus confluentus*. One of the Indians carried a forked stick, while the other had the liver of a recently killed antelope. The serpent was gently but securely held to the ground by means of one of the forked sticks while the assistant impaled the liver upon another. The snake was then excited by thrusting the liver towards its head, where it soon buried its fangs; this was repeated several times, when, finally, the reptile, becoming obstinate and refusing to bite the object again, was killed.
>
> The liver was then carried to camp and placed upon a pole where the rays of the sun hastened decomposition. The time necessary for this operation depends upon the state of the atmosphere; but usually a day is sufficient for all purposes. When the liver became putrid, it was taken down and crushed into a plastic mass in a small tin vessel, after which the arrows were dipped into it and laid away to dry.[13]

Apaches used the same method according to one source. The Paiutes filled the heart cavity of a large mammal with a mixture of ground rattlesnake fangs and poison sacs and a horned toad or two and smeared arrows with the matter after decomposition. The Indians of Sonora used a cow's liver pâté doctored with centipedes, scorpions, and rattlesnake venom. Some Nevada Indians boiled a dozen rattlesnake heads and red ants in a jar to obtain their poison. The Shoshonis and Bannock Indians preferred the blood of an antelope that had died from rattlesnake bite. The Blackfeet and Assiniboin forced a rattlesnake to strike wood bark and applied the venom directly to their arrows. Charles Smiley, an educated Dakotan from the Sisseton Agency, reported that his people used various herbs and plants pounded into a mass with the gums and fangs of a rattlesnake. This preparation was then applied to arrows and also to bullets. According to Smiley, a hunter using a bullet thus prepared did not have to aim at the object but merely had to raise his gun and pull the trigger, because the bullet was sure to kill.

Over great distances the ability to communicate quickly was important, and tribes employed a number of methods. In the foothills, on benchlands, and atop buttes, they often used smoke signals. One of those commenting on this form of communication was George Custer, who called it "as perfect a system of signals as ever were introduced into civilized warfare."[14] Another method was to shoot lighted arrows into the air. As strange as it may seem, a number of whites mentioned Indians using bugles in battle. At Beecher Island warriors responded to the shrill peal of an artillery bugle. Under assault in Nebraska in 1864, J. E. Richey reported that one of his attackers was an accomplished bugler, noting, however, that the calls were not those used by the army.

STRENGTHS AND WEAKNESSES

Indian warriors of the West did have some weaknesses. First was the lack of discipline. Their stress on individual performance meant that they could only make and execute the simplest of plans. Second, they lacked good security. Soldiers repeatedly surprised them in their camps—on Tongue River, at the Washita, at Red Forks of the Powder River, at Summit Springs, and many other places. Third, those who lived on the plains and mountain plateau were vulnerable in winter, when they had to split into small groups because of difficulties of subsistence. Also, their ponies grew weak because of short rations, sometimes reduced to feeding on twigs from cottonwood trees. They also had a few tactical shortcomings. In the early years when the bow and arrow was the principal weapon for many, a battle in rain could spell disaster. Bow strings expanded when wet, decreasing the tension needed to launch arrows with force and accuracy. In the case of rifles, warriors also had a tendency to fire high but corrected the fault with experience. Generally, Indians were adequate marksmen because they had limited ammunition and learned to fire only when they expected results.

Perhaps the Indians' greatest weakness in warfare was the fact that there were no noncombatants among tribesmen. Women and children and the elderly were often caught in the cross fire. In trying to protect their families, fighting men were unable to divert their full energies to the task at hand. On campaign, war was not the army fighting another army; it was the army fighting a people.

In summary, at the height of the Indian wars, the Plains Indians and other equestrian tribes of the West were more than able opponents for the U.S. Army. A veteran who signed himself "Observer" put it aptly in a letter to the *Army and Navy Journal* in 1878 when he wrote, "The Indian horseman of to-day is superior to the white man because he subsists himself and horse more readily; because in a fight he carries about his horse and person less impediments, and because he is a more skillful marksman while his horse is in motion."[15]

The Army

THE PROBLEM OF DISTANCE

The first problem the U.S. Army faced was the great expanse of the American West.[16] In the beginning the land mass lacked established transportation routes, few rivers being navigable, and railroads had yet to penetrate the region. Too few troops had too many acres to cover, and chasing nomads meant riding in endless circles with the dim hope of engagement driving them on. Perhaps Frederick Benteen put it best when he wrote his wife that in so vast a country, a chase after Indians had one chance in a thousand of being successful. Not untypical was Company K of the Seventh Cavalry that traversed over three thousand miles in sixteen months during the campaign of 1885–1886, an average of over six miles a day. Initially, because much of the territory had not been explored or mapped, commands often had little knowledge of where they were going or how to avoid ambush or find good camping places. In the West it was often fifty to two hundred miles between watering holes, and in certain regions the water was so impregnated with alkali that it was dangerous to drink.

Marching long distances also meant problems of supply, and the U.S. soldier had to have a lot of extra items from bullets to horseshoes. For many years troops carried one hundred pounds of clothing, equipment, and rations. Cavalry also had to have grain for their horses, and units often kept close to their supply trains, which restricted their mobility and efficiency. As the period progressed, technology resulted in lighter equipment, decreasing the weight of the soldier's load. In 1877 Lieutenant W. B. Weir recorded that his infantryman's full field equipment now weighed 41.77 lbs., distributed as follows:

TABLE 8: INFANTRYMAN'S FULL EQUIPMENT, 1877

60 rounds of ammunition and belt	5.40 lbs.
overcoat	5.25 lbs.
blanket (gray wool)	5.13 lbs.
rubber blanket (ground cloth)	3.00 lbs.
Springfield rifle and sling	8.40 lbs.
extra	2.00 lbs.
full canteen (one quart)	3.84 lbs.
five rations: 3/4 lbs. meat and 1 lb. hardtack per day	8.75 lbs.

Great distances also created a problem of command. In his report on military operations for 1867, Department of the Platte commander Christopher C. Augur noted that the extent and variety of duties required of the troops had caused their separation into small commands and that their being scattered over the country had had very destructive results on the discipline and instruction of both officers and men. He did acknowledge, however, that the circumstance did enlarge their experience, develop individuality, and contribute to a correct knowledge of the country. Stationed on the northern plains, the Seventh Infantry was better than many regiments, because it managed to keep its companies together and develop an esprit de corps. Only the Thirteenth Infantry, serving in Apache country, and the Fourth Cavalry were fortunate enough to stay together during this period. Complicating the whole picture was the army's bifurcation of authority at its highest level. The commanding general of the army was in charge of discipline and military control, while the secretary of war conducted the army's fiscal affairs through its staff departments. And all these ultimate decision makers were sometimes thousands of miles away from troops in the field, a problem later remedied to a degree when telegraph lines and railroads reached the West.

CLIMATE

Creating other problems were the extremes of heat and cold experienced on the plains and in the mountains. Extremes were not only from season to season but from day to day. The records for one locality show a change of one hundred degrees in twenty-four hours during a week in December. Another, in the same week, experienced a change of seventy degrees in twelve hours. Between March and June a detachment could suffer both from frozen limbs and heat exhaustion, all the time wearing the same uniform. Because tribes were especially vulnerable in the winter, November to February campaigns became more frequent in the coldest climates. Devastating to the Cheyennes and Sioux were Ranald Mackenzie's attack on Dull Knife's Cheyenne Village on November 25, 1876, and Nelson Miles's attack on Crazy Horse's village on January 8, 1877.

TRAINING

One of the frontier soldier's deficiencies was his lack of training.[17] This was due to the fact that he devoted most of his time to nonmilitary duties. In 1879 a correspondent of the *Omaha Herald* succinctly described the predicament: "The regular soldier on the frontiers is no more nor less than a beast of burden, and what is still worse, he is treated as such. He is exposed to continual hardships and fatigue, he has to work in the sun and in the rain. From sunrise to sunset it is work, building houses, stables, etc. The finishing of one building here is the beginning of another. Strangers and visitors from the East, often take them for convicts."[18] As one veteran put it, the posts on the immense plains were "like men-of-war moored in mid-ocean to catch pirates, with a crew of sailors busily engaged in civil handicrafts."[19] Writing a few years later Captain Guy V. Henry pointed out that cavalrymen were even more put upon, because they had to perform all the labors and care for their horses besides.

After the Civil War, training became more important than ever because the skills of recruits were less applicable to military service. The number of whites who possessed prior familiarity with firearms diminished as the East industrialized, and farming families provided fewer recruits because of the manpower needed to work the soil. To improve the situation the army instituted small arms practice in 1872. Regulations required each soldier to fire ninety rounds annually at a rifle range and participate in drills on estimating distances. Beginning in 1874 the army issued 120 cartridges per man for target practice, but it was not until after the Nez Percé War of 1877 that enlisted men received any instruction whatsoever in the theory of marksmanship.

The result was that the soldier during the peak years of the Indian wars was not a very good marksman. In 1893 Captain James Parker of the Fourth Cavalry observed that the lack of success of his branch of the service in the Indian wars had often been rationalized on the grounds that the enemy had possessed superior weapons. He declared that in truth the Model 1873 Springfield was the best military rifle in the world, but the Indian was simply a better shot. According to Parker, when the warrior fired his weapon, he fired it to kill, each cartridge representing a life.

It has been fashionable to blame Custer's defeat on poor marksmanship. It is true that about fifteen percent of those in the Seventh Cavalry were generally unskilled recruits, and many of the rest were ill prepared for battle through neglect of target practice. However, in his latest work, *Archaeology, History, and Custer's Last Battle*, Richard Fox does not attribute Custer's ultimate defeat to troopers' poor firing and riding skills. Rather he finds the key in the shock firepower of Henry repeating rifles brought by Sioux to bear on Calhoun's line, whose disintegration spread to the rest of the command. Thus, in the case of the Custer fight, poor training among the troops seems to have been less a factor than concentrated short-range firepower on the Indian side.

With its performance criticized in the Sioux Campaign of 1876 and the Nez Percé War of 1877, the military hierarchy began a period of self-examination and reform. In 1879 the army raised the requirement to twenty rounds monthly and began a policy of awarding prizes and furloughs to the best shot in each unit. In 1880 the service inaugurated a formal program of competitions at posts, progressing to department and divisional levels. Winners competed at Creedmore, on Long Island, New York. By 1890 the army believed that its men were the world's superior military marksmen.

HORSES

One of the keys to survival for those who inhabited the plains was a good horse. Army troopers soon learned to value their mounts. Soldier John Brooks was not in a minority when he said, "I took better care of my horse than I did of myself." A. J. Davis observed that, "A cavalryman is nothing away from his horse, and what steed was there ever who won a battle by himself. Like the centaur of old, we are one."[20] In 1883 cavalry commander A. G. Brackett reported that a trooper often stole food for his horse and in many cases shared his scant ration of bread with him. Some old hands used mules and horses to keep sentry for them, the animals neighing when their sense of smell told them that Indian horses were in the vicinity. Private George Edwards had a horse named Ike that would wake him up when Indians were in the area.

A well-trained animal could be the difference in battle or a tight place, and the soldier spent a great deal of time training his mount to respond quickly and appropriately. Here are some tips for managing and training horses that come from the cavalrymen who rode them:

Never use a whip from a horse that is to be shot from, else, when a gun is raised to fire, he will imagine it to be the whip, and is sure to be unsteady.

To overcome the stubbornness of a horse that has thrown himself down, do not flog him. Twisting or biting his tail is the usual way to manage him. A tuft of grass set-ablaze and placed under his nostril will cause him to rise.

In crossing a deep river with a horse, drive him in, and then follow, grasping his tail. Should he turn his head and try to change his course, he may be directed by splashing water in his face.

To accustom a horse to firing, station a few men at a little distance from, and on both sides of, the stable door, and cause them to fire pistols as the horses are led into the stable to be fed; for the same object, a gun may be fired during the hour of feeding.

Army horses were grain-fed, which put them at a disadvantage on a long campaign, and though Indian warriors always had more than one pony to ride, the cavalry mount had little time to rest. The animals also carried heavy loads, burdens that were doubly difficult to bear when traveling over rugged terrain on meager supplies. Moreover, picketed cavalry horses did not get much chance to graze for additional food intake. The result was that U.S. horses sometimes broke down after long marches, and cavalrymen found themselves becoming infantry. Two well-known examples of this were the forces led by Colonel Nelson Cole and Lieutenant Colonel Samuel Walker in the Powder River Expedition of August–September 1865, and George Crook's "starvation march" in western South Dakota in August–September 1876.

TACTICS AND METHODS

One major shortcoming of the U.S. Army in the nineteenth century was its failure to develop a course of instruction to train its rank and file in methods of Indian warfare. During the Indian wars the army issued four manuals on infantry tactics. The standard volume at midcentury was the *Scott's Infantry Tactics* (1814). *Hardee's Light Infantry Tactics* appeared in 1855 (after Hardee became a Confederate, the army reissued his book as *U. S. Infantry Tactics*), and in 1862, the army issued *Casey's Infantry Tactics*. Because of book shortages, all three of these manuals were official. In 1867 Brevet Major General Emory Upton came out with his *New System of Infantry Tactics*, which underwent several revisions and remained the standard volume until 1891. In writing about infantry tactics, Captain Charles King pointed out that the manuals had been prepared by four officers "eminent for everything but Indian fighting."[21]

The standard cavalry manual was that authored by General Philip St. George Cooke in 1861. Cooke devoted some attention to Indian fighting. Upton's *Cavalry Tactics*, which appeared in 1874, did introduce more maneuverability into formations, establishing a "set of fours" or "squads" as the smallest unit. The manual prescribed an interval of five yards between skirmishers when fighting on foot and a spacing of fifteen yards between squads. This replaced the old close-order drill, in which men fought shoulder to shoulder, a style made obsolete by improved weaponry and totally unsuited for guerrilla warfare in rugged terrain.

Nor did the U.S. Military Academy or army journals deal with the subject of Indian warfare. However, a few officers did write about it, notably Randolph Marcy, whose volume, *The Prairie Traveler: A Handbook for Overland Expeditions*, appeared in 1859. Near the end of the period, in 1881, Edward S. Farrow published a series of articles on "mountain scouting" in the *Army and Navy Journal*, which, slightly revised, appeared in book form in 1902. Farrow devoted a chapter to Indian fighting and presented valuable information throughout on getting along in the wilderness.

From time to time, officers and others offered their opinions on how to conduct Indian warfare. Some suggested that at a minimum, the army should only enlist good riders. Others suggested that soldiers be given the horses, arms, and dress of hunters and taught to act independently. The key was to keep within supporting distance of one another, with each man selecting his own vantage-ground and fighting according to his own knowledge and inclination. One officer argued that those engaged in Indian warfare should always live in the field, relying on their own resources for subsistence. All of them should be expert marksmen, selected from the general service because of their skill with rifle and pistol and paid a higher wage than other enlisted men. Jim Bridger believed that the best way to succeed in Indian warfare was for a party of men to follow on foot, week after week, subsisting as Indians did, eventually to overtake and surprise them in their villages. An article in the *Army and Navy Journal* of May 31, 1873, suggested a similar tactic in attempting to quell the Modoc uprising.

Because of an official lack of interest in the subject matter, officers in the field were free to develop their own methods, and the best of them began to experiment with varying results. Pioneered by General Sheridan in 1867, one of the first successful tactical developments was to attack fixed camps in winter, when ponies were weak. Another was to use converging columns to trap Indians and force them into battle. Commanders also began to use trackers to hunt their prey, and some of these developed what appear to be from today's perspective almost supernatural skills. In 1869 the *Army and Navy Journal* printed an account by an officer serving in Dakota Territory in which he described the abilities of a scout named Hack and how he worked his magic. On the way to the Niobrara River the men crossed the tracks of an Indian pony, which they followed for a few miles. Suddenly, the scout turned to the officer and said: "It is a stray, black horse, with a long, bushy tail, nearly starved to death, has a split hoof on the left fore-foot, and goes very lame, and he passed here early this morning." Astonished and incredulous, the officer asked him the reason for knowing these particulars, and he replied: "[He] was a stray horse because [he] did not go in a direct line. [The horse's] tail was long, for he dragged it over the snow. In brushing against a bush, he left some of his hair, which shows its color. [The horse] was very hungry, for, in going along, he has nipped at those high, dry weeds, which horses seldom eat. The fissure of the left fore-foot, left . . . its track, and the depth of the indenture shows the degree of his lameness. And his track shows [that] he was here this morning, when the snow was hard with frost."[22] Such information gleaned from keen observation could sometimes make or break a campaign.

Among innovators George Crook stands out. Often using Indians as scouts, he was among the first to employ them as auxiliaries, effectively using Crows and Shoshonis at the Battle of the Rosebud, and Pawnees and Winnebagos in the attack on Dull Knife's village on the Red Forks of Powder River. Although Crook obviously recognized scouts' worth as guides and trackers, he also coldly calculated the psychological benefits that accrued from their use. "Nothing breaks them up," he wrote, "like turning their own people against them." He explained: "They don't fear the white soldiers, whom they easily surpass in the peculiar style of warfare which they force upon us, but put upon their trail an enemy of their own blood, an enemy as tireless, as foxy, and as stealthy and familiar with the country as they themselves, and it breaks them all up. It is not merely a question of catching them better with Indians, but of a broader and more enduring aim—their disintegration."[23] Crook also advocated reliance on mule trains as the means of achieving mobility.

As the years passed, soldiers developed the caution that reduced vulnerability. To prevent surprise attack in transit, they learned to put out flankers on front, rear, and sides. They camped in depressions so that enemies approaching on most nights would be easily discernible targets framed against the sky. To keep from falling asleep, one sentry rubbed tobacco juice into his eyes. On campaign they slept with shoes on and pistols in their holsters. When camping in Indian country, they formed their wagons into a circular or elliptical corral, securing the main opening and spaces between with chains or ropes. Horses and mules spent the night inside, tied to wagons, fed with grass cut earlier with knives or scythes and brought into the corral in blankets.

Guards learned to move fifty yards after darkness fell and never to move between the fire and the horizon, where they became a tempting target. When on picket a guard learned that a wolf call made by an Indian had no echo. Small scouting parties quietly moved from their first camp where they had earlier made coffee and left their fires burning to go a mile farther to sleep in the shelter of dense brush, their horses' reins fastened to their arms. To confuse the enemy, they walked backward out of camp. Tired of losing their horses in sudden night or early morning raids, the army experimented with hobbles, finally settling on a metal one as the best of its genre. One enterprising unit taught its grazing horses to run to the post when stampeded.

Frontier soldiers learned that motion, not plainly caused by the wind, meant life. They learned to distinguish between whites and Indians at a distance, because warriors rode bareback, making a distinctive movement with knees and heels when riding at top speed. They understood that a man kicks prairie grass forward as he walks, and, because of the semicircular sweep of its front feet, a large-hoofed animal drags the grass backward as it moves ahead. They learned to eat coyote, prairie dog, cactus, and rotten horseflesh, sprinkling the latter with gunpowder as it cooked to take away the odor. They drank the blood of horses to survive in the heat of the desert. They came to prefer dry hardwood fires, as they generated little smoke. On a cold, windy day they sought a canyon before building a fire. When Indians set fire to the prairie, they set their own, beat it out, and occupied the burned ground before the other blaze arrived. They cleared muddy water by pouring it through a cone of twisted grass. When it rained, veterans got their army blankets and rolled them as they walked, knowing that when saturated they would contain two gallons of rank but precious liquid that could be squeezed out and drunk. A cavalryman learned to jump off his horse in subzero weather and run beside him to keep from freezing.

To keep their horses quiet when Indians were near, the men had them lie on the ground and covered their heads with cavalry jackets or held their noses. Troops learned to fire low to have a better chance of inflicting a fatal abdominal wound rather than missing the head or heart. They learned that Comanche arrows carried about seventy yards, and their pistols one hundred, so they kept that distance.

Finally, a few troops learned to imitate the Indian's way of fighting. At the Battle of Mud Springs in February 1865, Iowa and Ohio volunteers engaged a large party of Cheyennes and Sioux for several hours. The volunteers' commander, Colonel William O. Collins, described the sparring: "We found it necessary to imitate the Indians, get under banks and creep up to favorable position, watch for an Indian's head, and shoot the moment it was shown and pop down at the flash of his gun. The men got quite handy at this game and soon made any ground occupied by Indians to[o] hot for them. It was common to see a soldier and an Indian playing pop up in this manner for half an hour at a time."[24] General John Gibbon noted that the elbow touch formations recommended in manuals by William J. Hardee and Silas Casey were "utterly thrown away" in the Indian fights for more practical maneuvers.[25]

Two Indian war veterans have left us with accounts of personal experience in Indian warfare that are rare in the literature. The first is a description of how it feels to be shot, recorded by Captain Henry Romeyn, who was wounded at the Battle of Bear Paw in October 1877. The officer lay hidden in the long grass as the battle progressed. When he stood up to see what was going on, a warrior singled him out and fired. Romeyn described the sensation: "I felt as if a red hot iron bar had been driven through me. I stood rooted in my tracks for a moment, gasped and felt the air coming in at my back. The next instant my mouth filled with blood, and then I knew I had been shot in the lung. I walked seventy-five yards and then fell."[26]

In the 1870s the standard treatment for a gunshot wound was to cover the entering and departing orifices with a layer of lint an inch and a half square, saturated with cold water. Then comrades laid on a piece of oiled silk, twice the size of the lint, retaining it in place by a pocket handkerchief or some other means. This dressing remained until the parts became stiff and painful—two to six days, according to the season—and were then removed. The next application was either a similar dressing of water or a bread-and-water poultice, usually renewed once or twice a day. If it was an arrow, the men learned to pull it out immediately, because blood moistened and loosened sinew that bound the point to the shaft, and the missive would remain deep in the wound. Surgeons devised a number of instruments to remove embedded arrows. The method was to insert a forceps or steel rod with a wire loop or snare into the dilated wound. After encasing or entangling the arrow head, the surgeon withdrew both shaft and instrument. Abdominal wounds were especially deadly, and Mexicans often wore protective folds of blankets around their middles when fighting Apaches. Of eighty arrow wounds tracked in a study by surgeon J. H. Bill, twenty-nine were fatal.

The other rare description is found in the *Army and Navy Journal*, written by a soldier who was with Custer's command at the Battle of the Washita in 1868 and recorded how it feels to be scalped:

As we ran through . . . [the village], a big red jumped out at me from behind a tent, and before I could shorten up enough to run him through with my bayonet, a squaw grabbed me around the legs and twisted me down. The camp was full of men fighting, and everybody seemed yelling as loud as he could. When I fell, I went over backward, dropping me gun, and I had just got part way up again, the squaw yanking me by the hair, when the Indian clubbed my gun and struck me across the neck. The blow stunned me; the squaws kept screeching and pulling my hair out by handfuls. I heard some of our boys shouting close by, and the squaw started and ran, one of the boys killing her not three rods off. The Indian stepped one foot on my chest, and with his hand gathered up the hair near the crown of my head. He wasn't very tender about it, but jerked my head this way and that, like Satan. My eyes were partially open, and I could see the bead-work trimming on his leggings. Suddenly, I felt the awfullest biting, cutting flash go round my head, and then it seemed to me just as if my whole head had been jerked clean off. I never felt such pain in all my life; it was like pulling your brains right out; I didn't know anymore for two or three days, and when I came to I had the sorest head of any human being that every lived. If the boys killed the viper they didn't get back my scalp; perhaps it got lost in the snow. I was shipped down to Laramie after a bit, and all the nursing I got hain't made the hair grow out on this spot yet.[27]

STRENGTHS AND WEAKNESSES

During the Indian wars the army enjoyed one advantage besides generally better technology. Because of the structure of Euro-American society, soldiers accepted discipline, making it possible to devise long-range plans and carry them out. However, the frontier army in the nineteenth century did not utilize all its insufficient force to implement its strategy. When the troops did take to the field, significant numbers remained behind to protect government property. Furthermore, in the case of the cavalry, one fourth of those who went into battle served as horse-holders. General Sherman tried to compensate for this by having the less courageous identified and assigned to this duty.

Perhaps the greatest problem confronting troops in the field was the difficulty of separating warring Indians from the peaceful. Conventional tactics did not permit the army to do this. What happened was that punishment fell on both the innocent and guilty, making new enemies and strengthening the opposition. But far and away the army's greatest weakness was its prevailing belief that Indians were inferior and that Euro-American pluck and ingenuity would triumph in every situation. From John Grattan to William Judd Fetterman to George Forsyth to George Armstrong Custer, soldiers believed that they could meet and defeat any Indian force they might encounter. The price of arrogance was often defeat and sometimes death.

5. Indian and Army Life

Indians of the West

WOMEN

Among the Indians of the West men and women had clear divisions of responsibility. Men hunted, waged war, sat in council, instructed their sons, and protected their families and the tribe. Women raised the children; maintained, organized, and transported lodges; helped butcher meat; prepared meals; made clothing and containers; decorated skins with quilling and beadwork; hauled wood and water; made and tended the fire; and did the packing for moving. Both valued each other's roles.[1]

HABITATIONS

Indians in the West fashioned a variety of shelters. Mandans lived in earth lodges, circular in shape with floors excavated slightly below ground level. Covered with brush and dirt, underlying structures consisted of four or more center posts supporting rafters. Apaches and Basin and California peoples made wickiups of bent saplings covered with brush. Navajos lived in hogans made of logs, brush, and a covering of earth. Pueblos lived in adobe apartments, while Northwest peoples built houses of planks. Those who followed the buffalo lived in conical "tipis," a Sioux word meaning "used for dwelling." Made of fifteen to eighteen dressed buffalo skins, tipis were about fifteen to twenty feet in diameter and weighed from 125 to 150 pounds. Poles that formed the supporting tripod, usually about twenty in number, averaged about twenty-five feet in height and were tapered from two to six inches at the base. In early days some tribes, such as the Pawnees, lived in earth lodges in permanent villages for four or five months a year and then moved onto the plains in tipis.

CAMPS

Plains Indians did not like to sleep without some sort of cover. On the open prairie, they would pull the tops of long grass together to make a sort of cocoon and crawl in. Camps were many and varied, from an overnight bivouac of a few boys on a hunting or horse-stealing expedition to great sprawling tribal assemblies. Leaders chose camps according to the proximity of wood, water, and grass, the last two being most important. For larger encampments tribes followed a general plan, in which tipis were raised in a rough circle or semicircle with a kind of central plaza. In the center were the lodges of the medicine chief and the sweat house. The head of the band determined the location of the camp, halting his pony to jab the butt of his lance into the earth. To the rear of the shaft, his women erected his shelter, the lesser chiefs following as a location pleased them. The entrance to the camp and the doors of all tipis faced east. Among the Sioux the Unkpapas were guardians of the entrance, their names being derived from "unkapea" meaning "the opening to the camp."

Summer camps were often happy affairs, but winter ones were usually tests of survival. As winter neared, the big camps broke up into tribal units and journeyed to points previously selected, no two occupying the same place. Leaders chose winter camps that were sheltered from blizzards and had sufficient cottonwoods, willows, and light growth to feed ponies when the grass was gone. Starvation for humans and animals at these winter camps was a possibility. Sometimes bands lost all their ponies from lack of forage and had to beg mounts from other groups, even from those who at other times were considered their enemies. Those asked usually complied, even if quantity or quality was not up to standards.

FOOD

Some Indians in the West were part-time farmers. The Pawnees had gardens in the river bottoms where women grew corn, beans, and squash. At least twice a year, the band went on bison hunts. The men in all the tribes did the hunting. Over the years they acquired many skills in snaring, disabling, and dispatching game. Studying each animal's habits, they learned to approach without giving warning by donning animal skin disguises, waiting for prey at water holes, and stalking against the wind. On the plains and in the mountains they pursued buffalo, elk, deer, moose, bear, wolves, coyotes, mountain lions, and wildcats for their meat, fur, or hides. They favored larger game because it meant more meat for the effort, a buffalo yielding half a ton to a deer's one hundred pounds. Tribesmen dried their meat to preserve it, making pemmican for easy transport. In hard times dogs became the meal, and a few tribes required a young puppy feast as part of their honoring ceremonies. In the Great Basin and other marginal areas, rabbits and other small animals were valued. Along the streams, women gathered black cherries, chokecherries, buffalo berries, gooseberries, strawberries, Juneberries, wolfberries, wild plums, grapes, wild potatoes, turnips, artichokes, and turkey peas. The Sioux ate all birds except eagles and turkeys. Fish were the most important items of diet among Northwest Coast and Plateau tribes, but many of the Plains Indians did not consider them fit to eat. In the Great Basin and California, people ate more wild plants than any other food, but all the Indians in the West made use of varieties from roots and tubers to greens, fruits, seeds, and nuts. One trick was to find a mouse's cache of dried beans. Insects were eaten by some, such as California tribes who ground grasshoppers into flour. Hide scrapings warded off starvation in winter.

BUFFALO

The most important animal to Plains Indians was the American bison or buffalo. Multiplying to perhaps as many as sixty million by the seventeenth century, the big, mobile mammals roamed the Great Plains from the Gulf of Mexico to the Canadian woods and from the Rocky Mountains to the timbered belt along the Mississippi. Some even spread into the Ohio Valley and parts of the Old South. The buffalo dominated tribal life. Plains Indians lived in, walked on, and ate parts of its body. They had ceremonies to attract and honor it.

Though it is common knowledge that the Plains Indians made good use of many parts of the buffalo, probably few of us could have imagined the full extent of the animal's versatility in supplying the Indians' needs. Table 9 reveals an astounding array of uses.

The coming of whites in the nineteenth century spelled the end of the buffalo culture. One of the first recorded kills of a buffalo was that of Joseph Field of the Lewis and Clark expedition, who dispatched his animal near Sioux City, Iowa, on August 23, 1804. The overland migrations of the 1840s and 1850s divided buffalo country into northern and southern segments, and at the mid–nineteenth century George Catlin wrote that the once vast herds were rapidly wasting away, destined in a few years to live only in books or on canvas. His prediction was close to the mark. After 1870 cheap transportation provided by new railroads into Kansas in-

TABLE 9: USES OF THE BUFFALO

Rawhide	*Buckskin*	*Bones*
containers	cradles	fleshing tools
shields	moccasin tops	pipes
buckets	winter robes	knives
moccasin soles	bedding	arrowheads
drums	shirts	shovels
splints	belts	splints
mortars	leggings	sleds
cinches	dresses	saddle trees
ropes	bags	war clubs
sheaths	quivers	scrapers
saddle blankets	tipi covers	quirts
stirrups	bridles	awls
bull boats	backrests	paintbrushes
masks	tapestries	tableware
parfleche	dolls	toys
lariats	mittens	jewelry
Skull	*Blood*	*Hoofs & Dewclaws*
Sun dance	soups	glue
medicine prayers	puddings	
other rituals	paints	
Hair	*Horns*	*Meat*
headdresses	arrow points	immediate use
pad fillers	cups	sausages
pillows	fire carrier	cached meat
ropes	powder horn	jerky
ornaments	spoons	pemmican
hair pieces	ladles	
halters	headdresses	
bracelets	toys	
Muscles	*Fat*	*Tail*
glue preparation	tallow	medicine switch
bows	soaps	fly brush
thread	hair grease	decorations
arrow ties	cosmetic aids	whips
cinches		
Paunch Liner	*Tongue*	*Stomach Liner*
wrappings (meat)	choice meat	water containers
buckets	comb (rough side)	cooking vessels
collapsible cups		

Tendons	*Scrotum*	*Stomach Contents*
sinews—sewing	rattles	medicine
bowstrings	containers	paints
Bladder	*Chips*	*Brains*
pouches	fuel	food
medicine bags	diaper powder	hide preparation
rattles		
Hind Leg Skin	*Teeth*	*Beard*
spoons	ornamentation	ornamentation
preshaped moccasins		
Gall	*Liver*	
yellow paints	tanning agents	

creased the market for hides. Eastern tanners purchased them by the millions, and swarms of eager hunters hunted the plains to fulfill the new demand. By 1879 the buffalo was nearly extinct.

The last great buffalo hunt in the United States took place in June 1882, when a Sioux hunting party of two thousand men, women, and children came to Hiddenwood Creek, near present-day Hettinger, North Dakota, where the last of the northern herd had moved in from Montana and Wyoming. In three days they killed five thousand buffalos. The next year, about twenty miles farther south, another Sioux hunting party killed the final one thousand buffalos in that herd. That left only a few isolated groupings and piles of bones that eventually became fertilizer or ingredients in the making of bone china. By 1889 fewer than 1,100 buffalos remained in the United States and Canada. From 1883 to 1900 ranchers preserved a few buffalos, and the Canadian and American governments initiated conservation measures. In the United States some herds survived in the National Bison Range in western Montana and in Yellowstone National Park.

DANCE AND MUSIC

Dancing and music were an integral part of military, religious, and social activities, whether directed toward communal welfare or individual glory. Dictated by tradition, they were mainly symbolic. Participants sometimes wore costumes or special clothing, and some dances were for one sex only. In the Southwest prairies and woodlands, most group dancers moved in a circle, while participants in the Plains, Great Basin, and Plateau regions preferred straight-line dancing. Pueblo rhythms were slow, almost hypnotic, and those on the Plains sometimes approached frenzy. In general

American Indian dancers lifted the heel and the ball of the foot high, coming down with great force and rapidity. Changes in position were gradual, but shifts in attitude were sometimes quick and violent. Women employed several steps, including the shuffle, the glide, and the hop. Percussion instruments and chanting usually accompanied dancing. Performers did not use harmony in singing or playing. Drums, rasps, rattles, and clappers were common, but the only Indian instrument that could play a melody was the flute, used mostly by young men for playing love songs in courting. Whistles were important in the sun dance.

Perhaps the most famous dance in Plains Indian history was the Ghost Dance, originated by the Paiute Indian Wavoka and spread by the Sioux medicine man Short Bull. Having witnessed the Ghost Dance at Pine Ridge Agency in fall of 1890, Lieutenant Marion P. Maus reported his understanding of it in an article in *Harper's Weekly*:

It seems generally believed that the Indians [after continuing to dance for many months] will all fall into a trance, and when they awake they will find the whites will have been buried, with all their civilization, many feet beneath the surface of the earth, never to rise again, and the Indians, with all the dead restored to life, will remain upon the earth—renewed and made many times more beautiful—alone to enjoy it. No more reservations, no more white men, no more soldiers to disturb them; the prairies will be covered with grass waist-deep; the forest and mountains alike will abound in buffalo, elk, deer, and antelope, more abundant than ever.[2]

Influenced by Christian ideas of the Second Coming, this dance led to army interference and ultimately to the death of Sitting Bull and the tragedy at Wounded Knee on December 29, 1890.

RELIGION

The diversity seen in habitations, principal food sources, languages, and mores also characterized tribal religions.[3] However, some broad generalizations are possible. Certainly, ideas about the supernatural permeated Indian cultures. Nearly all Indians believed in a general power or impersonal force, something similar to electricity, that ran throughout nature and could be utilized with the right knowledge and equipment. This was not the sole god of the whites but rather an indwelling spirit in everything. The Sioux called it Taku Wankan (The Something Mysterious), the Omahas referred to it as Wakonda, and the Hidatsas named it Mahupa. However, when Euro-American contact occurred, many began to adopt the white man's idea of a single, anthropomorphic god, due to the powerful technology of the intruders and their success as worshipers of the deity. For example, in time, the Sioux name for the great power evolved from Taku Wankan to Wakan Tanka (The Great Mysterious Being).

At the same time, most conceived of other supernatural forces of many sorts. There were spirits of fields, trees, lakes, and other aspects of nature, who could withhold favors if the people misbehaved or reward them for patience and perseverance. Some Indians named these spirits, some did not. In any event supplicants were practical, seeking help from all sources to increase possibilities for success. They looked for assistance in everyday doings as well as in life's crises: hunters wanted spiritual aid for success in hunting, warriors for help in war, growers to ensure good harvests. Most often power came through a vision, usually in the form of an animal helper, but sometimes as the sun, stars, or other natural objects. Probably the best-known vision in the Indian wars is that which came to Sitting Bull after he offered one hundred pieces of flesh in a sun dance held nineteen days before the Battle of the Little Bighorn. The Unkpapa leader saw U.S. troops falling into the Indian camp, a portent of a great victory to come. Usually those requesting help made contact with spirits by acts of purification such as bathing, sweating, and fasting. They usually made offerings of tobacco but often sacrificed food, clothing, and adornment of various kinds.

North American Indians perceived a spiritual connection between humans, animals, and other living things. Some mythologies reported that in the beginning all were human, and some later metamorphosed into their present forms. Being a part of the cosmos, they possessed magical powers that could be transferred to humans. To obtain favor, some imitated animals in dress and actions and carried parts of them on their persons as totems. The grizzly bear, the buffalo, and the eagle were especially valued among the Plains Indians.

Some tribesmen asked shamans or priests for help. The former claimed to contact the spiritual world and manipulate the supernatural, while the latter presided over rituals and conducted ceremonies that promised to bring the desired results. Pueblos and Northwest Coast Indians depended on priests, and Plains Indians consulted shamans or medicine men. Army officer John G. Bourke, writing in *The Nation* in 1890, noted that medicine men of American tribes were not the frauds and charlatans that many whites believed. They were repositories of all the lore of their people and very formidable opponents. To counteract their influence Bourke recommended that young Indians then being educated at Carlisle and Hampton should be taught an elementary course in electricity and chemistry and the use of the solar spectrum, the microscope, the telescope, and other instruments. This would give them powerful knowledge of the way in which the world works, rendering them independent of tribal medicine men.

Many tribes held special ceremonies to invoke the aid of the supernatural. Secret societies conducted some, while whole tribes participated in others. Some were held at regularly appointed times, such as the solstice ceremonies of the Hopi, but others convened when an individual wished to fulfill a pledge or undergo rigors for some end. The Navajos and Apaches had extended curing rituals and elaborate public ceremonies to celebrate girls' puberty. Plains tribes had many ceremonies for communal and personal well-being and to honor the way of the hunter. The sun dance was the most spectacular, with about twenty tribes participating, usually during the summer hunt when all the bands had assembled. Its purpose varied from earth renewal to vengeance. Common features were preparation of a special enclosure, raising of a central pole, dancing lasting one to four days, and dramatic climax rites. Dancers often blew whistles, and some practiced voluntary self-laceration.

A reporter for the *Omaha Herald* described the preparations for the sun dance at Spotted Tail's camp in 1878: "The candidate for honors cuts two longitudinal slits down each breast. One end of a lariat is passed under the strip between the incisions and tightly tied and the other end is made fast to the top of a high pole. The candidate then throws himself backward with his weight upon the lariat, and the dance goes on until the flesh gives way. Should he fail to break loose in the manner prescribed, or should he faint during the operation he is forever disgraced."[4]

Some men were hoisted twenty feet in the air to hang until their weight caused them to rip free. Lurid accounts of the self-torture led to the prohibition of the sun dance on the reservations in 1883, but some tribes continued the practice in secret.

Some tribes had objects that had great spiritual significance. Among the Sioux it was the Sacred Calf Pipe, brought by White Buffalo Woman as a direct link to the Buffalo People. The Cheyennes had the Sacred Arrows and the Sacred Hat, which in dangerous times accompanied them into battle. The Pawnees had a sacred bundle that contained two ears of corn and was renewed annually. In early times the Skidi Pawnee sacrificed a maiden to the Morning Star to guarantee a bountiful corn crop and success in the bison hunt.

Although Indian religious practices might have appeared strange to Euro-Americans, tribesmen found white beliefs hopelessly confused. Take the example of the Brulé chief Spotted Tail, whose musings appeared in the *Army and Navy Journal* in 1878:

Some years ago a good man, as I think, came to us. He talked me out of all my old beliefs, and after a while, thinking that he must know more of these matters than an ignorant Indian, I became a Methodist. Not long after he went way and another man came and talked, and I became a Baptist; then another came and talked and I became a Catholic; then another and I became a Presbyterian, and now another has come and wants me to become an Episcopalian. . . . All these people tell me different stories, and each wants me to believe that his special way is the only way to be good. I always believed in the Great Spirit and talked to him in my own way. These people don't want me to change my belief in the Great Spirit, but to change my way of talking to him. White men have education and books and ought to know exactly what to believe and what to say, but hardly any two of them agree on anything. I have about made up my mind either that they all lie, or that they don't know anything more about religion than I did before they came to me.[5]

Chief Joseph, on the other hand, was quite clear in his mind about the white man's religion. When asked if he wanted schools among his people, prior to the Nez Percé Indian War, he said no. When asked why, he replied. "It would bring the churches." When asked to explain, he exclaimed, "No! no! It will teach us to quarrel about God, as the Catholics and Protestants do. We fight each other, but we don't want to learn to fight about God."[6]

DEATH AND MOURNING

Agricultural and hunting tribes often had different conceptions of the afterlife. Those who were hunters usually imagined a happy land following death, one plentiful in game. Colonel Henry Carrington interviewed one of Red Cloud's followers in 1866 concerning the afterlife and reported that it was a physical paradise where every desire was promptly met. "If a man wants food," he stated, "it is at hand; water springs up for ready use; ponies and game abound; blossoms, leaves, and fruit never fail; all is perennial and perpetual."[7] There were exceptions, however. Among the Plains tribes the Blackfeet and the Gros Ventres held a melancholy view of a future state. All was unreality. They were doomed to hunt shadow buffalos with arrows that turned to blades of grass and to see their animal traps vanish upon their approach. Agricultural groups tended to believe in a subterranean realm of the dead, where Mother Earth regenerated life, a quiet and rather gloomy netherworld.

The practice of mutilation by some tribes had a relation to life in the hereafter. Henry Carrington stated that cutting arm, calf, and thigh muscles and other maiming performed by the Sioux and Northern Cheyennes following the Fetterman fight were for the purposes of disabling their enemies for eternity. According to Carrington, persons so mutilated were supposed to have lost the power of walking, running, climbing, and using weapons in the spirit-land. Thus, while the pious roamed the happy hunting grounds of paradise with no desire ungratified, bad Indians and the red man's foe suffered ceaseless unfulfilled longings. Carrington also reported that the Plains Indians feared hanging, for a warrior dispatched in this manner could never put his feet down and could only hover, not partaking of eternal rewards. Some also believed that those who suffered mutilation were destined to wander forever as ghosts and werewolves.

Tribes had different ways of treating the death of a loved one. Following the death of a Sioux family member, survivors allowed friends, relatives, and others to take their best things. Grievers dressed in ragged clothes and rubbed their faces and bodies with dirt. Women usually cut themselves with knives. Relatives clothed the body of the deceased elaborately, wrapping it in the best blankets and cloth. They usually placed the corpse on a scaffold inside a lodge, in the open, or on a platform in a tree. Elevating the body protected it from scavengers and carnivores. The exception was when a warrior had been killed in battle. Then it was customary to place the body against a tree or rock in a sitting position, always facing the enemy, to indicate his courage even in death. The mourning period lasted for twelve months, and years later relatives gathered the bones for burial underground or placement in rock crevices. Among others who practiced aerial sepulture were the Chippewas, Mandans, Gros Ventres, and Arapahos. The Plains Cree interred their dead at a depth of about five feet when the ground was not frozen, and otherwise they utilized the scaffold. Tribes on the Pacific slope preferred cremation. Northwest Coast Indians often placed their dead in little cabin-shaped mortuary boxes before placing them on raised posts, in trees, or in caves. Occasionally, Northwest Coast Indians put bodies in canoes, supporting them on posts or lodging them in the forks of trees.

The Army

THE LAND

Those who came west to serve in the frontier army often commented on its vastness and speculated on its meaning.[8] Such a man was G. M. Jones of Company B, Nineteenth Kansas Cavalry, who reached the plains in 1868. Fifty years later the memory haunted him. "Who can forget the impression made on the mind by that vast wild country?" he wrote. "I was born in February, 1850, and to my inexperienced boy mind, it seemed that when the Great Creator finished up the world, he had left on hand a vast lot of raw material, and no other place to put it, so spread out and dried it and made that vast region reaching to and including the Great Divide. Considering its wild and almost untamable nature, what else could it produce other than the unthinkable red skins that we were chasing."[9]

First, newcomers had to adjust to extremes of heat and cold. In August 1866, a soldier stationed at Fort Wallace, Kansas, conducted some experiments concerning the heat. At seven in the morning his thermometer, hanging inside a frame building, showed 98 degrees Fahrenheit. At 2 PM, he put the glass in the sun on the south side of the structure, and in fifteen minutes it registered 125 degrees. Notwithstanding, the men of his company worked steadily laying stone. One Arizona soldier wrote about the effects of 114 degree heat at Fort Mojave: "Yesterday I experimented with two fresh laid eggs. One was exposed to the sun all day and when broken showed a trifle of the white cooked. The other was broken in a saucer at noon and exposed to the sun for six hours. The white lost all its water and the yoke nearly all, but it dried out rather than cooked. . . . Iron rods exposed to sun will blister the hand. Water from the pipes that are just below surface of parade ground will scald delicate skin."[10]

Temperatures recorded at Fort McDowell, Arizona Territory, from June 16 to August 7, 1884, showed only one day below 100 degrees Fahrenheit, with the highest reading at 116 degrees. More than one soldier agreed that Fort Yuma, Arizona, was the hottest post in the West. In his book, *Adventures in Apache Country*, published in 1869, humorist J. Ross Brown described the results of a summer's heat: "Everything dries; wagons dry; men dry; chickens dry; there is not juice left in any thing, living or dead, by the close of summer. Officers and soldiers are supposed to walk about creaking; mules, it is said, can only bay at midnight; and I have heard it hinted that the carcasses of cattle rattle inside their hides, and that snakes find a difficulty in bending their bodies, and horned frogs die of apoplexy.

Chickens hatched at this season, as old Fort Yumers say, come out of the shell ready cooked and bacon is eaten with a spoon."[11]

On the other hand, the soldier serving in the American West had to be prepared for the other extreme as well. For example, at Fort Sanders, Wyoming Territory, the temperatures from December 27, 1881, to January 1 were as follows: December 27, plus thirty-five degrees Fahrenheit; December 28, minus fifteen degrees; December 29, minus forty-five degrees; December 30, minus thirty-eight degrees; December 31, minus twenty-five degrees; and January 1, plus fifteen degrees.

And on the plains there always seemed to be the wind. One soldier with imagination and a classical education described it thus: "The demon Aeolus, with his legions of howling devils, rushes in . . . [and] shrieks, wailing, roars, terrible imprecations fill the air, with a running accompaniment of rattling shingles, banging shutters, slamming gates and the 'devil tattoo' of sand which drives against the window panes that stand between the crouching inmates and Pandemonium without."[12] And sometimes it was hail. The *Army and Navy Register* reported in 1888 that a hail storm near Fort Custer, Montana, had been severe enough to knock a soldier who was herding government stock off his horse, kill a large number of calves and colts, and literally beat to death an old Indian woman who had been caught while out gathering wood.

If the climate were not bad enough, there were creatures, mosquitoes in particular, that could make life miserable for the initiate. According to a Texas soldier, they were so large as to be frequently mistaken for curlews. One Wyoming victim referred to them as "Platte Valley birds."[13] "Bars are no protection," another soldier declared, "as they easily tear them, or lift up the edge and come under."[14]

Another more dangerous discomfort was the rattlesnake. Lieutenant William Bisbee found them plentiful on his way to Fort Phil Kearny in July 1866, reporting that "killing the reptiles with whips and revolvers was one of our daily amusements."[15] In *Following the Guidon*, her reminiscence of army life in the American West in the 1870s, Elizabeth Custer commented that when she accompanied her husband on a camping trip, "They were everywhere. It was impossible," she said, "to exaggerate the numbers of them that surrounded us. . . . The snakes swarmed over the route or march. They lined the way when we went for a hunt or a pleasant ride."[16] One afternoon in 1879, soldiers at Fort Fred Steele, Wyoming Territory, killed seventy-three rattlesnakes a short distance from the post. Even more upsetting was the tendency of the serpents to seek shelter in human habitations. A soldier from Fort Harker, Kansas, told of killing three rattlesnakes found warming themselves by the fire in his log and sod cabin in February 1867. A soldier who served in the Apache campaigns in 1885 noted the rattlers in Arizona often crawled under the men's coats at night.

With the difficulties of climate, the presence of pests, scorpions, and venomous serpents, and the possibility of engaging in battle with skilled and ferocious opponents, no newly inducted soldier was enthusiastic about his assignment, and many were apprehensive. Veterans made the most of this and offered a great deal of advice, some of it spurious, some of it useful. Here is an example of both that appeared in the *Army and Navy Journal* in 1869, authored by "CIAUS," under the headline "Good Advice for a Soldier Going to Fort Riley, Kansas":

Altogether we have to advise each of the fellows who are to come here this fall, to do as follows:

1st. Make your will.

2d. Get your life insured. We could recommend a certain company on Broadway, but then people might think this was an advertisement.

3d. Bring enough money to pay your own funeral expenses.

4th. Have a first-class obituary of yourself prepared for insert in the [*Army and Navy*] *Journal,* by some New York Bohemian, for people out here haven't the time or the genius to write them.

5th. Don't ever expect to return, but say your adieus as you would if you had been selected for a "forlorn hope."

6th. Get your regimental adjutant to intercede to prevent you [from] being sent here. Argue that these fellows can't be expected to have any desire for a return to society. They (we) might as well stay because they (we) are used to it.

You will find this arrangement will work beautifully, it being already in practice in about four artillery regiments.[17]

SHELTER

The first order of business was to build forts on the frontier, where men and horses might be protected, supplies stockpiled, and soldiers trained. In the beginning, men camped in tents. The common A-tent was in use for many years. It had no ventilation except from the front door. The wall-tent used by officers was more roomy and less uncomfortable. In summer its occupants could raise its walls for air and in winter use a small stove for heating, after cutting a ceiling hole for the stove pipe. The Indian tipi suggested the arrangement of the Sibley tent, which had a single pole in the center, standing on a tripod. Beneath it a small stove was placed, with a pipe leading up to the opening in the top. Men learned to pile up snow on the sides of the tent as insulation to survive in winter.

Early forts might not have been that accommodating. For example, the initial barracks at Fort Dodge, Kansas, in December 1865 consisted of holes in the ground on the banks of the Arkansas River. About four feet above the high-water mark, they were about six feet in length, eight feet wide, and three feet high. Men cut bunks or beds out of the dirt on each side. The distance between bunks was about two feet. The men roofed their beds on a level with the top of the ground with brush, gunny sacks, and dirt.

When finally built, forts followed a pattern. The center of the typical post was the parade ground, a quadrangle with a row of officers' quarters on one side and some barracks on the other. Behind were kitchens and behind them latrines. In front of the guardhouse were the flagstaff and an obsolete saluting gun. In the area was the headquarters building and nearby, usually away from the quadrangle, were quartermaster and ordnance storerooms. Beyond them were the stables and quartermaster corral. Usually somewhat apart from other structures was a row of noncommissioned officers' quarters, known as "suds row," because many wives served as laundresses.

A sutler's store, which developed into the official canteen, later PX, sold goods to all who had the money. The sutler usually had rooms for an officers' club and enlisted men's bar. Completing the scene were a hospital and dispensary and perhaps a chapel. In the barracks men slept in iron bunks and kept their belongings in footlockers. Officers often lived in duplexes. Housing being chosen by rank, the arrival of an important newcomer might mean a shift all the way around. Officers' wives usually brought furniture with them, supplementing it with packing boxes covered with cloth or less-than-finished furniture made by company carpenters. A short distance from the post was the cemetery. The remains of men who died in the service were to receive perpetual care, so when posts were abandoned, the army moved the remains to active posts or national cemeteries.

Some of the living quarters at the early posts were quite primitive. An anonymous officer at Fort Harker, Kansas, left us with an especially descriptive account of how it was to live in a house with a mud roof:

Our own dwelling, twelve feet square, is made of rough logs, so upright and plastered with mud; the roof is a heterogeneous mass of mud, sticks, straw and boughs. The former, owing to its profound respect for the law of gravitation, would persist, at first, in falling in clods at all hours. It dropped upon our plates at dinner and into our mouth in dreams, till finally, a bright idea striking us, we stretched a piece of tent cloth above our bed and defied the mud. It snowed the night of our experiment, and a bushel or so of snow sifted into the tent cloth. Toward morning came thaw. We were dreaming ourselves a victim of the Spanish Inquisition, and they were trying on us the torture of the shaven head and ice-cold drops of water. Just as we were about to renounce Protestantism in toto, we were awakened to a sense of the reality. The water was dripping from our cotton roof in quarts, and as we wrung ourselves out, a few clods of mud fell with a loud thump, in the opposite corner, as if to remind us that in an un-civilized country man can never war successfully with the elements.[18]

ENLISTED MEN

Those who served in the frontier army were not greatly admired by the gen-eral populace. In 1874 a Chicago newspaperman wrote that the majority of enlisted men in the army were simply human driftwood, men who had fled from the law to enter the service under assumed names. Disappointed, dis-heartened, and ambitionless, they had found relief in the lazy life of the sol-dier. As with most comments concerning the men of the regular army, there was a bit of truth in the criticism. Some were loafers and men with a past, but others were immigrants and boys from the town or farm out for adventure and to improve their lot. Half the men in the army recruited from 1865 to 1874 were foreign-born. Nearly twenty percent were Irish and twelve percent German. According to one of their own, John Burkman, a German transplant who enlisted in the Seventh Cavalry in 1870, they were "Jist privates . . . jist rough, strong young fellows ready to march all day, tired, hungry, thirsty, to go here, go thar, without understandin' why or nothin' except to shoot and shoot to kill. And yet to ourselves we seemed important."[19] African Ameri-cans also found continuous and honorable employment in the army at a time when there were few opportunities elsewhere. The so-called buffalo soldiers that made up the Ninth and Tenth Cavalry and the Twenty-fourth and Twenty-fifth Infantry served with distinction.

For a short period during the Civil War, enlisted ranks included former Confederate prisoners, called "galvanized Yankees." Confederates who wished to leave confinement had four choices: They could ask to be ex-changed, wait to be paroled, go north to work on government fortifica-tions, or enlist. Contrary to popular belief, if they chose the soldier life there was no assurance that they would not be sent to engage in battle with

TABLE 10: A PRIVATE'S EXPENSES, 1871

For retained pay	$1.00
For Soldiers' Home	.125
For blacking, two boxes at 15 cents	.30
For "cleaning stuff," such as tripoli	1.00
For soap for personal	.25
For towels, four per year at 30 cents, per month	.10
For laundress	1.50
For shaving and hair cutting	.75
For blacking, clothes, brass, and brushes (wear and tear per month)	.50
For regulation cap, two per year at $3 per month	.50
For altering two suits of clothing per year at $5.50 per year	.90
For altering three pairs of boots per year at 75 cents, per month	.18
For stockings, one pair per month	.30
For handkerchiefs, six per year at 50 cents per month	.25
For gloves (white), two pairs per month at 30 cents	.60
For gauntlets, two pairs per year at $2 per month	.35
For tobacco, one pound	.70
For paper, envelopes, and postage stamps	.40
TOTAL	$9.70

their former comrades. Many chose this avenue of escape from prison, and the army ultimately created six regiments of these troops, with Union officers in command.

To join the army, an applicant had to meet some minimum requirements. In 1864 an enlistee had to be eighteen to thirty-five years of age, at least five feet three inches in height, able-bodied, sober, free from diseases, of good character and habits, and possess a competent knowledge of English. In 1873 the standard height for cavalry was not less than five feet five nor more than five feet ten.

In the 1850s army pay for enlisted men varied from 5 to 10 dollars per month. In 1861 the amount rose to 11. During and after the Civil War the rate of pay was 16 dollars per month, but from 1871 to 1891, compensation was set at 13 dollars for thirty days' service. In 1877 General Sherman noted that the clerks who worked for the army were all enlisted men and could earn between 100 and 175 dollars for the same job in civilian life. From this pay the enlisted man had many items to purchase and such other expenses as alterations to his uniform and a contribution to the Soldiers' Home, where veterans might receive nursing care. At a time when Congress was considering reducing the pay to 11 dollars, the *Army and Navy Journal*, in an article written by G. V. W. of Harrisburg, Pennsylvania, printed a breakdown of the typical private's expenses (see table 10).

The author of the tabulation noted that the figures did not take into account the inflated prices charged at many points on the frontier, which sometimes doubled the amounts shown.

The commanding officer of the garrison determined the work order, which he published in general orders. Here is a typical schedule for a post in the mid-1870s, based on records at Fort Abraham Lincoln:

5:45 (AM)	Assembly for buglers
6:00	Reveille and roll call
6:30	Breakfast
7:30	Fatigue call
8:00	Sick call
8:55	Assembly of buglers
9:00	Recall for fatigue details
10:00	Drill
11:00	Recall from drill for infantry and artillery
11:30	Recall from drill for cavalry
11:45	First sergeant's call for morning reports
12:00 (PM)	Lunch. Recall from fatigue on days when no drills are held
1:00	Drill for target practice (Monday, Wednesday, and Friday)
2:00	Fatigue call (except Friday and Saturday when troops cleaned the barracks and other facilities in preparation for weekly Sunday inspection)
4:15	Recall from fatigue duty
4:30	Stable call (care for horses). No evening mess call, except by gongs or triangles.

Five minutes before sundown:

	Assembly of entire garrison in dress uniform for retreat and roll call
8:55	Assembly for buglers call
9:00	Last call (for soldiers in company formations in front of quarters)
9:30	Lights out

As a general thing, soldiers wore their fatigue uniforms and worked at almost anything except soldiering. They built quarters, made roads, cut wood, herded cattle, and cleared the land. Fort Robinson, Nebraska, was an example of a military post built solely by soldier labor. According to one officer, the only expenses to the government were incurred in purchasing the nails, strap-hinges, window sashes, and glass. One observer characterized the soldier in 1867 as a woodchopper, baker, mason, carpenter, brickmaker, artisan, wheelwright, and journeyman laborer. Not surprisingly, officers and men complained that they were not doing the things that they had enlisted to do. As one disillusioned soldier said, "Making dirt shovelers of soldiers may make them a source of profit in time of peace, but it is equally sure to make them worthless in time of war."[20]

OFFICERS

Officers on the frontier had to travel light, prepared to move to the next assignment. In 1868 a veteran offered good advice to those going west. He recommended that each should bring with him a good mess chest well furnished for four or six persons, a good roll of bedding, a mattress, a few comfortable camp chairs, and a trunk filled with a good supply of clothes for at least one year. Before leaving he should give his measurements to a good tailor and boot maker so that he could replenish his wardrobe by order at any time. Also recommended were a table spread or two, a few curtains, some cloth suitable for covering furniture, and a roll of carpeting. In conclusion, he stated that an officer would never regret bringing any small articles of luxury that his taste suggested, for he would find very little difficulty in taking them with him from station to station. At the post other furniture could be improvised, such as a gun box for a settee, a cracker box for a washstand, a pine bunk for a bedstead, and blankets for curtains.

Officers' pay did not permit a luxurious lifestyle. According to one officer, "As the pay is so little, and the chance for distinction so slight, the only thing that tempts an American gentleman into the Army is a love for the profession of arms strong enough to induce him to forego all hope of worldly prosperity."[21] Another drawback was the lack of opportunities for promotion, especially in the post–Civil War army. In 1883 a first lieutenant of artillery prepared a chart projecting a dismal future for officers in his branch of the service. Generally, officers entering in 1861 became captains in 1871 after ten years of service. Those entering in 1864 had to wait nineteen years, while those who received commissions in 1867 averaged twenty-eight years, and the unfortunate officer who became a lieutenant in

1870 could expect to wait thirty-two years before becoming a captain. Nor were chances for promotion better in the infantry and cavalry.

Officers, too, received their share of criticism from the civilian sector. In 1878 a Massachusetts congressman opined on the floor of the House that officers spent their time in putting two lumps of sugar on a table and betting drinks as to which lump a fly would first land on. To which an artillery officer responded in the *Army and Navy Journal* of August 31, 1878, "Let some member of Congress swap places with some one of the Army officers for a while, and he will find out that it is easier to make eloquent speeches to languishing brunettes than it is to listen to the midnight howling of hungry coyotes."[22]

ARMY LIFE IN GENERAL

There were times when food was bad, and there was little of it. One soldier who served at Fort Shaw, Montana, in the 1870s remembered that when his comrades came in exhausted and hungry from their incessant labor, they began crying from sheer rage at the poor quality of the food set before them. Their provisions, he declared, "consisted of condemned stores left over from the late unpleasantness and we didn't receive half enough to eat of what their [sic] was."[23] One officer noted that it did not take much to make an aristocrat in the frontier army. A man might put on airs if he was the fortunate possessor of a cabbage or a mess of potatoes, while others were without these toothsome comestibles.

Soldiers often supplemented their rations with wild game and fish. For example in 1885, Fort Laramie soldiers caught 150 large fish with a net in the Laramie River. And when times were hard, they ate practically anything, including prairie dog. A little poem entitled "Epitaph of a Soldier," appearing in the army newspaper *The Frontier Scout*, advised against such a diet. It read:

Here lieth a soldier that vanished in fog;
By eating too much of a prairie dog;
He swallowed all but intestines and hair—
Of the course of this mortal, oh, reader, beware.
He griddled him quickly upon the coals,
As ancient did martyrs, alas poor souls;
Then ate him, the blood running out of his mouth,
This gallant and chivalrous son of the South.
Oh, sad it will be when the nights are so dark,
To hear round his sepulcher prairie dogs bark.

Bewailing their friends he voraciously swallowed,
And who into death he so speedily followed.[24]

The real problem with the army diet was the lack of fresh fruits and vegetables during winter months, which meant scurvy. As a substitute, the government issued what was termed "desiccated" vegetables—onions, cabbage, beets, turnips, and green peppers that had been steamed, pressed, and dried. They were made into cakes twelve inches square and one inch thick and packed in foot-square sealed cans. So finely compacted, they weighed as much as wood. Used mostly for soups, the vegetable cakes were very convenient for soldiers on a scout, because they were easily carried in saddlebags. In the absence of vegetables, medical staff had to improvise when scurvy broke out. The post surgeon at Fort Sedgwick, Colorado, had the men gather a bushel of prickly pear cactus. After removing the bristles, they made the cactus into a sort of applesauce that provided the necessary vitamin c to cure them. Food on campaign was skimpier. One veteran described his rations in the field in Texas as sow belly, beans, and black coffee boiled in stagnant water, scented with dead buffalo, and cooked on fire made with buffalo chips.

On the other hand, life was sometimes good. In 1928 General Hugh Lenox Scott reminisced about his days at Fort Totten, North Dakota, in 1878–1879 where soldiers raised wonderful crops of potatoes, cabbages, tomatoes, carrots, beets, and onions. They traded them for loads of Red River catfish and pike. During the summer Sioux women brought in wild raspberries and gave them half an oilcanful for twenty-five cents. This enabled Scott to live better and cheaper than he had lived anywhere since.

HEALTH

One of the dangers of serving on the frontier was death from disease. Circular No. 8 of the Surgeon General's office in 1875 reported that the death rate in the army was more than twice that among citizens of the territories of about the same age living under nearly the same conditions. The average death rate from disease for men in the army was twelve and three-eighths per thousand compared to that of five and three-fifths per thousand civilians.

Periodicals of the period often contain laments for the deaths of friends and loved ones. An example is found in the *Army and Navy Journal* on February 29, 1868, telling of tragedy at a post in Colorado:

We of the frontier had, during the Summer our dark days. That scourge of Yellow Jack, the cholera, gave the post a visit and laid low not only some of our most respected officer friends but also some of the purest and best of those sharers of our joys and sorrows. Long will the lamented McGill and his lovely wife be remembered— buried in their lonely graves by the Arkansas; also the genial-hearted Helm, in his resting place at Zarah; Mrs. Douglas, at Dodge; Mrs. Sternborg, at Harker, and others, who cheering the life of the garrison by their presence, died deeply and widely lamented. God keep both you and us, my friends, from another such season.[25]

Nor was death often dignified. Frontier conditions sometimes prevented proper interment. Such was the case of soldiers on patrol near Wilson, Kansas, in 1867. When thirteen men died of cholera, their comrades placed them in ponchos and blankets. Burial was short and quick. "We just dug holes and buried them," wrote an attending private, "as we didn't have any coffins and no doctors."[26] Some complained of the treatment of sickness. Former soldier Alex Dahlgren declared, "Hospital facilities were primitive but then sickness was a thing of taboo and our Army Surgeon diagnosed anything that didn't call for the knife or saw as malingering."[27] And there was always the chance of violent death in a land far from home. General Sherman in his annual report for 1877 stated that during the past two years the ratio of officers and men killed in the Indian wars in proportion to the number engaged had been equal to or greater than the ratio of loss on either side in the Civil War or in the current Russian-Turkish campaign.

It is not surprising because of life on the frontier that many did not reenlist for further duty. One ex-soldier described the enlisted man's life as a "hang-dog, demoralizing life, unfitting a man for any respectable civil position, destroying all self-respect, sinking all that makes a man a man."[28] Many felt like Private Charles Lester of Company H, Fourth Infantry, who wrote his sister in April 1867, "I have sixteen months to serve yet and when it is up they can go to the devil; they wont get this chile again."[29] Many in fact did not wait until their term of enlistment had ended, instead they gave the army "the grand bounce," deserting in droves. Of the 255,712 men who enlisted between 1867 and 1891, 88,475 deserted.

However, it is not well known that many of them found life no better on the outside and enlisted again, this time under an assumed named. One man made this a way of life. Paul A. Kirshner enlisted July 3, 1883, in Company C, Tenth Infantry and deserted May 6, 1884. On July 1, 1884, he enlisted as Robert Louis Hoffman, Company C, Fifth Infantry, deserting October 15, 1884. His next enlistment was on November 25, 1884, as Paul G.

Wagner, Battery I, Second Artillery, deserting on January 27, 1885. He enlisted on February 10, 1865, as Henry H. Hansen, in Mounted Service, deserting March 8, 1885. His final enlistment was on May 23, 1885, as Robert L. Ross, in General Service. He deserted and was apprehended at David's Island, New York Harbor, on June 1, 1885, and received a ten-year prison sentence. When coupled with death and discharge, desertion raised the annual turnover rate from twenty-five to forty percent.

Contributing to the rate of desertion and the failure of many to reenlist was the military system of punishment. Basic to army law were the Articles of War, a lengthy list of permissions and prohibitions with which each man had to become familiar before taking his final oath of allegiance. To etch them in the collective memory, the army required that they be read and published for each company every six months. Another source of law was the post regulation. A commanding officer might declare some "hog ranch" or Indian camp off-limits or limit the amount of liquor enlisted men could purchase from the sutler. Those who ignored post regulations usually found themselves in the guardhouse. Post records show that the most common crimes were losing or selling government property, absence from drill or without leave, using abusive language, stealing, brawling, neglect of duty, being drunk while on duty, and, of course, desertion. Punishments for these crimes were often severe. According to the offense, legal punishments were imprisonment, confinement on bread and water, solitary confinement, hard labor, the wearing of ball and chain, forfeiture of pay and allowances, discharge from the service, reprimands, and, in the case of noncommissioned officers, reduction to the ranks. Before the Civil War, deserters might be flogged or branded, and between 1865 and 1870 tattooing was a legal punishment.

WOMEN OF THE POST

Women living at frontier army posts fell into six categories: the wives and daughters of officers, the wives and daughters of enlisted men, the wives and daughters of civilian employees, the female servants of officers' families, company laundresses, and hospital matrons. Of all these women only laundresses and hospital matrons had legal status. The rest were defined as "camp followers" and subject to the supervision of the post commander.

Officers and their wives had the best housing available at the post, starting with commanding officer and descending in order to the lowest junior lieutenant. Most officers employed cooks and maids, sometimes brought with them from the East and sometimes detailed from the enlisted ranks.

Their comrades called the latter "strikers" or "dog robbers." Because of the help with domestic duties, officers' wives occupied much of their time with reading, needlework, and social activities. Many of them kept diaries, and it is their writings that record what life was like at a frontier military post. Some of them, such as Margaret Carrington and Elizabeth Custer, were wonderful chroniclers whose work is still read and admired. Known as K.O.W. (a correct abbreviation being unthinkable), the commanding officer's wife set the tone and organized theatricals, teas, and dances. One who had little time or affection for those who topped the military caste system was cashiered officer Duane Merritt Greene, who in 1880 authored a venomous little book, *Ladies and Officers of the United States Army, or American Aristocracy: A Sketch of the Social Life and Character of the Army*. He is highly critical of the way these women exerted their power, noting that the selections of officers for important courts-martial were often arranged by wives who wanted to see one another.

In any event these women learned to be self-sufficient and suffered many hardships. According to one source, the answer to the question "Where is your home?" brought the response, "With my husband." As Frances Carrington observed, what "could not be done," had no place in the Army Code.[30]

The American army inherited the institution of laundresses from the British. An act of March 12, 1802, allowed women to accompany the troops in the capacity of washerwomen in the ratio of four women to each one hundred men. Over the years the proportion changed to one laundress for every nineteen and one-half men. It was a captain's privilege to appoint the laundresses, just as it was his right to pick the first sergeant. Subject to military law, laundresses received quarters, fuel, and the services of the post surgeon. Their pay was set by the post Council of Administration. At Fort Laramie in 1867 officers paid four dollars per month and enlisted men one dollar. In the early days the army ration included a portion of whiskey, and some laundresses became addicted. Along with women servants, single laundresses were popular at dances, theatricals, and other performances given by the men, and many of these women soon found a matrimonial partner. Housing for married laundresses was known as "Soapsuds Row."

Conflicting views of laundresses come down to us from the past. Some saw them as an unrefined and bickering lot, sometimes derelict in their duty and often morally deficient, living together in squalid quarters among too many of children of dubious parentage and often becoming embroiled in fights that ended only when the officer of the day intervened. One anonymous writer to the *Army and Navy Journal* put his views in verse:

And yet methinks where fight is,
Twere better be at forts;
And not at Laundress Row, where fights
Oft end in law and courts.[31]

A more generous characterization was that penned by General George Forsyth who wrote: "They were good, honest, industrious wives, usually well on in years, minutely familiar with their rights . . . which they dared to maintain with acrimonious volubility, as they became martially inclined, and they were ever ready for a fight, yet they were kind at heart if rough in manner, always ready to assist in times of distress."[32] Though all the women at the post understood the military caste system and did not fraternize between strata, they were unusually close. Laundresses often acted as midwives and nurses for each other and officers' wives, and the latter often went to them for advice in the handling of husbands and children. In 1878, after several attempts by the army, Congress agreed to end the enrollment of company laundresses, but a proviso permitted previously employed women to continue.

CIVILIANS

The sutler's store was the center of social and economic activity at the frontier military post, and the man who ran it was usually educated, well-mannered, and skilled in business, often a friend of generals and politicians, unmistakably powerful, and occasionally corrupt. In the beginning, sutlers were camp followers who provided services to armies in the field, but a few isolated posts such as Fort Laramie had one in residence. Sutling reached its peak during the Civil War, but abuses by those attached to regiments caused the army to abolish the sinecure on July 28, 1866. In July 1867, however, pressure by those serving on the frontier resulted in creation of a similar position, called post trader, to serve garrisons west of the 100th meridian. Extended to all installations in 1870, the post tradership became an extremely lucrative business, reaping fortunes for many in the next decade.

In addition to a monopoly to sell to troops on the military reservation, these entrepreneurs sold to Indians, transients, emigrants, and settlers; held contracts for wood and hay; raised cattle and horses; provided credit and banking services; and secured additional government jobs through appointment or election, such as postmaster or county commissioner. The 1880s saw the decline of business. Success or failure depended on the ability to sell alcoholic beverages to the troops, and when a presidential order prohibited the sale of hard liquor in 1881, income dropped. This was followed by a ruling that the post trader could not also hold a license to trade with the Indians. At the same time, the post canteen (later called the PX) came into existence, offering stiff competition in isolated areas. Run by noncommissioned officers, these alternative places of entertainment offered goods for sale at cost, gymnastic exercise, billiards, and other games. By October 7, 1890, sixty-eight canteens had been established.

In the end the post trader found himself only one of many businessmen who could provide goods and services to American soldiers. The urbanization of the West finally made the trader's presence at military posts unnecessary, a fact announced by a U.S. Army spokesperson in 1893 following a five-year study. Once it started, the demise progressed rapidly. On March 4, 1889, there were eighty-five post traders; by the fall of 1892 only fifteen remained.

In comparing the lives of Indians and soldiers in the nineteenth century, several generalizations emerge. The Indian lived off the land, using that which was available, and the soldier had to bring his supplies and equipment with him; consequently, while the first was generally self-sufficient and mobile, the latter was dependent and plodding. The Indian had buffalo in many places, the soldier only his supply wagon. The Indian learned wilderness skills from childhood, the soldier, especially in the later years, probably after enlistment. Because he knew the land, the Indian made the best use of terrain in war. In the long run the soldier withstood winters better, finding shelter in the garrisons, where the food might not be especially good or healthful but was usually available in sufficient quantity to see most of the men through. And if soldiers had women and children with them, they were protected in the forts.

6. The Indian Wars in Literature and the Arts

Early Literature

Over the years the Indian wars have been the subject of novels, poems, paintings, films, and other creative works. They have greatly influenced the way that Americans perceive the Indian wars, Native Americans, the frontier army, and leaders on both sides.

POETS

Poets played a part in shaping Euro-American views. Alexander Pope (1688–1744), the English poet and essayist, authored a couplet that gave the Indian a new epithet. Using poetic conceit he wrote in "Essay on Man" (1773–1774), "Lo! the poor Indian, whose untutor'd mind, sees God in clouds, or hears Him in the wind." Soon frontiersmen, in derision, began calling their antagonist, "Lo, the Poor Indian," or "Poor Lo." In 1855 the American poet Henry Wadsworth Longfellow (1807–1882) wrote the epic poem "Hiawatha," also much parodied, that described the life of an Ojibway warrior who acquired wisdom in many adventures; performed many deeds against his father, West Wind, to avenge his mother; and became the leader of his people. Both works presented the idea that other simpler cultures were more fulfilling, virtuous, and happier than contemporary society. European intellectuals, following the lead of Jean Jacque Rousseau (1712–1778), saw the Indian more favorably: perfect in bodily form, brave, honorable, fair, and dignified. Frontiersmen often took the opposite view, hence the ridicule.

NOVELISTS

The most influential novelist of the nineteenth century to write about Native Americans was James Fenimore Cooper (1789–1851). Throughout the writings of officers, their wives, and contemporary journalists, we read of "Cooper Indians." In his book, *My Life on the Plains*, published in

1874, George Armstrong Custer wrote that much of the criticism he had received following the Battle of the Washita had come from people whose ideas about Indians were of a sentimental order. He blamed romantic novelists in particular for filling the popular mind with false and ill-judged notions of Indian character and named James Fenimore Cooper as the worst offender. Cooper's most famous novels in which Indians are portrayed have been given the general title of "The Leatherstocking Tales" and feature that indomitable trapper, hunter, and scout, Natty Bumpo, who is variously called La Longue Carbine, Hawkeye, the Pathfinder, the Deerslayer, and Leatherstocking. In four of the novels Bumpo is accompanied by his Delaware friend, Chingachgook, and in one of the books he has a second companion, Uncas, the son of his Indian associate. Included in the series are *The Pioneers* (1826), *The Last of the Mohicans* (1827), *The Prairie* (1827), *The Pathfinder* (1840), and *The Deerslayer* (1841).

For artistic purposes, Cooper divided his Indians into two categories: those that were good, and those that were bad. Of the four Indian nations treated in the five novels, two of them, the Iroquois and the Sioux, are evil. At various times Bumpo calls them miscreants, liars, vagabonds, varlets, knaves, devils, furies, rascals, snakes, cheats, beasts, and thorough savages, and characterizes them as perverse, wicked, crafty, ruthless, treacherous, thievish, deceitful, and greedy. Conversely, the Delawares and the Pawnees possess only virtue. In *The Pathfinder* Bumpo declares, "If you crave to see a truly honest man, you must go among the Delawares to discover him," and in *The Prairie* he calls the Pawnees "a valiant and honest tribe." In Bumpo's two companions, Chingachgook and Uncas, Cooper invests all the strengths and virtues of their tribe. Uncas in particular is without flaw, Cooper telling us that his sympathy to the tender feelings of others "elevated him far above the intelligence, and advanced him probably centuries before the practices of his nation." In *The Last of the Mohicans*, Cooper created one of the great villains in American literature, the Iroquois Magua, the personification of treachery and evil who is responsible for the death of Uncas. However, Cooper's readers seemed to remember only his good Indians, and the appellation "Cooper Indian" came to mean noble red man. Cooper characterized all Indians as courageous, stoic, and merciless in war. Because they were one of the creations of the Supreme Being, their lives could not be taken without some sufficient cause. Finally, according to Cooper, the Creator meant for whites and Indians to live apart. Many of these ideas supported or perhaps even helped to formulate nineteenth-century Indian policy, and the idea of separate ness remains today. It is interesting to note that a careful reading of Custer's writings shows that he also found his opponent to be courageous, stoic, merciless in war, and incapable of being incorporated in white culture.[1]

Writing in the last quarter of the nineteenth century was Charles King (1844–1933), a graduate of West Point in 1866 who finished his career with a credit of seventy years of active service that began with the Indian wars and continued through the Spanish-American War to World War I. He authored sixty-five books, fifty-two of them novels, and almost single-handedly created the twentieth century's image of the Indian-fighting army. His first published work was *Campaigning with Crook* (1880), the story of his service in the 1876 Sioux War. His first novel was *The Colonel's Daughter*, published in 1883 by J. B. Lippincott, and was an immediate literary success. Perhaps lacking imagination, King stuck faithfully to what he knew and had experienced. Some have criticized his heroes and heroines as being unduly pure and his villains as unnaturally evil, but he did not exaggerate the brutality and difficulties of the period. As social documents, his novels deserve a lasting place in the history of the Old Army.

A major literary figure who addressed the Indian problem at the turn of the century was Hamlin Garland (1860–1940). Short stories written mainly between 1895 and 1905 were collected in *The Book of the American Indian* (1923). *The Captain of the Gray-Horse Troop* (1902) is the story of an army officer who acts as an Indian agent and comes to appreciate the Indian's apprehension of nature's unity while valuing the white man's methods in breaking down nature into controllable entities. His is the only serious attempt to reconcile the rationalistic and intuitive approaches of the two cultures.[2]

HISTORIANS AND ANTHROPOLOGISTS

Another influential nineteenth-century image maker was Helen Hunt Jackson (1836–1885), author of *A Century of Dishonor* (1881). Published four years before her death, the nonfiction book aroused the nation to the Indian's plight. The thesis was that the United States had followed an Indian policy that defied basic principles of justice and international law. Jackson described Indian maltreatment from the American Revolution to the more recent handling of the Nez Percés and the Northern Cheyennes. She urged that Indians be given individual title to their land to give them the incentive to labor in their own behalf. A year after its appearance, the powerful Indian Rights Association was born. The climate she created was largely responsible for the enactment in 1887 of the Dawes Act, which attempted to provide a means for Indian citizenship and absorb the Native Americans into the body politic. In 1884 she published *Ramona*, a sentimental novel that depicted Indian life in California as it had never been.

Another important nineteenth-century thinker was Lewis Henry Morgan (1818–1881), sometimes called the "father of anthropology," who authored the book, *Ancient Society, or Researches in the Lines of Human Progress from Savagery, through Barbarism to Civilization* (1877). Under the influence of Darwinian evolutionary theory, he developed the idea that cultures evolve in the same six successive stages from savagery to civilization. This theory made it possible to formulate Indian policy that was paternalistic in nature but withheld full rights of citizenship. In other words, it was not possible for primitive societies to become integrated into what was considered by Western intellectuals to be the final stage of improvement.

Modern Literature

HISTORIANS

Publishing in the first three decades of the twentieth century were a number of historians, ethnologists, and English professors who recorded the stories of participants in the Indian wars. Foremost among them was George Bird Grinnell (1849–1938), whose studies of the Cheyennes, *The Fighting Cheyennes* (1915), and *The Cheyenne Indians* (1923), created a standard rarely matched. Using reminiscences of Indian wars veterans, Cyrus Townsend Brady (1861–1920) produced two important volumes, *Indian Fights and Fighters* (1904) and *Northwestern Fights and Fighters* (1907).

English professor Walter Campbell (1887–1957), writing under the pseudonym Stanley Vestal, interviewed Sioux warriors and authored several popular works, including *Sitting Bull: Champion of the Sioux* (1932) and *Warpath and Council Fire: The Plains Indians' Struggle for Survival in War and in Diplomacy* (1948). Journalist E. A. Brininstool (1870–1957) interviewed frontier veterans and published their stories in such works as *Troopers with Custer* (1925) and *Fighting Red Cloud's Warriors* (1926). Later writers, such as lawyer J. W. Vaughn (1906–1968) in *With Crook at the Rosebud* (1956), *The Reynolds Campaign on Powder River* (1961), *The Battle Platte Bridge* (1963), and *Indian Fights: New Facts on Seven Encounters* (1966), pinpointed sites and derived strategy based on metal detector research. Popularizers Fairfax Downey in *Indian-Fighting Army* (1941), Paul Wellman (1898–1966) in *Death on the Prairie* (1934) and *Death in the Desert* (1935), and Ralph K. Andrist in *The Long Death* (1964) wrote general works on the Indian wars that created interest.

The best-selling book in the 1970s on the Indian wars was Dee Brown's *Bury My Heart at Wounded Knee* (1971), which tells the story from the Indian viewpoint. Brown (b. 1908) also writes western fiction, *Yellow Horse* (1956) and *Action at Beecher Island* (1967) being notable. Establishing himself as the leading professional historian writing about the Indian wars was Robert M. Utley (b. 1929), whose two survey volumes, *Frontiersmen in Blue: The United States Army and the Indian, 1848–1865* (1967), and *Frontier Regulars: The United States Army and the Indian, 1866–1890* (1973) became the standard works.

WESTERN NOVELISTS

In the twentieth century the western emerged as a genre, complete with stock characters, stereotypes, and formulas.[3] In outlining the ten common plots, Frank Gruber has listed number seven as "The Cavalry and Indian Story," and it is difficult to visit a bookstore or supermarket today without finding a wide selection of paperbacks devoted to mythologizing that era.

Among the best of those written during the last half century or so are *Bugles in the Afternoon* (1944) by Ernest Haycox (1899–1950) and *Sergeant Rutledge* (1959) by James Warner Bellah (1899–1976). Perhaps the best craftsman of the writers of westerns, Haycox tells the story of the Little Bighorn through the eyes of a soldier who did not make it to the battlefield. Bellah's short stories on the Indian wars appeared regularly in the *Saturday Evening Post* during its heyday and were anthologized in the collection *Reveille* (1962). Published serially in the *Post*, *Sergeant Rutledge* was the first novel to tell the story of the black soldier in the West. Bellah's short stories were the basis for the movies, *Fort Apache* (1948) and *She Wore a Yellow Ribbon* (1959). Among books from the 1960s, *Distant Trumpet* (1960) by Paul Horgan (b. 1903) stands out: It is a story of how an officer serving in the Southwest chooses honor over his emotions. Michael Straight, an English-educated American, penned two excellent novels dealing with Red Cloud's War and the aftermath of the Sand Creek Massacre: *Carrington* (1960) and *A Very Small Remnant* (1963). Will Henry, a pseudonym for Henry Wilson Allen (b. 1912), wrote probably the best novel on the Nez Percé Indian War in *From Where the Sun Now Stands* (1959). Another important writer of the decade was Frederick Manfred

(1912–1995), whose novel *Scarlet Plume* (1964) is set during the Minnesota Uprising of 1862.

In the 1970s two other novelists of the Indian Wars emerged. Three-time recipient of the Bronze Star, Oliver Patton, produced three adult novels: *The Hollow Mountains* (1976), *My Heart Turns Back* (1978), and *Western Wind* (1980), stories of the Indian wars in which heroes and heroines undergo suffering and tests of character before achieving their goals. Arkansan Douglas C. Jones produced the most imaginative Indian wars fiction with *The Court-Martial of George Armstrong Custer* (1976). In the novel Custer survives the Battle of the Little Bighorn to hear his peers condemn him but wins acquittal. In the 1990s, Billings, Montana, author Terry C. Johnston (b. 1947) dominates the market. Based on careful research and field study, his novels follow the adventures of Seamus Donegan, sometimes scout, sometimes sergeant. In *Sioux Dawn* (1990), *Red Cloud's Revenge* (1990), and *The Stalkers* (1990), Johnston can be considered king of the Indian wars' fiction writers.

INDIAN NOVELS

Two excellent novels that deal with the Indian side of the wars in the West are *Blood Brother* (1947) by Elliot Arnold (1912–1980), the story of Chiricahua Apache chief Cochise and Indian agent Tom Jeffords; and *Cheyenne Autumn* (1953) by Mari Sandoz (1907–1966), an epic account of the Northern Cheyennes' attempt to return from Oklahoma to Montana in 1878–1879. In *Conquering Horse* (1959), Frederick Manfred (1912–1995) stands alone in imagining the life of Plains Indians at the time of the introduction of the horse around 1800.

The debilitating effects of life on the reservation are ably covered by Oliver LaFarge (1901–1963) in *Laughing Boy* (1929), winner of the Pulitzer Prize in 1930. No one has better captured the despair of the American Indian, both rejected and suffocated by an alien culture. Perhaps James Welch's *The Death of Jim Loney* (1979) equals the power of *Laughing Boy* in depicting the male side, but LaFarge treats the reaction of the two sexes to their predicament, one able to adapt, the other doomed.

INDIAN WRITERS

In the recent past, Indian writers have exploded on the scene. Sioux Vine Deloria Jr. (b. 1933), continues to offer critiques of tribal and national affairs that began in such books as *Custer Died for Your Sins* (1969), *We Talk*

You Listen (1970), and *God Is Red* (1973). At the same time, Indian novelists have begun to sell well in midstream markets. The first was N. Scott Momaday, a Kiowa, who won the Pulitzer Prize for *House Made of Dawn* in 1969. The appearance of *Winter in the Blood* (1975) established Blackfeet/Gros Ventre writer James Welsh (b. 1940) as an important interpreter of Indian life. In *Fools Crow* (1986), he chose to deal with the historic past, treating life of a band of Blackfeet in Montana in the 1870s and the impact of white settlement. Chippewa Louise Erdrich's (b. 1954) three novels— *Love Medicine* (1984), *The Beet Queen* (1986), and *Tracks* (1988)—treat multiple relationships between Indians, whites, and mixed bloods during the period 1912 to 1982. Rounding out the circle of best-known Indian novelists is Leslie Marmon Silko (b. 1948), whose *Ceremony* (1977) is a story of a Pueblo World War II veteran who heals himself by immersion in the ritual life of the Laguna. Her recent novel, *Almanac for the Dead* (1991), is an indictment of white society and predicts an Indian revolution in the Americas and sees a corrupt world rushing to Armageddon.

The Arts

WESTERN FILMS

Films have contributed greatly to the public's perceptions of the Indian wars. Although some have kept close to the facts, others have veered widely from the truth. Historians generally object to filmmakers' tendency to simplify explanations of historical processes but laud their creation of visual authenticity when it appears. In such cases the visual power of the movies rises above errors of chronology and character. It is also important to remember in viewing films that even the most accurate often are vehicles for commentary on the contemporary scene by those who made them. Nowhere is this better seen than in films made about George Armstrong Custer. In the 1941 film *They Died with Their Boots On*, Custer (Errol Flynn) sends the Seventh Cavalry to certain death in order to save Terry and Gibbon. Made at a time when the United States was about to enter World War II, the need for personal sacrifice was never more present in the public's mind. Conversely, in the 1970 film *Little Big Man* Custer's actions in attacking the Indian village manifested a destructive racism that directors of the film believed abided in American society, revivified in the Vietnam War.[4]

Such subtexts are present in the three John Ford-John Wayne films, generally recognized as being the best about the Indian-fighting army: *Fort Apache* (1948), *She Wore a Yellow Ribbon"* (1949), and *Rio Grande*. *Fort Apache*, with Henry Fonda (Colonel Thursday) as the commanding officer and John Wayne (Captain York) as his immediate subordinate, is perhaps the first anti-western, the first to attack prevailing myths about the building of the West. As with real officers before him, Fonda's ignorance and arrogance predetermined his downfall. His counterpoint is John Wayne, who personifies the bravery, skill, persistence, and good humor of many regular army soldiers who garrisoned the frontier.

Filmed mostly in Monument Valley, Utah, *She Wore a Yellow Ribbon* is about the passing of a heroic age and the passing of command from one generation to another. Captain Nathan Brittles (John Wayne) is the transmitter of the skills and values that had established a fragile safety for frontier inhabitants. He challenges and trains Lieutenants Cahill and Pennel, emphasizing negotiations over force. Made following World War II, it was a time when veterans needed to pass on their skills to the young so that world peace would be maintained. *Rio Grande* (1950), on the other hand, was a film released during the first months of the Korean conflict, when negotiations were no longer possible. Colonel Kirby York (John Wayne) frets over the State Department's refusal to allow him to cross the Rio Grande (translate Yalu River in Asia) to destroy the enemy. Two films of special merit in the 1960s were *Sergeant Rutledge* (1960), starring Woody Strode as a black soldier-hero who shows compassion for those who have harmed him, and *Distant Trumpet* (1964), in which Troy Donohue and Suzanne Pleshette portray the difficulties in living at an isolated frontier post.

INDIANS IN FILMS

In early movies Native Americans were featured as a menace, portrayed exclusively as attackers in such memorable films as *Stagecoach* (1939). In the watershed film *Broken Arrow* (1950), based on the novel *Blood Brother*, James Stewart plays a scout who marries an Indian woman and sympathizes with the Apaches. His blood brother is Cochise, played by Jeff Chandler, who turns out to be a stronger advocate for peace than his friend. Subsequent films defended the Indian, the most complex of which is probably Samuel Fuller's *Run of the Arrow* (1956). Based on the Mari Sandoz novel, *Cheyenne Autumn* (1964) was an attempt to retell from the Indian point of view the Cheyenne outbreak of 1878–1879. Critics deplored the "Indian" casting of Gilbert Roland, Ricardo Montalban, Dolores Del Rio, Victor Jory, and Sal Mineo. In the 1970s two films, *A Man*

Called Horse (1970), based on a Dorothy Johnson story, and *Little Big Man* (1971), based on a Thomas Berger novel, used white captivity as a device to show the Indian way of life. In the first, aristocratic captive Richard Harris survives and becomes a tribal leader, and in the second Dustin Hoffman rejects white society to fight for his new Indian family. *Little Big Man* and *Soldier Blue* (1970) portrayed the U.S. soldier as brutal, racist, and potentially genocidal. At the same time, Hollywood projected a new Indian image in films such as *Tell Them Willie Boy Is Here* (1969) and *Flap* (1969). However, non-Indians continued to play principal Indian roles.

Dances with Wolves, directed by Kevin Costner in 1990, was an important breakthrough: It was the first movie to use Native Americans to play each and every Indian part. Floyd Westerman is Chief Ten Bears, Graham Greene is Kicking Bear, Rodney A. Grant is Wind in His Hair, Wes Studi is the Pawnee chief. Including extras, four hundred Native Americans made their appearance in the film. *Dances with Wolves* was also the first commercial production in which an Indian language, in this case Lakota, is the one most spoken. English subtitles are provided throughout, marking another first.

The movie contrasts white and Indian values in the mid–nineteenth century. The protagonist is the young army officer played by Costner, Lieutenant John Dunbar, who in 1863 through a brave act finds himself able to choose his next assignment. His choice is Fort Sedgwick on the frontier, identified as the last outpost of civilization. Upon arriving Dunbar finds the fort abandoned, but true to his military training remains at his station and in time becomes acquainted with his neighbors, a wolf named Two Socks and a band of Teton Sioux. Acquaintance leads to friendship and friendship leads to commitment. Dunbar gradually adopts the Sioux way, finding the values that he needs to build a new life. Writing in his journal, Dunbar notes that Sioux live in harmony, which contrasts with the ultimate white disharmony, the Civil War, that has turned brother against brother. Several times whites are shown killing animals for commercial gain beyond the need of their own survival or simply for fun. When the Sioux take human or animal life, it is to protect their families and homes or provide food. Finally, Dunbar has to decide between life in one world or the other, but circumstances make it impossible for him to enjoy either. In the end he leaves his Indian friends to return to his own culture, where he is hunted as traitor, to explain his actions and attempt to bring understanding concerning the true nature of the red race.

Understandably, Sioux peoples rejoiced in the film. The Lakota men and women are brave, wise, and trusting, and they act for the good of the whole group. But the enemies of the Sioux in the movie, the Pawnees, are as stereotypically villainous as any of their celluloid predecessors. The killing of a Pawnee chief by Costner and his Indian comrades is one of the highlights of the film. *Dances with Wolves* is, in effect, a Cooper film with one tribe possessing all the virtue and the other none of it. It is interesting to note that in Cooper's *The Prairie*, the Sioux were the evil tribe and the Pawnees the exemplary one.

Television and video documentaries are new mediums for discussion and portrayal of the Indian wars. "Kenny Roger's The Real West," and "How the West Was Lost" are two recent television series that drew wide audiences. Featuring western historians, interpreters of Indian history, and other experts, these programs emphasized multiple points of view. Paul Steckler's "Last Stand at the Little Bighorn" (1992), shown on PBS's *American Experience*, was a sincere attempt to tell a balanced story of the Battle of the Little Bighorn from white and Indian perspectives. In the video market, the Old Army Press of Fort Collins, Colorado, continues to produce solid historical treatments, such as *A Good Day to Die!* (Battle of the Little Bighorn), *Fort Laramie, Crossroads of the West*, and *Forts on the Santa Fe Trail*. Of special merit is the two-volume video set, *America's Great Indian Leaders and Great Indian Nations*, produced by Questar Video, Inc., of Chicago.

WESTERN PAINTERS

The Custer fight has been depicted more than any other event in western history.[5] Don Russell in a less-than-exhaustive search logged 848 pictures relating to the battle and more than 300 Last Stands. William de le Montagne Cary (1840–1922) produced the first depiction of Custer's Last Stand in a woodcut for the July 19, 1876, issue of the *New York Graphic and Illustrated Evening Newspaper*. Cary had been with Major Reno's escort for the Northern Boundary Commission in 1874 and knew his troopers. John Mulvaney (1844–1906) was one of the first artists to paint the scene on canvas. In 1881, after visiting the site and interviewing Sioux, he painted an eleven-by-twenty-two-foot oil, *Custer's Last Rally*.

The most popular Custer rendition, however, was that originated by Cassily Adams (1843–1921) in 1886. His twelve-by-thirty-three-foot painting entitled *Custer's Last Fight* was shown in the East and then purchased by Anheuser-Busch, Inc., of St. Louis. In 1896 Busch decided to use the image to advertise his beer and hired F. Otto Becker (1854–1945) to copy the painting for the smaller lithograph format. In doing so, Becker took more than ordinary liberties with the picture, so many that some consider it a different work of art. The lithograph had tremendous circulation and is the single picture most responsible for the public's view of Custer's demise. Busch presented the original canvas, minus two original side panels, to the Seventh Cavalry. The painting eventually ended up at Fort Bliss, Texas, where fire destroyed it on June 13, 1946.

A painter who devoted himself almost exclusively to the Indian wars was Charles Schreyvogel (1861–1912). He became an instant success in 1900 when his painting, *My Bunkie*, received the highest prize of that year's National Academy exhibition. Among his finest paintings are *The Silenced War Whoop*, *Attack at Dawn*, *A Sharp Encounter*, *Defending the Stockade*, and *Custer's Demand*. In recognition of his skill, Theodore Roosevelt gave Schreyvogel a presidential permit to visit army posts and Indian reservations. Schreyvogel depicted Native Americans as dignified and worthy antagonists, bold and courageous men fighting for their land and families. Because he did most of his work on big canvases, he did not produce a large body of work; consequently, he is less known than some others of his era. Another artist sympathetic to the Indian was Henry F. Farny (1834–1916). Two of his most famous works are *A Dance of Crow Indians* (1883) and *The Song of the Talking Wire*. Another artist who specialized in military subjects was Rufus Fairchild Zogbaum (1848–1925). Much of his best work is assembled in his *Horse, Foot, and Dragoons* (1888) and in Charles Kings's *A War-Time Wooing* (1888) and *The Iron Brigade* (1902).

Edgar Samuel Paxson (1852–1919) was a painter who spent many years in the West. He moved to Montana in 1876, serving with the militia during the Nez Percé Indian War in 1877. In 1879 he moved to Deer Lodge, Montana, where he began painting signs, houses, theatrical backdrops, and western subjects. Apparently visiting Custer Battlefield as early as 1877, he began work on a painting that took him over twenty years to finish. Many notable Indians posed for the painting, including Sitting Bull, Gall, Two Moon, and Rain-in-the-Face. E. S. Godfrey provided Paxson with copious notes on what the officers were wearing that day. Completed in 1899, the six-by-ten-foot oil, *Custer's Last Stand*, now resides in the Whitney Art Gallery, Buffalo Bill Historical Center, Cody, Wyoming.

The two best-known western artists of the period were Frederick Remington (1861–1909) and Charles Russell (1864–1926). Remington produced three thousand pictures that cover almost every phase of western history. The New York–born and Yale-educated Remington went to the West at the age of nineteen and eventually bought a little cattle ranch in Kansas. He returned to the East in 1884, where his artistic breakthrough came on January 9, 1886, his sketch appearing on the front page of *Harper's Weekly*. Four years later he could report that in that year alone *Harper's Weekly* had published 119 of his illustrations, *Harper's Monthly* 36, and *Century Magazine* 18. Remington continued to spend his summers in the West and was at Wounded Knee in 1890, riding with Lieutenant Edward Casey and his Cheyenne scouts. By 1895 he was recognized as the foremost practitioner in western art. Remington returned often to the Indian wars for his subjects. Among his best works were illustrations for E. S. Godfrey's account of the Custer fight in the January 1892 issue of *Century*. These include *Indians Watching Custer's Advance*, *Dismounted*, *Boots and Saddles*, and *Unhorsed*. Remington was an excellent writer as well. *Pony Tracks* (1895) contains his articles on the Sioux War of 1890–1891. At his request his epitaph read, "He knew the horse." His New York studio has been reassembled in the Whitman Gallery of Art at the Buffalo Bill Historical Center, Cody, Wyoming.

Charles Russell migrated to Montana at the age of sixteen, where he worked at cowboy jobs. After his marriage in 1896 to Nancy Cooper, he settled down to work full-time at his art. By 1903 he had a studio in Great Falls, Montana, and a national reputation. Among his Indian wars pictures are *Painting the Buffalo Robe*, *Indian Warfare*, *A Desperate Stand*, and *Custer's Last Stand* (1903), which illustrated *Adventures with Indians and Game* by William A. Allen. Russell was also a colorful writer, and his "Rawhide Rawlins" stories are important in western literature. His last book was *Trail's Plowed Under*, published posthumously in 1927. Collections of his work may be seen at the Charles M. Russell Museum in Great Falls and the Montana State Historical Society in Helena.

Billings artist James. K. Ralston made his reputation as a faithful chronicler of the Indian wars and ranching culture. Based on thirty-nine separate documented instances, *After the Battle* is the most ambitious of the dozen oils he completed on Custer subjects. Unveiled in 1955 at the seventy-ninth anniversary of the battle, the four-and-one-half-by-eighteen-foot painting may be seen in the museum at the Little Bighorn Battlefield National Monument.

INDIAN ART

Painting on animal hides was an early form of artistic expression and a means of recording special events among hunting tribes. In the nineteenth century warriors sometimes drew their sketches in captured army ledger books. Imprisoned Cheyennes became famous for their ledger art, a term that came to encompass all paper drawings. Howling Wolf (1849–1927) in particular perfected the genre while in prison at Fort Marion from 1875 to 1878 and continued his work until his death in 1927. Well known to Indian wars enthusiasts are the drawings of the Sioux warrior, Red Horse, whose forty-one "picture-writing" renditions of the Battle of the Little Bighorn have been widely reproduced.

7. Conclusions

According to Don Russell the total number of engagements fought against Indians by the regular army between 1776 and 1891 was 1,240, not counting those that happened during the War of 1812 (which was largely an Indian war), the Mexican War, or the Civil War. Between 1848 and 1861, 206 fights occurred, and 938 between 1865 and 1891. Many others were fought by volunteer troops or civilians. Casualties for the regular army were 186 killed between 1848 and 1861 and 923 killed between 1865 and 1891. Also during this later period 1,061 officers and men were wounded. According to the *National Tribune* there were 415 fights with Indians between 1859 and 1891 that were classified as outbreaks, and the U.S. Army has recognized thirteen campaigns. The estimated number of Indians killed is 5,519, but recent scholarship seriously questions this figure as highly overblown.[1] Although these conflicts were of major importance, diseases brought from Europe—smallpox, measles, and cholera—killed more Indians and destroyed more of their culture than the wars and removals put together. Also more Euro-Americans died from these plagues than from any other cause. But for the writers of American history the deaths from disease have held less interest than deaths in battle. Historians and ethnologists, such as George Grinnell, George Hyde, Stanley Vestal, Paul Wellman, J. W. Vaughn, and Robert Utley, have immortalized participants in the Indian wars and chronicled their deeds, and today's motion pictures continue to tell a romanticized story of personal bravery and cultural subjugation. Its appeal remains because it is an American epic, embodying grand themes and great heroes.

In looking back one hundred years from the end of the conflict, it is easy to see that the army was less successful than it had hoped.[2] Joined to lumbering supply trains, its stolid columns crept about the western landscape looking for a foe who could strike and disappear in a flash. Many forays exhausted grain-fed cavalry horses and concluded with troops expending as much energy to keep from starving as in chasing Indians. The inability to separate guilty Indians from those who were not was a major weakness. Some critics pointed to a lack of preparedness. In 1885 an officer of thirteen years' experience told a newspaper reporter that the current failure in the Apache campaign reflected lack of troop training and ignorance of the topography.

Reasons for the decline in America's armed forces after the Civil War are specific. Reduced to a force of fifty-four thousand, the army had to oversee Reconstruction and guard remote western military posts. Throughout the 1870s General Sheridan transferred troops from the South to the frontier and back again over the new network of railroads. As lines of transportation and communication expanded, the numbers of men needed to carry out short-range objectives decreased. At the same time eastern humanitarians lobbied for a reduced military presence, and the Panic of 1873 led Congress to make deeper cuts. Nor could the army fight back. In later years its main job was on the frontier, isolated from the rest of the population. This separation was costly in terms of public and governmental support: out of sight out of mind. It was a forgotten war. As Robert Utley has pointed out, the army's frontier employment made it unfit for orthodox war, while its preoccupation with orthodox war made it unfit for frontier duties. However, although the frontier army performed at a standard less than anticipated, it did accomplish its overall mission: It upheld American dominion within the territorial limits of the United States from foreign encroachments and against Indian nations.

The Indian wars experience was important for the U.S. Army in that its lack of success in some areas caused reforms that strengthened it. After inspecting the army in the late 1880s, Lord Wolsey reported that, man for man, it was the best in the world. Certainly it was a different army, one better trained in the use of firearms and less trained in masonry and carpentry. Between 1889 and 1891 the changes came swift and sure. Among them were separate theoretical instruction for each arm of the service, practice maneuvers, improved recruiting practices, examinations for promotions, and standardized punishments. Canteens, gymnasia, and riding and drill halls were also established. By 1891 the army had abandoned one fourth of all the posts that had existed in 1889.

One of the interesting spin-offs of the Indian wars was the empathy that it created between warriors on both sides. Officers often voiced compassion for those whose cultures they believed doomed. Most of them concluded that both sides shared responsibility for the wars' causes. One of the most articulate was General George Crook. In addressing the 1884 graduating class at the U.S. Military Academy at West Point, Crook expressed his views concerning Indian capacities and rights. Drawing from thirty years of experience, he proclaimed:

> The savage is hemmed in by civilization, and he sees that the inevitable must be faced. He is more ready to abandon his old habits and accept civilization, than civilization is to accept him. With all his faults, and he has many, the American Indian is not half so black as he has been painted. He is cruel in war, treacherous at times, and not overly clean, but so were our forefathers. His nature, however, is responsible to a treatment which assures him that it is based upon justice, truth, honesty and common sense; it is not impossible that with a fair and square system of dealing with him, the American Indian would make a better citizen than many who neglect the duties and abuse the privileges of that proud title.[3]

Crook acted on these views in 1879. Two years earlier the Poncas had been forcibly removed from their reservation on the Dakota-Nebraska line and sent to Indian Territory. Early in 1879 Chief Standing Bear and thirty of the tribe headed for home, where troops under Crook took them into custody. Believing in the injustice of the affair, Crook sought legal assistance. Newspaper editor Thomas Henry Tibbles along with several interested lawyers obtained a writ of habeas corpus from the U.S. District Court, and a trial was scheduled for April 30. The government argued that because Indians were neither persons nor citizens under the law, they had no right to file suit. However, Judge Elmer Dundy ruled that Indians were indeed persons with legal standing and that their forced removal had deprived them of personal property. It was a landmark case that Crook precipitated. In December he served on a commission that recommended the Poncas remain in Nebraska, receive monetary compensation for their losses, and be given additional funds for schooling and farming supplies. In retrospect, while Crook was one of the Indians' worst enemies on the battlefield, he was one of their best friends in court. Also in 1879 Crook verbally defended both Dull Knife's band of Cheyenne fugitives and the embattled Bannocks, some of whom had scouted for him against the Sioux. When Crook died on March 21, 1890, the Apaches reportedly wept and wailed.

For Euro-American veterans the Indian wars accomplished several things. For William Bisbee, a lieutenant at Fort Phil Kearny, and later a general in the war in the Philippines, it meant the opening up of the country so that citizens might build cities and towns and convert the land "to the want and conveniences of mankind."[4] To R. D. Wilson it meant freeing millions of acres of the best land in the United States for cultivation and stock growing. To many entrepreneurs the army's presence in the West meant the opportunity to make a good living providing the military with clothing, shoes, wood, hay, grain, horses and other livestock, groceries, and specialized labor.

The army's Indian opponent was a keen observer and a master of concealment and surprise. His was the war of the hunter. Like the animals he stalked, he made a careful and patient study of surrounding conditions and the habits of his antagonist. Using elements of surprise, ambush, and stealth, he struck swiftly and with all the force at his command. "Let the Indian select time and place for the encounter," wrote veteran Josiah Hubbard, "and the chances of success were in his favor."[5] And the Indian soon learned to play the government both ways. As Eugene F. Ware observed, the "Indian idea was to have the Government feed the old people, women, and children, while the . . . [warriors] would ravage the country."[6] In describing Indian methods of warfare, Henry Carrington put it best when he declared, "The Indian comes as the hornet comes, in clouds or singly, yet never trying to sting until his ascendancy is assured, and his own exposure the slightest." Carrington then added a precise summary of Indian strategy, tactics, abilities, and mores: "In ambush and decoy," Carrington wrote, "he is splendid; in horsemanship; perfect; in strategy, wise; in battle, wary and careful of life; in victory, jubilant; in vengeance, terrible and fiendish."[7] The Indian lost not because he lacked courage or technical skill, but because he lacked the resources and numbers of his enemies. His greatest weakness was that his society was not designed to sustain prolonged warfare. In addition, tribes fought among themselves, precluding united resistance.

Defeat was devastating to Native Americans.[8] First, they lost much of their land. This was exacerbated by some key pieces of legislation passed in the late nineteenth and early twentieth centuries. In 1887 the Dawes Act authorized individual allotments of as much as 160 acres. After being held in trust for twenty-five years, the government conveyed title to a "certifiably competent" allottee, who at that moment became an American citizen free to do what he wished with his property. This and succeeding refining legislation resulted in the purchase of most allotted land by whites. The Indian Reorganization Act of 1934 halted sales and extended the trust period. At the beginning of contact with whites, Native Americans controlled 1.934 billion acres in what is now the continental United States. Today 40 million acres remain within reservations and 12 million in individual Indian ownership. The net loss has been 1.882 billion acres.

In 1946 legislation created the Indian Claims Commission to hold hearings and make economic awards to redress past fraud, injustices, and violations of treaties. The Utes were the first to file, asking for compensation for sixteen million acres in Colorado, taken without adequate payment. Within four years they had won an award of $31.7 million, encouraging other tribes to apply. Eight hundred and fifty claims have been filed to date. The latest significant award has been for the Black Hills, where Congress gave the Sioux $115 million. The Sioux, however, have refused to receive payment, holding out for return of the land.

The effect of white contact on the Indian population was also severe. The Indian population decreased from about 600,000 in 1800 to 250,000 in 1900. At the same time, non-Indian residents grew from about 5,000,000 to over 75,000,000. At the end of the nineteenth century, the Indian population had reached its low point. It then began to slowly increase to its present level: The 1990 census indicated that there are 1,873,536 self-declared Indians in the United States. Of this number, 1,175,173 are tribally enrolled, and 685,464 live in areas governed by tribes.

Perhaps even more devastating than the loss of land was the suppression of Indian culture after 1883. In banning the sun dance and other ceremonies, the U.S. government violated religious freedom, one of this country's great democratic principles. Steps have been taken to recognize and protect Indian traditions. In 1978 Congress passed the American Indian Religious Freedom Act for the purpose of "protecting, preserving for American Indians their inherent right of freedom to believe, express and exercise their traditional religion, [which includes] but is not limited to access to sites, use and possession of sacred objects."[9]

The loss of Indian lives and land and the suppression of Indian culture resulted in widespread anger and resentment. Tribal reaction to the end of nomadic freedom and the repression of traditional culture seems to follow a pattern discerned by contemporary psychologist Elisabeth Kubler-Ross in those having suffered great loss. The first stage is denial, seen in the Ghost Dance movement that promised a return to previous conditions. The second stage is anger, which appeared in the 1970s with the Second Wounded Knee and other acts of violence. The third stage is bargaining, evidenced in the refusal of the Sioux to accept the sizable appropriation for loss of the Black Hills and calling for a return of the land itself. Step four is grieving, seen in the present repatriation movement to return Indians' remains and belongings from museums and other institutions to the tribes and in such events as the Wounded Knee commemorative ride. The fifth step, acceptance, is still to come.

In recent decades the Little Bighorn Battlefield has become a stage on which Indian peoples can act out their feelings. The theme of repression has been dramatized through demonstrations by Indian activists, principally by American Indian Movement (AIM) leader Russell Means. The history of protests began at the one hundredth anniversary of the battle on June 25, 1976, when Means and two hundred followers arrived on the scene dragging an American flag upside down. At one point Means threatened to burn down the park visitor center because it contained Custer memorabilia. Negotiations avoided violence. The last protest of note occurred in 1988 and ended in the placement of a plaque within the grassy area next to the soldier monument on Custer Hill. The text proclaimed honor for Indian patriots who had successfully fought to save Indian women and children from mass murder and secure their people's homeland.

Little Bighorn Battlefield National Monument has also been the scene of attempts at reconciliation. The initial ceremonial attempt at the battlefield was in 1926, when Brigadier General E. S. Godfrey, with naked sword, led five troops of the Seventh Cavalry to meet an Indian column led by White Bull, son of Sitting Bull. At their meeting the warrior raised his open hand in the sign of peace, and the old soldier sheathed his sword. Godfrey presented White Bull with a large American flag, and according to one historian the chief cherished it until the day of his death. The most recent attempt at reconciliation was in 1986 when remains of troopers found on the battlefield through archaeology were reinterred in a public ceremony. A Sioux speaker noted that the battle site was not alien ground but steeped in tribal history and pride, and a white speaker reminded listeners that those who had faced each other more than a century before had fought side by side in recent wars. A new sign of the increasing power of reconciliation was the passage of federal legislation in 1993 changing the name of the National Park Service area from Custer Battlefield National Monument to Little Bighorn National Battlefield and authorizing a major new monument on site to honor Indian dead.

A strange bedfellow of reconciliation is appearing on the scene: cultural heritage tourism, a new significant segment of the travel industry that promotes visits to historic sites, especially in the American West.[10] The most recent example is a proposal by the citizens of Wallowa, Oregon, for Nez Percés to return to the Wallowa Valley, which they left in 1877. In 1991, in an effort to attract tourists to an area depressed by partial shutdown of its timber industry, community leaders asked the Nez Percés to hold an annual powwow and friendship feast. The success of the event has caused townsfolk to raise money to purchase 160 acres on nearby Tick Hill for a permanent powwow site, campground, and interpretive center.

The profit motive has spurred some interesting recent uses of history. For several years the Crow tribe has been holding a pageant in which the Custer fight is represented with Crow men playing the part of their enemies and opponents in the battle—the Sioux, Cheyenne, and Arapaho. A few years ago the tribe opened a gambling casino about a mile from the battlefield, invoking Custer's name to encourage betting. Appearing in local newspapers has been an advertisement declaring that "Custer Would Have Had a Much Better Chance of Winning" if he had visited the casino instead of the Indian village.[11] More insidious have been proposals to privatize Little Bighorn Battlefield and build a theme park nearby.

Complicating the matter of reconciliation has been the emergence of a new school of historical writing that measures nineteenth-century actions in terms of late twentieth-century social values. Though often refreshing and providing new readings of an old text, at its worst it distorts history, selecting heroes and villains to meet the needs of the present.[12] Instead of providing balance in the telling of multiple viewpoints, it can become an exercise in self-flagellation, political posturing, or ethnic myth making. The key to meaningful reconciliation remains discussion and respect for differing views. It is important to confront the past so that some understanding may come of human unpredictability and duality, at once selfless and selfish, compassionate and unforgiving, and merciful and merciless. We need to become aware of our illusions.

There are things yet to be learned from the Indian wars. In 1879 Chief Joseph wrote an article for *The North American Review* entitled "Chief Joseph's Story," in which he appealed to the whites' sense of justice. "Whenever the white man treats the Indian as they treat each other," he declared, "then we shall have no more wars." This meant to Joseph, the right to freedom. As he put it, "Let me be a free man—free to travel, free to stop, free to work, free to trade, where I choose, free to choose my own teachers, free to follow the religion of my fathers, free to think and talk and act for myself—and I will obey every law, or submit to the penalty."[13] In 1884 officials permitted Joseph and 150 of his tribe to live on Colville Reservation in Washington. There the Nez Percé leader spent his remaining years, urging the young to pursue education and speaking out against gambling and alcohol abuse. When he died on September 21, 1904, the agency physician listed the cause of death as a broken heart.

1. Red Cloud (1821–1909). The Oglala chief was the only Indian leader to achieve his long-range objectives in war against the United States. His resistance to the attempt to utilize the Bozeman Trail led to its abandonment in the summer of 1868. During his warrior days, he counted eighty coups.

2. Sitting Bull (1834–1890) and One Bull (1853–1947). A warrior, visionary, and diplomat, the Unkpapa leader formed an alliance that resulted in the army's worst defeat at the Battle of the Little Bighorn. In remaining true to the values and principles that guided his people, Sitting Bull achieved greatness. One Bull, who became Sitting Bull's adopted son in 1857, was a participant in the Custer Fight and reservation leader in the twentieth century.

3. Quanah Parker (1854–1911). Born of a white mother and a prominent Kwahadie Comanche, Parker became a war chief in 1867. For the next nine years, he led the Comanches in battles with U.S. troops. Settling on the reservation in 1876, he became a spokesman for all his people, serving as a judge, religious leader, and negotiator with the federal government in land issues.

4. Geronimo (1829–1909). Perhaps more than any other Indian leader, this Chiricahua Apache did more with less in his resistance to white domination. In 1886 he was the last chief to formally surrender to the United States.

5. George (1839–1876), Tom (1845–1876), and Elizabeth Custer (1842–1933) in the spring of 1865. Soon to become the nation's most famous frontier couple, George and Elizabeth Custer captured the public's imagination through their adventures and writings. Tom rivaled his brother in daring-do, having twice received the Congressional Medal of Honor for bravery under fire.

6. Wesley Merritt (1834–1910), Philip Sheridan (1831–1888), George Crook (1828–1890), George Forsyth (1837–1915), and George Custer (1839–1876). Surrounding their commander "Little Phil," these young Civil War officers were destined to fight in some of the most famous engagements of the Indian Wars: the Battles of Beecher Island, the Rosebud, the Little Bighorn, and War Bonnet Creek.

7. Nelson A. Miles (1839–1925). Nelson Miles was the most ambitious and probably the most able of all frontier army officers. Besting Sitting Bull, Crazy Horse, and Geronimo, he became the commanding general of the army in 1895.

2. Places to Visit

Historic Sites and Museums

Visiting historic sites and museums is an important way to acquire an understanding of the Indian wars.[1] The centers of military activities were the forts, some large, some small, some walled, some not. Some were beehives of activity, and some were forever quiet. After the army left them, they occasionally became settlements themselves, or their buildings, sold at auction, became private dwellings in town or country. Today parts of most of the frontier posts established and occupied by the U.S. Army during the Indian wars have been preserved in federal, state, or city ownership. Some survive as parts of active military installations, some as units in other federal enclaves, and some as historic parks. Below are my own selections of historic forts that await your visit. In every case there are physical remains in the form of buildings, sometimes just a few. In many instances large numbers of important structures remain in good condition. Significant numbers of these have been refurnished with period furnishings and accouterments. All of them are fairly accessible; a few such as Fort Bowie, Arizona, require some hiking to enjoy. Most of them are publicly owned and equipped with museums and interpreters. Battlefields are classrooms for understanding the way that engagements progressed and concluded. The use of the terrain often made the difference between victory or defeat. In the case of the Indian wars, the places were often important camping sites, to which tribes returned again and again. The battlefields have been selected for listing because of their significance, their remains, and their accessibility to the public.

In addition to the museums and visitor centers mentioned as part of a fort or battlefield complex, several specialized facilities deserve mention. These are either separate museums devoted to the Indian wars or Indian heritage or that contain significant exhibits and artifacts. Finally, some properties that relate to the Native American side of the story did not fit into other categories and are presented as Indian heritage sites. They deal with individual homes that have been preserved, burial places, geographic landmarks important in tribal history, or sites or institutions that are being perpetuated that give special insights into social, economic, or spiritual life. To place these structures, sites, and museums in context, a short narrative history of the area precedes the listing. The histories follow the culture areas presented in Chapter 2; namely, California and the Northwest, the Great Basin, the Plateau, the Southwest, and the Great Plains.

For those who wish to join an Indian wars organization or seek guided assistance in visiting battlefields or historic sites, a few national groups conduct meetings and tours and publish newsletters. The Order of the Indian Wars (1–501–225–3996), P.O. Box 1270, Little Rock AR 72217, has a newsletter and an annual meeting in mid-September that features speakers and a tour of multiple Indian wars sites. The Council on America's Military Past (CAMP), 518 W. Why Worry Lane, Phoenix AZ 85201, has an outstanding newsletter, *Headquarters Heliogram*, that keeps the interested abreast of activities and events affecting historic military posts and a spring meeting of speakers and tours. Specializing in Indian wars tours is History America Tours (1–800–628–8542), P.O. Box 797687, Dallas TX 75379. Most publicly owned forts and battlefields have support groups that operate bookstores, provide financial assistance, and publish newsletters.

At the end of the Mexican War, the United States claimed a vast territory in the West, having acquired Texas, New Mexico, and California and having settled the Oregon boundary dispute. In this area lived nearly a quarter-million Indians. About one third of them occupied lands through which emigrants moved on their way to find new lives. Along the trails west and near pockets of settlements that developed because of the suitability of the land for farming, ranching, and mining, the U.S. Army found much of its business in the next half-century. The struggle that followed was for land and the dominance of culture. On the one hand, it was a story of dramatic conquest; on the other, it was the tragic story of the loss of freedom.[2]

California and the Northwest

On the Pacific Coast, the California Gold Rush brought miners into contact with a large population of semisedentary Indians that occupied the ore-rich mountains. Overrun, some groups simply disappeared, having been dispersed or eliminated. Many of those in northern California and southern Oregon fought back. The Rogue River War in Oregon began in 1855 when a group of volunteers attacked a camp of Indians, killing twenty-three women, children, and elderly men. In retaliation the Indians swept the valley, killing twenty-seven whites. The concluding engagement of the conflict occurred May 27–28, 1856. In the Battle of Big Meadows, the Rogue River Indians were about to overrun forces under Captain Andrew Jackson Smith, when reinforcements led by Captain Christopher C. Augur permitted a counterattack so devastating that the Indians surrendered within a month.

In Washington Territory the Yakimas reacted to an invasion of their lands by gold seekers headed for the newly discovered Colville diggings and to land-ceding treaties recently promulgated. In 1855–1856 Chief Kamiakin briefly united the Yakima, Walla Wallas, Umatillas, and Cayuses in resistance to white invasion on the west side of the Cascades. After some Yakimas killed six whites, volunteer units patrolled the region. The Oregon militia killed Walla Walla Chief Peo-Peo-Mox-Mox at a truce parley, taking his ears and scalp for display. In the spring of 1856, five hundred regular army troops under Colonel George Wright took the field, meeting no resistance. After volunteers killed forty Walla Wallas in July 1857, conditions returned to a pre-war status quo, with the Indians moving about the countryside and whites continuing to appear.

Trouble began again in May 1858 when 164 men under Colonel Edward J. Steptoe crossed the Snake River and advanced boldly into Indian country. On May 17 hundreds of Palouses, Spokanes, and Coeur d'Alenes ordered him back and then attacked as his force withdrew. Using his artillery to good effect, Steptoe held off the aggressors during the day and made his way back to Fort Walla Walla that night. Colonel Wright was the next to take the field. In

August he repulsed six hundred warriors, and in the Battle of Four Lakes on September 1 and the Battle of Spokane Plain on September 5, he defeated them soundly, the Indians making a negotiated peace. Wright ordered fifteen of those accused of depredations and other offenses hanged. This campaign forever broke the power of the Indians of the Columbian Basin.

In the Northwest George Crook began to make his mark. In the spring of 1866 the Yahuskin and Walpapi bands of Northern Paiutes left their reservation in southern Oregon and began raiding miners' camps, ranches, and stage stations. In response regular army troops moved in. Then lieutenant colonel of the Twenty-third Infantry, Crook took command of Fort Boise, Idaho, in December 1866 and immediately began a campaign that lasted for two years. In forty battles his troops killed 329 and captured 225. On July 1, 1868, Old Weawea and 800 Paiutes surrendered at Camp Harney, Oregon.

In 1872 the Modocs left their reservation in southern Oregon, where they had been kept in company with more numerous and unfriendly Klamaths, and returned to their homeland in the Lost River country of California. When troops tried to force them back, the Modocs took shelter in the lava beds, a natural rock fortress near the northern California border. There for six months they held out against more than twenty times their number, inflicting more casualties than received. During the siege the Modocs killed General Edward R. S. Canby and other peace commissioners under a flag of truce. A sergeant with the party retrieved Canby's false teeth from his body, which he still had in his possession fifty years later. The Modocs finally surrendered, and the army hanged four of their leaders, including Canby's assassin, Captain Jack. The Modocs heads were shipped to the Army Medical Museum in Washington, while the rest of the tribe went into exile in Oklahoma.

California

HISTORIC SITES

Lava Beds National Monument
Located in Siskiyou and Modoc Counties, California, the lava beds are accessible via California Highway 139 and secondary roads. For information write P. O. Box 867, Tulelake CA 96134.

After several unsuccessful attempts to keep the Modocs on a reservation north of their homeland, the army marched against the band in November 1872. Fighting started before discussions could begin, and the Modocs fled into the lava beds of northern California. There in the twisted mass of volcanic rock known as Captain Jack's Stronghold, the Modocs held out for six months. The first battle occurred on January 17, when seventy Modocs repulsed an attack by three hundred troops. At a truce meeting on April 11, the Modocs killed General Edward R. S. Canby and peace commissioner the Reverend Eleasar Thomas. Six days later troops stormed the stronghold but found it deserted. However, the army continued to pursue the Indians, who eventually surrendered. Captured on June 1, Captain Jack stood trial for his life at Fort Klamath. In October he and three other leaders were hanged. This national monument covers forty-six thousand acres and includes Captain Jack's Stronghold, the site of the army's base camp, the truce site, and the battlegrounds. A museum, markers, and self-guiding trails present the history and geology of the park.

MUSEUMS

Gene Autry Western Heritage Museum
Near the Los Angles Zoo, Griffith Park, 4700 Heritage Way, the museum is open year-round Tuesday through Sunday from 10 AM to 5 PM; (213) 667–2000.

Opened in 1988, the huge museum contains exhibits pertaining to the military and Indian history of the West and western film.

Southwest Museum
Located at 234 Museum Drive, Los Angeles, the museum is immediately east of downtown by way of the Pasadena Freeway. It is open from 11 AM to 5 PM, Tuesday through Sunday; (213) 221–2163.

Four main exhibit halls focus on the native peoples of the Southwest, California, the Great Plains, and the Northwest. Among its archival materials are the papers of George Bird Grinnell, the ethnologist, journalist, and historian of the Cheyennes.

Oregon

HISTORIC SITES

Fort Dalles
The site is located at 15th and Garrison Streets and 14th at Trevitt Streets, The Dalles. The historic house museum is open on weekdays between March and October from 10:30 AM to 5 PM and on weekends from 10 AM

to 5 PM. Off-season hours are from noon to 4 PM on Wednesday through Friday and on weekends from 10 to 4 PM; (503) 296–4547 or 296–6616.

The army established Fort Dalles in 1850 to protect the Oregon Trail and serve as a supply base in the Indian campaigns, especially the Yakima War (1855–1856). The last troops left in 1867. The only surviving building is a surgeon's frame quarters in the Gothic Revival style. Owned by the Oregon Historical Society, it now serves as a museum.

Washington

HISTORIC SITES

Fort Simcoe State Park Heritage Site
The fort is located on the Yakima Indian Reservation, seven miles west of White Swan at the western terminus of Highway 220. The interpretive center is open Wednesday through Sunday from April 1 to September 30 and the rest of the year by appointment; (509) 874–2372.

Established in 1856 and abandoned in 1859, Fort Simcoe was a participant in the 1858 campaign against tribes in eastern Washington. After the cessation of activities, the army transferred the post to the Indian Bureau for use as the Yakima Agency. In 1953 the state of Washington leased property from the Yakima Nation and began restoration. Now Fort Simcoe State Park, the post contains three officers' quarters (1857–1858), one of the four original blockhouses (1856), and the two-story commandant's house (1857–1858).

Vancouver Barracks
The complex is located east of the Vancouver Freeway, bounded on the south by East 5th Street and on the north by East Evergreen Boulevard, adjacent to Fort Vancouver National Historic Site; (206) 696–7655.

Known as Camp Vancouver (1849–1850), Columbia Barracks (1850–1853), Fort Vancouver (1853–1879), and Vancouver Barracks (1879–present), the military complex served as a headquarters and supply base through World War II, being deactivated in 1946. For most of the period of 1866 to 1920, it served as the headquarters of the Department of the Columbia. Stationed there were Ulysses S. Grant, Philip Sheridan, George Crook, O. O. Howard, and Nelson Miles. Remaining structures have been modified, but Officer's Row National Historic District is a string of twenty-one restored structures, including the Grant House, now a restaurant.

Fort Walla Walla

The post is located on the Veterans Administration Hospital grounds in the southwestern part of the city of Walla Walla.

Established in 1858, Fort Walla Walla was an important post in the Indian wars of the Northwest. Soldiers from the fort participated in the 1858 campaign in eastern Washington, the Modoc War (1872–1873), the Nez Percé War (1877), and the Bannock War (1878). Today many buildings remain from the historic period; however, many have been modified to suit the needs of the Veterans Administration. The post cemetery, which contains burials from the Nez Percé War, is within a city park, immediately south of the hospital.

The Great Basin

During the Civil War, California Volunteers extinguished the last flickers of resistance in the mountains of northern California and ruthlessly dealt with the Paiutes in Nevada and Shoshonis in Utah. At the beginning of 1863, Colonel Patrick E. Connor took to the field to punish Chief Bear Hunter's Western Shoshoni, who had been reacting violently to the influx of miners headed for Idaho and the spread of Mormon settlement from Salt Lake. Embarking on a winter offensive, Connor and his Third California Volunteers attacked the Shoshoni village on Bear River, near present-day Preston, Idaho, on January 29. Troops struck a devastating blow, killing 224 and capturing 164 women and children. This was only one of many engagements that took place in 1863 in the Cache, Skull, Cedar, and Utah Valleys. Connor and Governors James Doty of Utah and James Nye of Nevada followed these encounters with successful treaty negotiations, establishing a peace that lasted for several years.

Nevada

HISTORIC SITES

Fort Churchill State Historic Park

Go nine miles south from Silver Springs, Nevada, on Alternate 95. The park is open daily from 8 AM to 4:30 PM.

Established in 1861 after the Pyramid Lake War, Fort Churchill guarded overland travelers, the Pony Express, and the Pacific Telegraph. The army abandoned the post in 1872. The park contains the adobe ruins of the post and a visitor center that tells the story of the Pyramid Lake War and the fort's eleven-year history.

Fort McDermit

Take an unimproved road about two miles east of U.S. 93 and McDermit.

Established by California Volunteer troops in 1865, just south of the Oregon-Nevada boundary, Fort McDermit was involved in Crook's campaign against the Snake Indians in 1866–1868, the Bannock War of 1878, and in controlling the Indian agency located nearby. After abandonment in 1889, the Indian Bureau occupied the fort, operating a school in one of the buildings. Today, the remaining buildings, including two officers' quarters, serve as headquarters for the Fort McDermit Indian Agency.

Utah

HISTORIC SITES

Fort Douglas

Fort Douglas is located on the northeastern edge of Salt Lake City. The museum is open year-round Monday through Saturday from 9 AM to 5 PM and from 1 to 5 PM Sunday in June, July, and August; (801) 538–1050.

The army established Fort Douglas in 1862 to protect those traveling overland trails from Indian attack and to keep an eye on the Mormons. From this post, Colonel Patrick E. Connor led his California and Nevada Volunteers in the devastating attack on the Western Shoshonis at Bear River in January 1863. Fort Douglas remained an active military post until 1967. Most of the original acreage has been acquired by the state of Utah. Remaining from the 1880s are the headquarters building, several officers' quarters, post office, stables, and chapel. The U.S. Army Center of Military History operates the Fort Douglas Military Museum. A self-guided tour of the fort includes the original 1862 cemetery.

The Plateau

In August 1869, warriors of the Piegan band of Blackfeet shocked Montanans into action when they killed Malcom Clarke, a popular rancher who lived north of Helena. A clamoring citizenry forced a campaign, and in January 1870 Major Eugene M. Baker and his men rode north from Fort Ellis to punish Mountain Chief and his followers. Attacking the Chief Heavy Runner's camp on the Marias River on January 23, they killed 173 men, women, and children and captured another 140. Eastern humanitarians screamed massacre, while Sherman and Sheridan defended Baker's actions, stating that depredations had been committed by this group as well. Condemnation in the press led to the army's exclusion from participating in Grant's new Indian policy in any direct way and to the practice of appointing churchmen to serve as Indian agents.

Chief Joseph of the Nez Percés lived his early years in the quiet of the Wallowa and Imnaha Valleys of northeastern Oregon. However, in 1860, the discovery of gold brought thousands of adventurers into neighboring Idaho, and pressures by white interests resulted in a series of treaties and executive orders that reduced Indian holdings. A split in the tribe came in 1863 when those bands who had become Christianized signed a treaty reducing Nez Percé lands by seven million acres. Because the agreement deprived the Wallowas and allied bands of their traditional homeland, they refused to sign, becoming known as the nontreaty Nez Percé. In protest, Old Chief Joseph tore his copy of the treaty to shreds, destroyed his New Testament, and continued to oppose white settlement until his death in 1871. At this point, his son, Young Joseph, became the central character in the drama that was to unfold. Born in Wallowa Valley in about 1840, Joseph was known to his tribesmen as "Thunder Rolling in the Mountains." When he became an adult, he was very striking in appearance. About six feet in height, he was powerfully built, with strong features and a regal bearing.

Although the Wallowa Valley proved barren of gold, stockmen coveted its grassy meadows. Finally, officials ordered the nontreaty bands to occupy un-allotted lands inside the boundaries of the reservation, authorizing force if necessary. On May 14, 1877, General O. O. Howard gave the nontreaty Nez Percés thirty days to comply. Trouble began on June 13 a few miles from the reservation border, when three young men decided to avenge earlier griev-ances with white settlers. A two-day raid followed in which eighteen whites were killed, causing the nontreaty bands to flee. On June 17 Captain David Perry, two companies of the First Cavalry, and twelve civilian volunteers en-gaged the Nez Percés in the Battle of White Bird Canyon, suffering a resound-ing defeat and losing thirty-three soldiers. The Nez Percés did not lose a single warrior. In this battle, as in all those that followed, Joseph fought like any other warrior, leaving military strategy to others.

During the next four months, the Nez Percés fled twelve hundred miles over the Bitterroot Mountains, through Yellowstone National Park, and across the breadth of Montana. Of the 700 who began the journey, only 155 were able-bodied warriors. Major engagements included the Battle of the Clearwater, July 11–12; the Battle of the Big Hole, August 9; the Battle of Camas Meadows, August 20; the Battle of Canyon Creek, September 13; and the Battle of Bear Paw, September 30. On October 5, 418 Nez Percés surrendered to General Nelson A. Miles, just forty-one miles south of the Canadian border, ending what General William T. Sherman referred to as one of the most extraordinary Indian wars of record. Joseph's poig-nant surrender speech, when translated into English, ended with the oft-quoted lines, "Hear me, my chiefs, I am tired; my heart is sick and sad. From where the sun now stands, I will fight no more forever." Total casu-alties for the war were 127 soldiers, about 50 civilians, and 151 Nez Percés. Army officials estimated that the campaign cost $931,329.02.

Initially taken to Fort Leavenworth, Kansas, the Nez Percé prisoners were eventually sent to Indian Territory in Oklahoma. In 1884 officials per-mitted Joseph and 150 of his band to live on Colville Reservation in Wash-ington. For many years writers pictured Joseph as the Red Napoleon who had outwitted U.S. generals, a misconception created by General O. O. Howard, his pursuer, in several books. Only recently have historians more precisely defined Joseph's role as that of an orator, diplomat, and states-man. An inspiration to his people, he remains a symbol of the tragedy suf-fered by nineteenth-century Native Americans.

Problems in Idaho in 1878 and 1879 led to campaigns against the Ban-nocks and Sheepeaters. Violence erupted in March 1878, ninety miles southeast of Boise, Idaho, when a Bannock wounded two white men whose hogs had been feasting on camas roots, an Indian staple. After Buffalo Horn and two hundred warriors began raiding southern Idaho, white civilians organized a party of volunteers. They attacked the raiders on June 8, killing the Bannock leader. The remaining Bannocks joined with Paiutes from Malheur Agency under Oytes and Chief Egan. Combined, they numbered four hundred fifty fighting men. Captain Rueben F. Bernard and men of the First Cavalry surprised the Indians' camp on June 23. On July 8 a combined force under General O. O. Howard corralled the Indians on high ground next to Birch Creek, and Captain Bernard's cavalry pummeled them again. Outmaneuvering their pursuers by doubling back, the Bannocks and Paiutes appeared at the Umatilla Agency, near Pendleton, Oregon, where they engaged infantry under Captain Evan Mills in a six-hour fight on July 12. Chief Egan was a casualty, and his severed head became an exhibit in the Army Medical Museum in Washington DC. After their defeat, the Paiutes scattered, and the Oytes surrendered on August 12. The Paiutes lost their reservation, the government sending them to live with the Yakimas in Washington. The Bannocks, too, eventually gave up their arms. After incarceration at several military posts, they returned to their home on the Upper Snake in the summer of 1879.

Another Indian war began in May 1879, when whites accused the Sheepeaters in Idaho of several murders. Although probably falsely accused, this tribe of obscure origins, probably Shoshonis, fled into Salmon River Mountains, one of the most rugged and isolated regions of North America. Troops pursued them, and, while never mustering probably more than thirty fighting men, the Sheepeaters nearly trapped Lieutenant Henry Catley and fifty mounted men of the Seventh Infantry in Big Creek Canyon on July 29. Dogged pursuit by Lieutenant Edward S. Farrow and William C. Brown and the Umatilla scouts in August and September led to the band's surrender in early October. The Sheepeaters eventually ended up on the Fort Hall Reservation.

Idaho

BATTLEFIELDS

Clearwater Battlefield
The battlefield is located east of Highway 13 south of Stites.

On July 11–12, 1877, troops, packers, and civilian volunteers led by General O. O. Howard attacked the fleeing Nez Percés on the South Fork of the Clearwater River. While the military force eventually took possession of the Indian camp and captured some supplies, Chief Joseph and his tribesmen escaped to fight another day. Howard lost fifteen men and had twenty-five wounded, while the Nez Percés lost four men and had six wounded. The battlefield can be seen in panorama from atop Battle Ridge Road, reached from the Stites Grade Road.

White Bird Battlefield
The battlefield is located about sixteen miles southwest of Grangeville, just east of Highway 95.

Resentful at being forced to move to a new reservation, some of the non-treaty Nez Percés raided white settlers along the Salmon River on June 13–14, killing eighteen. On June 17, 1877, Captain David Perry with Companies F and H of the First Cavalry and twelve civilian volunteers engaged the five bands at White Bird Canyon. The Nez Percés won the engagement, not losing a man while killing thirty-three of Perry's men and forcing a hasty retreat to Grangeville. The battle caused the Nez Percés to flee eastward, beginning the twelve hundred-mile journey that would end just short of Canada in northeastern Montana almost four months later. A unit in Nez Percé National Historical Park, the battlefield retains its original setting. A wayside exhibit shelter overlooks the battlefield on new Highway 95.

MUSEUMS

Museum of Nez Percé Culture
A unit in Nez Percé National Historical Park, the museum is located ten miles east of Lewiston at Spalding. It is open daily from 8 AM to 6 PM, June through Labor Day, and from 8 AM to 4:30 PM the rest of the year; (208) 843–2261.

Exhibits explain Nez Percé belief and culture and tell about the Lewis and Clark expedition in the area. This is the information center for Nez Percé National Historical Park.

The Southwest

Among the first to feel the increasing tide of immigration to the California gold fields were the Yumas, who controlled the Yuma Crossing of the Colorado River. Initially, the Yumas benefited from the intrusion, charging travelers to raft them over the river. In August 1849, however, the first non-Indian ferry went into operation, and the Yumas resisted. U.S. troops occupied the crossing in 1850, and by the time the region had been acquired through the Gasden Purchase of 1854, the Indians had been subdued.

The army moved against the Jicarilla Apaches and the Utes in 1854 and 1855, defeating the Apaches at Cieneguilla and Rio Caliente in 1854, and the Utes at Poncha Pass in 1855. But similar offensives between 1857 and 1861 against the Gila and Western Apaches in the south and the Navajos to the west were less successful, providing little respite to the settlements.

Cochise, leader of the central band of Chiricahuas, parted ways with the Anglos in 1861, after being wrongly accused of raiding the Sonoita Creek ranch of John Ward and kidnapping his adopted son. After capture by Lieutenant George N. Bascom, who feigned friendship, Cochise escaped by cutting his way out of an army tent. The "Bascom Affair" set Cochise off on a series of raids that resulted in one hundred fifty deaths in two months. In reprisal Bascom hanged Cochise's brother, two nephews, and three others. The next year Cochise joined forces with his father-in-law, Mangus Coloradus, leader of the eastern Chiricahuas. Prior to this time, Mangus Coloradus had only raided Mexicans in revenge for wrongs done to his people. On July 15, 1862, the two chiefs attempted to ambush General James H. Carleton's advance command of California Volunteers at Apache Pass at the northern end of the Chiricahua Mountains. Howitzers enabled troops to rout the ambushers. On January 17, 1863, troops captured Mangus Coloradus under a flag of truce near Pinos Altos, New Mexico. On the night of January 18, he was shot trying to escape, or at least that was the official report. A prospector with the troops reported that he had been shot after objecting to soldiers burning his legs and feet with heated bayonets.

Carleton sent Kit Carson, colonel of the First New Mexico Cavalry, to control the Mescalero Apaches, a tribe that ranged from parts of Chihuahua, Coahuila, and northwestern Texas north to the thirty-fourth parallel and from the Rio Grande eastward beyond the Pecos River. After the abandonment of Fort Stanton in July 1861, the Mescaleros began raiding stock herds for subsistence, killing settlers in the process. Within a year Carson had captured about four hundred Mescaleros and sent them to a new reservation in the Pecos River Valley, known as the Bosque Redondo because of its distinctive circular grove of cottonwood trees. In November 1865 the Mescaleros bolted their inhospitable reservation and remained free for another eight years. In 1863 and 1864 Carleton also led a well-planned campaign against the Navajos, an important blow being delivered at Canyon De Chelly by troops under Kit Carson. The campaign ended for the Navajos in the "Long Walk" to Bosque Redondo in 1864 and the surrender of their principal leader, Manuelito, two years later. Permitted to return to their homeland in July 1868, the Navajos never again challenged the might of the U.S. government.

War began in earnest between the Western Apache and Anglos in 1863 when gold was discovered in Tonto territory. Conflict came to a climax on April 30, 1871, near Camp Grant in southern Arizona, where the Arivaipa band under Chief Eskiminzin had sought and received asylum. Blamed for killings fifty miles north, the Apaches were surprised in their camp by a group of Tucson Anglos, Mexicans, and ninety-four Papago warriors. Losing not a single man, they attacked and killed about one hundred Apache men, women, and children. Sold into slavery or given away to Papago families were twenty-nine captive children. The courts later tried the perpetrators, who gained acquittal after only nineteen minutes of deliberation.

Eastern protests of the butchery prompted President Grant to send emissaries Vincent Colyer, noted Indian reformer, and General O. O. Howard, Civil War hero and former head of the Freedman's Bureau. The new Department of Arizona commander was General George Crook, who had little use for Howard, but did not stand in his way. With the help of Thomas J. Jeffords, a close friend of Cochise, Howard met with the Apaches in the Dragoon Mountains in southwestern Arizona. Cochise agreed to occupy a reservation of his own choosing, a tract including most of the southwest corner of the territory. Two years after his death from stomach cancer in 1874, the government moved the Chiricahuas to the San Carlos reservation.

It was left to General George Crook to deal the Western Apaches the final blow. In November 1872 he launched a campaign lasting for nearly eighteen months, involving twenty skirmishes, and ending with the Apaches' surrender. In a reminiscence, Charles King described Crook's relentless method of pursuit:

> From October '72 until April '73, this marvel of a general was in the heart of the Arizona mountains with his troopers at his back; darting from range to range, marching night and day, striking right, left, front and rear; breaking up rendezvous, burning rancherias, scaling the highest peaks, charging into the blackest caves, tracking the fleeing foe, creeping among them in the darkness, dashing in upon them with the dawn, bringing terror and dismay to the bands that had never known a conqueror, and never quitting his relentless pursuit until he had, indeed, swept the Apaches from the face of the earth, or herded them, humbled and subdued, upon their reservation.[3]

With six thousand Apaches on the reservation, Crook was a hero.

Victorio led the Eastern Chiricahuas after the death of Mangus Coloradus. He raided until 1865, when he agreed to settle down on a reservation. The Chiricahuas camped peacefully at Ojo Caliente or Warm Springs waiting for the government to act. The decision did not come until 1877, and it was not to their liking as they received orders to move to the barren San Carlos Reservation. Refusing, the Chiricahuas left to raid in Mexico. They returned to Warm Springs in 1878 but left again when troops arrived to force them to San Carlos.

By 1879 Victorio had entrenched himself and a large number of followers south of the Rio Grande in Mexico, where raids continued unabated. On October 14, 1880, U.S. and Mexican forces cornered the band near the Tres Castillos Mountains in Chihuahua, south of El Paso, Texas. Sending the Americans on their way, the Mexican troops attacked, killing all but seventeen, Victorio among them. Leadership of the remaining Chiricahuas fell to Nana, who soon terrorized part of Texas, southwestern New Mexico, and northern Chihuahua. In six weeks from mid-July to August 1881, his little band of thirty or forty warriors killed an equal number of Americans and fought a dozen skirmishes with troops, winning most of them. Having had enough of war in 1883, he surrendered to General Crook and went to San Carlos.

In April 1877 Geronimo was arrested at Warm Springs by Indian agent John Clum and taken to San Carlos with 110 of his band. Four years later he left the reservation, operating chiefly in the Sierra Madre of Mexico and in southeastern Arizona and southwestern New Mexico. In the summer of

1881, a medicine man incited Apaches to a religious fervor that led to a fight with Colonel Eugene A. Carr's troops on Cibecue Creek in which the Indian scouts sided with their tribesmen.

In 1882 Crook returned to his old job as commander of the Department of Arizona. In the spring of 1883, he led one of the most remarkable Indian expeditions of record into the Sierra Madre of Mexico. The force consisted of Crook, one company of cavalry, and nearly two hundred Apache scouts. At great personal risk and with his professional career on the line, Crook succeeded in persuading Victorio and Geronimo and their Chiricahuas to return to San Carlos. It was an extraordinary feat.

In speaking of his method of fighting the Apaches, Crook later said, The only thing to be done is to run them down and make them surrender. . . . Chasing these redskins with the limited facilities at our disposal is something like trying to run down a flock of crows with cavalry. They have to be chased through mountains, valleys, forests and plains with often nothing but an old and indistinct trail to indicate the direction in which they have gone. They can travel ten miles where our cavalry can travel one, and they know every inch of the country. No more troops are needed—the present force is amply large enough. If the force were ten times as large the result would be the same.[4]

Geronimo took his time returning to the reservation, arriving in February 1884, but in May 1885 he took to the war trail once again. Crook followed with columns into the Sierra Madre, and by March 1886 he had persuaded the malcontents to come in for peace talks. All but Geronimo and his few followers returned. The latter backed out at the last moment, as bootleg whiskey and rumors of plans to kill him caused him to flee. When his superiors failed to back his surrender conditions, Crook asked to be relieved, and on April 28, 1886, he assumed command of the Department of the Platte for the second time. His replacement, Nelson A. Miles, was able to bring a successful conclusion to the campaign, when Lieutenant Charles Gatewood met Geronimo in his mountain retreat and convinced him to surrender.

On September 3, 1886, Geronimo had the distinction of being the last war chief of the Apaches to surrender formally to the United States. Sent to prison in Florida, Geronimo returned to Fort Sill, Oklahoma, five years later where he earned money selling photos of himself and small bows and arrows with his name on them. Crook died of heart failure on March 21, 1890, at his Chicago headquarters while exercising with dumbbells.

Apaches on the reservation mourned his death. At the time he was waging a political battle to have the long-time Apache prisoners of war released from imprisonment and sent to live in Oklahoma.

Arizona

HISTORIC SITES

Fort Verde State Historic Park
Take exit 279 from I-17. The visitor center is open daily from 8 AM to 5 PM; (602) 567–5276.

Camp Verde (1866–1891) protected the settlers in the Verde Valley of central Arizona and served as General George Crook's base of operations against the Yavapai in 1872–1873. The government sold the post's buildings at pubic auction, and only four survive: the administration building, which houses a museum, and living quarters for the post commander, the post surgeon, and the bachelor officers, all of which are refurnished.

Fort Apache
Take Highway 73 seven miles south of Whiteriver to the Fort Apache Indian Reservation headquarters and then to the nearby site. Call (602) 338–4625 to schedule a tour of the Indian village.

The post (1870–1924) guarded the Fort Apache Agency of the White Mountain Apache Reservation. Here General Crook organized his first company of Apache scouts, one of the tactical innovations that made him one of the most successful commanders in the Indian wars. Many buildings remain, including the adjutant's building that now serves as the U.S. Post Office and the log cabin reputedly used by Crook during the Apache wars. The Fort Apache Cultural Center exhibits Indian and military artifacts and interprets the history of the White Mountain Apaches. Nearby is an 1880s Apache Indian Village.

Fort Bowie National Historic Site
From Wilcox, travel southwest on Highway 186 and pass through Dos Cabeza. Twenty-two miles down the road is a graded gravel road that leads six miles to Fort Bowie. From the parking area in Apache Pass, a 1.5 mile foot trail leads to the ruins on site. Open all year-round; (602) 384–2272.

Garrisoned in 1862, Fort Bowie served for thirty-two years as the center of military operations against the Chiricahua Apaches. Established in the

Chiricahua Mountains, it guarded the eastern entrance of Apache Pass, a key to unimpeded transportation in the region. From here George Crook and Nelson Miles led expeditions that ended the power of Cochise, Mangas Colorado, Natchez, and Geronimo. Today rock foundations and adobe vestiges mark the site of the original fort, while rock foundations and wall fragments dot the slope below Bowie Peak. Still visible are the stone corrals. A small adobe museum is on site, where books, postcards, rest rooms, and drinking water are available.

Fort Huachuca

Fort Huachuca is located on the Fort Huachuca Military Reservation in the town of Fort Huachuca. For information call the Sierra Vista Chamber of Commerce at (602) 458–6940 or (800) 288–3861.

The army established Fort Huachuca in 1877 to protect settlers against the Chiricahua Apaches. Here Captain Henry W. Lawton organized the special force that chased Geronimo and his followers through the Sierra Madres during the summer of 1886. The original buildings, including adobe officers' quarters built in the 1880s, have been remodeled to serve the needs of their present tenant, the U.S. Army Strategic Communications Command. On site is an excellent museum covering the history of the post. Black regiments served here during the late 1800s, commemorated by "Buffalo Soldier Days" in late May.

BATTLEFIELDS

Cibecue Creek Battlefield

The battlefield is located on the Fort Apache Indian Reservation on an unimproved road, about two and one-half miles south of Cibecue.

The invasion of settlers and miners created Indian resentment, fanned by the teachings of Medicine Man Nakaidoklini. Fearing the worst, the Indian agent at the White Mountain (Fort Apache) Reservation called for military support. On August 30, 1881, Colonel Eugene A. Carr, with eighty-five men and twenty-three Apache scouts, arrested the medicine man at his camp on Cibecue Creek. Moving two and one-half miles down creek, they camped, where Nakaidoklini's disciples attacked them. In the battle some of the army's Apache scouts fled, shooting a captain and six soldiers before joining their tribesmen. The medicine man was killed by his guard, while Carr repulsed his assailants. The next day, while Carr fought a force of about five hundred, other warriors attacked Fort Apache, but it held. Today, the site of the battlefield remains in its natural setting within the Fort Apache Reservation.

MUSEUMS

The Heard Museum

The museum is located at 22 East Monte Vista Road, Phoenix. It is open Monday through Saturday from 10 AM to 5 PM, Wednesday until 8 PM, and Sunday from noon to 5 PM The museum features baskets, jewelry, kachina dolls, pottery, and textiles of the Southwest. Included are an authentic Navajo hogan, an Apache wickiup, and a Hopi corn grinding room.

INDIAN HERITAGE SITES

Cochise Stronghold

Cochise Stronghold is ten miles west by dirt road from Highway 666 at Sunsites. For information call the Pearce Chamber of Commerce at (602) 826–3535.

In the Dragoon Mountains was the place where the Chiricahua Apache leader Cochise and his followers sought refuge and kept U.S. Army forces at bay. In 1860, when falsely accused of a kidnapping by a young officer, Cochise broke away. After the army hanged those left behind, Cochise took to the warpath, raiding the Overland Trail, killing perhaps one hundred fifty travelers in a few months. Finally, in 1872 Scout Tom Jeffords convinced the chief to surrender. Within two years Cochise was dead. His friends hid his remains in the canyon. There is a picnic area at the canyon mouth and hiking trails throughout the area. The site is now part of the Coronado National Forest.

Hubbell Trading Post National Historic Site

The trading post is located on Highway 191 in Ganado in the eastern part of the Navajo Reservation. It is open daily from 8 AM to 5 PM; (602) 755–3254.

The National Park Service operates this facility. Built in 1883, the trading post remains in operation as it did in the nineteenth century. In a separate building, weavers ply their craft. Another building has exhibits on the role of the trader in the economy of the Old South.

New Mexico

HISTORIC SITES

Fort Stanton

Take an unimproved road about fifteen miles northwest of Las Cruces.

Founded in 1855 to control the Mescalero Apaches, Fort Stanton became the guardian of the tribe's reservation in 1871, to which the Jicarilla Apaches came in 1883. The reservation became a virtual replacement depot for the hostile Apaches, and many joined Victorio's band in 1879. His death in 1880 made the task of patrolling the reservation easier. The army abandoned Fort Stanton in 1896, which became a U.S. Public Health Service facility three years later. Today it is a state sanitarium. Many stone buildings from 1868 remain, remodeled for use as homes, wards, and offices. Grouped around three sides of the parade grounds are the commanding officer's house, other officers quarters, and barracks.

Fort Union National Monument
Fort Union is eight miles north of I-25, at the end of New Mexico 161, near Las Vegas. The park is open daily from 8 AM to 5 PM, except January 1 and December 25; (505) 425–8025.

Established in 1851 to guard the Santa Fe Trail, Fort Union served for four decades as the bulwark of frontier defense in the Southwest, providing a base for campaigns against the Apaches, Utes, Navajos, Kiowas, and Comanches. Constructed in three stages, from log fort (1851) to star-shaped earthen fortress (1861–1862) to sprawling adobe post (1863–1869), it became one of the largest U.S. military installations on the New Mexico and Arizona frontier. Remaining are an eighty-acre collection of the ruins of rock and adobe structures, preserved as an outdoor museum. Ruts of the Santa Fe Trail can be seen nearby. Administered by the National Park Service, the park has a visitor center and interpretive personnel.

Texas

HISTORIC SITES

Fort Concho
Fort Concho is located at 213 East Avenue D, San Angelo TX. It is open Tuesday through Saturday from 10 AM to 5 PM and Sunday from 1 to 5 PM

Fort Concho (1867–1889) guarded the San Antonio–El Paso Road and the Goodnight–Loving Cattle Trail, deep in Kiowa and Comanche country. Serving there were Ranald Mackenzie, Wesley Merritt, Anson Mills, and Benjamin Grierson. Troops under Mackenzie participated in the Battle of Palo Duro Canyon on September 27, 1874, and in the campaign against Victorio in 1879–1880. Today San Angelo preserves much of Fort Concho as an historic site. Designated a National Historic Landmark, Fort Concho contains two dozen original and reconstructed buildings, including the Robert Wood Johnson Museum of Frontier Medicine. Other structures have exhibits on Indian campaigns. Reenactors perform at special events.

Fort Davis National Historic Site

Located on Highway 17 just north of the town of Fort Davis, the park is open daily from 8 AM to 5 PM; (915) 426–3202.

The army established Fort Davis in 1854 to protect gold seekers headed for California along the San Antonio–El Paso Road from the Kiowas, Comanches, and Mescalero Apaches. Confederates occupied the post in 1861–1862 but then withdrew upon the approach of California Volunteers. The post remained deserted for five years, until Lieutenant Colonel Wesley Merritt and the buffalo soldiers of the Ninth Cavalry reactivated it. From then until 1885 Fort Davis was home to the black regiments, with details of the Ninth and Tenth Cavalry and the Twenty-fourth and Twenty-fifth Infantry serving there from time to time. Soldiers built a new post near the mouth of the canyon, completing it in the early 1880s. In the summer of 1880, Colonel Benjamin Grierson led forces from Fort Davis against Victorio, defeating the Apache leader and his followers in two battles in July and August and forcing the band into Mexico. Abandoned in 1891, Fort Davis is now a unit in the National Park System. The restored barracks serves as a museum and visitor center. Costumed rangers give tours during the summer, and the staff performs a military dress parade daily at 11 AM and 4 PM

Fort McKavett State Historic Site

The fort is located forty miles northeast of Sonora in the small town of Fort McKavett. The visitor center is open daily from 8 AM to 5 PM

The army established Fort McKavett in 1852 to help guard the Texas frontier. Evacuated in 1859, it was used intermittently by the Confederates during the Civil War. Reoccupied in 1869 by troops under Colonel Ranald Mackenzie, the post became important in the Red River War (1874–1875) and the Victorio Campaign (1879–1880). Abandoned in 1883, the fort is now the town of Fort McKavett. The post hospital serves as a visitor center.

BATTLEFIELDS

Adobe Walls

The site is located in Hutchinson County on an unimproved road, about seventeen miles northeast of Stinnett.

The Adobe Walls were the remains of a trading post built on the Canadian River by William Bent in the 1840s. In late November 1864, Kit Carson's force of about four hundred California and New Mexico Volunteers, Utes, and Jicarilla Apaches found Chief Little Mountain's village of about one thousand Kiowas camped on the site. In the battle that followed, the Kiowas received aid from other Kiowas and Comanches camped nearby, but Carson's two mountain howitzers made the difference. After burning the camp, Carson and his troops returned to Fort Bascom, New Mexico, leaving three dead. Indian casualties numbered sixty. Almost ten years later, on June 27, 1874, the site was the scene of one of the most famous of all encounters. Taking refuge in two stores and a saloon recently constructed by hunters and traders from Dodge City, Kansas, twenty-eight buffalo hunters held off a large number of Kiowas and Comanches for two days until others arrived to rescue them. Owned by the Panhandle-Plains Historical Society of Canyon, Texas, the site is marked, but all signs of the buildings have disappeared.

Palo Duro Canyon Battlefield State Park
The battlefield is located in Armstrong County, about twenty miles southeast of the town of Canyon.

On September 27 Colonel Mackenzie led troops in an attack on Comanches camped in Palo Duro Canyon on the Staked Plains. Troops captured the pony herd of fourteen hundred animals before retreating in the face of a strong counterattack. This decrease in mobility was important in the Comanche's decision to seek peace. The site is accessible by foot only, but may be viewed from the south rim of the canyon about ten miles northwest of Wayside.

The Southern Plains

For decades the Comanches successfully defended their homeland in western Kansas, Oklahoma, and Texas from other tribes, the Spanish, the Mexicans, and the Texans, before being confronted in the mid-1850s with white populations intent on wresting a living from the soil or beating a path to the gold fields of Colorado. Depletion of game led to conflict along the western frontier all the way from Texas to the Northern Plains. Initial white response occurred on May 11, 1858, when veteran Indian fighter Captain John S. "Rip" Ford and one hundred Texas Rangers attacked a Comanche village in the Canadian River valley near the Antelope Hills. For seven hours they battled three hundred warriors, who finally fled, leaving seventy-six dead.

In the fall Major Earl Van Dorn commanded the "Wichita Expedition." In a surprise attack on the morning of October 1, 350 men of the Second Cavalry charged the Indian village on Rush Creek, killing 56 warriors and 2 women and destroying 120 lodges and many supplies. Campaigning resumed in the spring of 1859, when 58 Indian scouts and 428 men of the Second Cavalry left Fort Radziminski. On May 13 an advance party under First Lieutenant William B. Royall attacked a small village on Crooked Creek, capturing 37 and killing 49 warriors and 8 women. Second Cavalry casualties included 1 killed and 13 wounded. Despite this success, and a comprehensive campaign during the summer of 1860, the Comanches and Kiowas remained a threat that would continue for another two decades.

Farther south, raiding by the Cheyennes in response to increased traffic on the Smoky Hill Trail brought Colonel Edwin V. Sumner into the field. On July 27, 1857, his troops caught the Cheyennes on the Solomon Fork in western Kansas. Facing three hundred warriors with an identical number of cavalry, "Bull" Sumner ordered his men to charge with sabers. The Cheyennes who had dipped their hands in a magical lake to repel bullets but not swords gave ground, and the soldiers pursued them for seven miles. After the meeting with Sumner, the Cheyennes became more tolerant of white intrusion.

Action on the Southern Plains escalated in 1864. By the Treaty of Fort Wise in 1861, the Southern Cheyennes and Arapahos had agreed to settle on a reservation but continued to raid occasionally as usual. Governor John Evans of Colorado and his territorial military commander John M. Chivington pushed for war to settle the matter. What turned out to be the beginning of what Eugene F. Ware called the Indian War of 1864 occurred on April 22, when a detachment of the First Colorado Volunteer Cavalry skirmished with Cheyennes at Fremont Orchard on the South Platte, about sixty miles northeast of Denver. The bloody encounter fueled fears that a general uprising of Plains Indian tribes was forthcoming. Thereafter, the Colorado militia began skirmishing with Indians wherever they found them. As the year progressed, the number of incidents increased, and both sides responded vigorously. At the end of the fall of 1864, a momentous event occurred in southeastern Colorado that would have a great impact on those who lived on the Central and Northern Plains the following year.

On November 29 the hostile spirit found full expression. In a dawn attack Colonel John Chivington and his force of Colorado Volunteers stormed Black Kettle's band of Southern Cheyennes camped on the upper reaches of Sand Creek. Believing themselves to be under the care of the military at Fort Lyon, the Indians were taken completely by surprise. When the fighting was over some two hundred were dead, mostly women and children. The volunteers later dangled scalps and severed genitals before cheering crowds in Denver. While nine chiefs died in the battle, Black Kettle escaped. The result of the barbaric act at Sand Creek was to enrage the Indians of the plains. The warriors of the Cheyennes and Arapahos and their close allies, the Sioux, began preparations for requital. When word of the slaughter reached the East, investigations followed, including one by a congressional joint committee. Although roundly condemned, Chivington escaped punishment, having left the army.

Following the massacre at Sand Creek, the Cheyennes and their Sioux and Arapaho allies gathered to seek vengeance. The first target was Julesburg, Colorado, the division headquarters of the Overland Stage Company and an important station of the Pacific Telegraph. On the morning of January 7 the avengers lured a small force from nearby Fort Rankin. In the ensuing fight the warriors killed four noncommissioned officers and eleven enlisted men, while the rest attacked Julesburg. In response General Mitchell led six hundred forty men on an unsuccessful twelve-day hunt for the raiders, covering three hundred sixty miles to the south and west. Failing contact, he ordered his troops to set fire to the prairie, which had little effect except perhaps to deepen the hate the Sioux and Cheyenne already had for the whites.

On the morning of February 2 the raiders returned to Julesburg, this time to finish what they had begun. Some witnesses claimed that between fifteen hundred and twenty-five hundred warriors participated in the second attack. Troops from the post skirmished with the attackers but were unable to drive them away. When it was over what had been Julesburg lay in smoldering ruins. Moving northwest, warriors attacked the telegraph station at Mud Springs on February 6, eventually engaging one hundred sixty troops from the Eleventh Ohio and the Seventh Iowa in a fight on Rush Creek on February 8. After two days of exchanging fire, the raiders withdrew, leaving in their wake burned ranches and plundered settlements. Moving through the Black Hills, the avenging warriors joined with their North Cheyenne kinsman and Sioux tribes to continue the war on the Northern Plains at Platte Bridge Station and elsewhere, returning south in the fall of 1865.

Quiet remained on the Central Plains until the summer of 1867, when General Winfield S. Hancock led an expedition to intimidate the Cheyennes and Arapahos. Instead of frightening them, Hancock aroused a people who had not yet forgotten Sand Creek. After bullying a delegation of chiefs at Fort Larned, he moved to a nearby village of Sioux and Cheyennes, whose fearful members fled in the night. When these Indians or others raided north across the Smoky Hill Trail, Hancock burned the captured village. The result was a summer of killing, pillaging, and attacking supply trains and ranches along the Platte, Arkansas, and Smokey Hill Rivers. Hancock's chief subordinate, Lieutenant Colonel George Armstrong Custer, spent months in a futile chase, wearing out his men and horses. Hancock's abortive campaign led to new initiatives for peace. Commissioners, including three generals, appointed by the president negotiated a treaty at Medicine Lodge Creek, Kansas, in the fall of 1867. The treaty created a large reservation in Indian Territory for the Cheyennes and the Arapahos and another for the Kiowas, Comanches, and Kiowa-Apaches. The government expected Indians to build a new life through agriculture.

Soon tribes on the Southern Plains reacted to the advance of the Kansas Pacific Railroad, which scared game away and attracted white settlement. Raids along the Saline and Solomon Rivers in 1868 brought troops into the field. Because troops were so few in number, General Sheridan authorized recruitment of fifty frontiersmen for use as scouts, placing them under the command of Major George Forsyth. On September 17 Forsyth's scouts encountered six hundred to seven hundred Dog Soldiers and Oglalas on the

Arikaree Fork of the Republican River in eastern Colorado. Digging in on a small island in the middle of the river, the scouts withstood attack after attack during the next two days, perhaps the most remembered charge being one led by the fabled Northern Cheyenne warrior Roman Nose, who suffered a mortal wound. Several days before, Roman Nose had participated in a Sioux feast during which he had eaten a piece of fry bread that had been removed from the fire with a metal fork, violating his taboo. Believing that he would die in the next encounter, he did not participate in the early fighting at Beecher's Island. However, late in the afternoon, after repeated urging by other warriors, he mounted his warhorse and led a charge in which he was shot through the body, dying the next day. He remains a symbol of the proud spirit of the Fighting Cheyennes. For seven more days the scouts subsisted on rotting horseflesh before help came from Captain Louis H. Carpenter's company of Tenth Cavalry. Lieutenant Frederick Beecher, nephew of the famous preacher, Henry Ward Beecher, died in the battle, as did five other men.

General Sheridan finally devised a plan whereby three columns would converge on the winter grounds of the Indians just east of the Texas Panhandle, one from Fort Lyon in Colorado, one from Fort Bascom in New Mexico, and one from Fort Dodge in Kansas. The Seventh Cavalry regiment under Lieutenant Colonel Custer fought the major engagement of the campaign. On November 29 Custer and eleven companies attacked Black Kettle's camp on the Washita River from four directions, killing more than a hundred, taking fifty-three women and children prisoners, and slaughtering nine hundred Indian ponies before neighboring Indian camps rallied. Five soldiers died in the village, and the loss of Major Joel Elliot and his detachment of fifteen men, which some believed had been abandoned, created animosity for Custer. This time Black Kettle was not so fortunate: he died with his wife in an attempt to escape. While some proclaimed another Sand Creek, army officers countered that the village contained ample evidence of depredations and four white prisoners, two of whom were killed by their captors during the fighting.

Another army victory was the Battle of Soldier Spring, on Christmas Day, 1868, in which Major Andrew W. Evans's New Mexico troops attacked a Comanche camp on the Red River. Early in 1869 Custer resumed the campaign against the Cheyennes. On March 15 he approached the village of Medicine Arrows and Little Robe on Sweetwater Creek, Texas, where two white women were known to be held captive. In a parley Custer took four chiefs hostage and demanded the release of the women. After

Custer threatened to hang three of the chiefs, the Cheyennes acquiesced and promised to go to their reservation. The Dog Soldiers, however, returned to their free ways. On July 11, 1869, Major Eugene Carr with the Fifth Cavalry and Pawnee Scouts under Major Frank North found them at Summit Springs, Colorado. In the fight that followed, Tall Bull and twenty followers died. From then on the Southern Cheyennes occupied reservations in Indian Territory.

After reservation Kiowas raided into Texas in 1871, General Sherman had their leaders arrested in a dramatic confrontation at Fort Sill. Satank died in an escape attempt, while Satanta and Big Tree received two-year prison sentences. After incarceration again in 1876, Satanta took his own life by throwing himself from the two-story window of a Texas penitentiary.

From posts in Texas, New Mexico, and Indian Territories in 1874, Nelson A. Miles led a campaign against Comanches, Kiowas, Cheyennes, and Arapahos. Five columns of troops converged on the Texas Panhandle. Consisting of forty-six companies in all, a force of over three thousand men, the blue coats precipitated seven major battles and seven minor skirmishes. The principal engagement among them was the Battle of Palo Duro Canyon, September 24, 1874, when Colonel Ranald S. Mackenzie and the Fourth Cavalry surprised the Indians' winter camp on the Stake Plains. The troops burned the fugitives' belongings and captured their horses, forcing many back to the reservation. The Southern Cheyennes' defeat at Sappa Creek by the Sixth Cavalry in April 1875 ended that tribe's power. By the end of 1879, buffalo had disappeared from the Southern Plains, ending the possibility of future outbreaks.

In the mid-1870s silver strikes in the San Juan Mountains in western Colorado led to further pressures on the Uncompahgre Utes to reduce their reservation, and the government was able to secure another four million acres for a token payment. In 1879, when the Indians refused to become farmers at the insistence of new Indian agent Nathaniel C. Meeker, the Indian Bureau called for troops to enforce the new pattern of living. The Utes responded by killing their agent and six of his assistants. On September 29 they attacked the approaching cavalry from Fort Fred Steele under Major Thomas R. Thornburgh, killing him and twelve others and wounding forty-three. The fight at White River resulted in the amassing of a huge force to handle the situation, but Chief Ouray was able to arrange a truce. When Ouray died the following year, the Uncompahgre lacked leadership. To punish the Utes the government seized their twelve-thousand-acre reservation and exiled them to two smaller tracts in nearby Utah. Many decades later they received compensation from the federal government for lands taken from them in the 1870s.

Colorado

HISTORIC SITES

Bent's Old Fort National Historic Site
Located eight miles northeast of La Junta on Highway 194, this National Park Service area is open year-round starting at 8 AM; (719) 384–2596.

Built on the Santa Fe Trail in the early 1830s by William Bent to trade with trappers and the Indians of the Central and Southern Plains, this huge adobe-walled fort was the center of life and business in southern Colorado for two decades. Bent abandoned the fort in 1849 following a cholera epidemic that decimated Plains Indians in the area. Others used the remnants of the fort in later years, and the walls finally disappeared in the first decades of the twentieth century. Reconstructed by the National Park Service in 1975–1976 to look as it did in 1845, the massive fifteen-foot-high quadrangle has twenty-four rooms, many of them refurnished, including a well-stocked trading post where visitors may purchase period items. Costumed personnel explain the fort's history, and each year living history reenactors meet for the Old Time Fourth of July at Bent's Fort.

Fort Garland
Located in Fort Garland on Highway 159, the post is open April 15 through October 15 from 9 AM to 4:30 PM; (303) 379–3512.

Established in 1858 within what was then New Mexico, Fort Garland remained a military post until 1883. Its purpose was to protect settlers in the San Luis Valley and keep Ute and Apache warriors from raiding the roads south to Taos. In 1866–1867, Kit Carson commanded the fort, which is now owned by the State Historical Society of Colorado. Restored buildings include officers' quarters, cavalry and infantry barracks, store rooms, guard rooms, and the adjutant's office.

BATTLEFIELDS

Beecher's Island Battlefield
The battlefield is located in Yuma County adjacent to the town of Beecher Island.

In response to a request of Sheridan for an independent command,

George A. Forsyth received permission to employ fifty frontiersmen as scouts. On September 17 his little force discovered about six hundred Sioux and Cheyennes on the Arikaree Fork of the Republican River. Digging in on a small island in the middle of the river, the scouts withstood attack after attack during the next two days, perhaps the most remembered charge being that led by the renowned Northern Cheyenne warrior Roman Nose, who suffered a mortal wound. For seven more days the scouts subsisted on rotting horseflesh before help came. Six soldiers were killed and fifteen wounded. The Cheyennes lost about twenty. This skirmish gripped the imagination of the American people, becoming a symbol of soldier pluck in the face of overwhelming odds, enshrining Forsyth as a national hero. A small state park encompasses the site of the stand by Forsyth's scout, but the changing course of the river has obliterated the island. A stone monument commemorates the battle.

Milk Creek Battlefield

The battlefield is located in Moffat County about twenty miles northeast of Meeker.

On September 29 troops under Major Thomas T. Thornburgh sent to punish the Utes who had killed agent Meeker and his family rode into an ambush. Corralling their wagons, Thornburgh's men held out for seven days until reinforcements from Fort D. A. Russell under General Wesley Merritt rescued them and defeated the Utes. Killed during the siege were Major Thornburgh and twelve others. The government imprisoned several of the Utes and sent the rest to a new reservation. The site remains relatively unchanged. A monument lists the names of the dead soldiers.

Sand Creek Battlefield

The battlefield is located in Kiowa County, eight miles north and one mile east of Chivington (U.S. 96).

On November 29 in a dawn attack Colonel John M. Chivington and his force of Colorado Volunteers swept down on Black Kettle's band of Southern Cheyennes. Believing themselves under the protection of troops at Fort Lyon, the Indians were not expecting trouble. The volunteers killed two hundred Cheyennes, mostly women and children, and displayed their bloody trophies in celebrations in Denver. Outraged, the American public demanded investigations, which soon followed. Chivington escaped retribution by resigning his commission. In retaliation the Cheyennes and Arapahos persuaded their Sioux allies to join them in a campaign of revenge.

The land along Sand Creek is undisturbed, utilized for grazing. A small monument stands on a hill above the battleground. A small fee gains access to this privately owned site. Some questions remain concerning the provenance of the site, and investigations are under way to determine its validity through research and archaeological investigation.

Summit Springs Battlefield

The battlefield is located in Logan and Washington Counties, about ten miles southeast of Atwood.

On July 11 Major Eugene A. Carr, with five companies of the Fifth Cavalry, scout Buffalo Bill, and three companies of Pawnee scouts under the North Brothers, caught Tall Bull's Cheyenne Dog Soldiers at Summit Springs. Killed in the surprise attack were fifty-two Cheyennes, including their leader, while troops captured seventeen women. Only one soldier was wounded. A small parking area allows the traveler to look out on the battlefield, used as ranch land by a private owner. Two markers provide information.

MUSEUMS

Colorado History Museum

Located at Thirteenth and Broadway in downtown Denver, the museum is open Monday through Saturday from 10 AM to 4:30 PM; (303) 866–03682. Among other exhibits are dioramas showing Indian life in Colorado.

Koshare Indian Kiva Museum

The museum is located at 115 West Eighteenth Street in La Junta. It is open daily from noon to 5 PM; (719) 384–4411.

The museum contains displays of the art and artifacts of the Plains and Southwest Indians. Home of the Koshare Dancers, a traveling group of Boy Scouts, the impersonators perform there on Saturday nights during the summer and the Christmas weekend.

Ute Indian Museum

Located at 17253 Chipeta 81401, Montrose, the museum is open May 1 to October 15, from 9 AM to 5 PM; (303) 249–4098. The six-acre tract was once part of a farm owned by Chief Oruay and his wife Chipeta, who are buried there. The museum traces the history of the Utes from before European contact to the present.

Kansas

HISTORIC SITES

Fort Hays

This fort is located at Frontier Historical Park, 1472 Highway 183 Alternate, Hays, Kansas. The remaining buildings of Fort Hays are near the intersection of Main Street (U.S. 183) and Business I-70 (U.S. 40) on the southern edge of the city. The museum is open from 10 AM to 5 PM weekdays and from 1 to 5 PM weekends.

Built in 1865 to protect travelers on the Smoky Hill Trail, settlers from the Indians, and workers building the Kansas Pacific Railroad, Fort Hays was General Hancock's supply base for his 1867 campaign and served as General Sheridan's temporary headquarters in 1868–1869. With the arrival of the railroad to nearby Hays City, the post became a quartermaster depot that supplied other forts throughout the West and Southwest. Miles and the Custers served here. Found in Frontier Historical Park, the four remaining structures are the two-story stone blockhouse, the guardhouse, and two frame officers' quarters. The Kansas State Historical Society preserves the buildings and maintains a museum in the blockhouse.

Fort Larned National Historic Site

Located six miles west of Larned on Highway 156, the National Park Service area is open year-round from 8 AM to 5 PM

The best preserved of all the old forts guarding the Santa Fe Trail, Fort Larned is a National Historic Site administered by the National Park Service. Built in 1860 to help guard the Santa Fe Trail (1822–1880), it was from here that Generals Hancock and Custer left in 1867 on their unsuccessful campaign against the Cheyennes and Sioux. In the mid-1860s the post became an agency for the Kiowas and Comanches. Troops left in 1878, and the fort became a ranch headquarters in the mid-1800s. With ten restored and refurnished buildings, Fort Larned is one of the most complete military posts remaining from the nineteenth century. Santa Fe Trail ruts are visible in the area.

Fort Leavenworth

Take U.S. Highway 73 to Historic Fort Leavenworth. The Frontier Army Museum is open all year Monday through Friday from 9 AM to 4 PM, Saturday from 10 AM to 4 PM, and Sunday from noon to 4 PM; (913) 684-3191.

Established on May 8, 1827, to protect caravans along the Santa Fe

Trail, it is the oldest continually active military post west of the Mississippi. The U.S. Army Command and General Staff College and the U.S. Disciplinary Barracks are part of the facility. On Reynolds Avenue is the Frontier Army Museum, organized around the theme of the army's role in westward expansion. Military uniforms of the Indian wars are featured. A living history unit performs at scheduled times. Home to George Custer, Douglas MacArthur, and Dwight D. Eisenhower, the Rookery (1832) is the oldest house in Kansas. Others associated with the post include Stephen Watts Kearny, Alexander Doniphan, Albert Sidney Johnston, William S. Harney, Edwin V. Summer, and Benjamin Grierson. The cemetery holds many burials from the Indian wars.

Fort Riley

To reach Fort Riley, take exit 301 from Interstate I-70 and turn left on Sheridan Avenue. The U.S. Cavalry Museum is open Monday through Saturday from 9 AM to 4:30 PM and Sunday from noon to 4:30 PM; (913) 239–2737.

The army established Fort Riley in 1853 as a staging area for soldiers who patrolled the Smoky Hill, Oregon, and Santa Fe Trails. Prior to the Civil War, its soldiers policed Kansas Territory to keep peace between pro- and anti-slave groups. Here in the fall of 1866 George Armstrong Custer arrived to take command of the Seventh Cavalry, then being mustered in. After the area's Indians had been subdued, the post took on new importance as headquarters for the U.S. Cavalry. Today it remains an active military post and home of the Army General School. The U.S. Cavalry Museum, located in the 1855 hospital, celebrates the long history of the American Horse Soldier from the Revolutionary War to 1950. Featured are weapons, uniforms, and original works by Frederick Remington.

Fort Scott National Historic Site

The entrance to the park is on Old Fort Boulevard in Fort Scott. It is open daily from 8 AM to 5 PM; (316) 223–0310.

Established on May 30, 1842, Fort Scott was a station for the First U.S. Dragoons, who proved an effective force in Indian control. Abandoned in 1853, it was reactivated for a few years in 1862, serving as a supply base, training center for black and Indian troops, and a prisoner of war camp.

A dozen historic buildings built between 1842 and 1845 have been restored and nine more reconstructed with federal funds. Furnished buildings include post headquarters, the hospital, guardhouse, bakery, dragoon barracks, officers' quarters, quartermaster's storehouse, powder magazine, and stables. Special events include the annual Good Old Days celebration in June.

BATTLEFIELDS

Punished Woman Battlefield

The battlefield is located twelve miles northeast of Scott City on the road to Scott Lake.

On September 27, 1879, Colonel William Lewis from Fort Dodge with five companies of cavalry and two of infantry chased the fleeing Northern Cheyennes into a narrow canyon on Punished Woman's Fork (now Beaver Creek) of the Smoky Hill River in central Kansas. About 5 PM the battle began, with sixty warriors holding their own against about two hundred soldiers. When Colonel Lewis received a bullet below the groin, from which he later died, the troops ceased their offensive. That dark and windy night, the Cheyennes escaped, slipping out through a small ravine to continue their way north in an attempt to reach their homeland. Now administered by the Kansas Historical Society, the battlefield remains in an unimpaired state, with a natural setting and wilderness ambiance.

Sappa Creek Battlefield

Twelve miles south of Atwood on Highway 25, turn east at the 212 mile marker and go three miles. At the second intersection turn right and proceed one quarter-mile to the Curtin Ranch.

On April 6, 1875, about one hundred Cheyennes fled the reservation in Oklahoma to join their relatives in Montana. The exodus followed an exchange of gunfire after the death of Black Horse, who had attempted to escape confinement. In pursuit Lieutenant Austin Henely and forty men from Fort Wallace found the village camped on Sappa Creek in northwestern Kansas. In addition to having lodges, the Cheyennes had dug holes in the high banks of a dry creek bed to make sleeping quarters for the destitute. On April 23 Henely attacked, his force augmented by twenty area buffalo hunters. Acting independently, the civilians took a position on the bluffs north and east of the village, using their Sharps rifles to kill indiscriminately. Henely reported twenty-seven killed, nineteen warriors and eight women and children. The Cheyennes claimed that seventy-eight died. Two soldiers lost their lives. The site of the battle is on private property.

INDIAN HERITAGE SITES

Quanah Parker Starr House

Located on Highways 62 and 115 in the center of Cache, the house is open by appointment. Call (405) 429-3238. This is the residence of the last chief of the nonreservation Comanches, who surrendered at Fort Sill in 1875. Built in 1890, the home contains mementos of his life.

Missouri

HISTORIC SITES

Jefferson Barracks Historical Park

Located at 533 Grant Road in St. Louis, the museum is open Tuesday through Saturday from 10 AM to 5 PM and on Sunday from 12 to 5 PM; (314) 544-5714. Group tours and educational programs are available on a reservation basis by calling (314) 889-2450, Monday through Friday.

Established in 1826 by troops under Colonel Henry Leavenworth and Captain Stephen Watts Kearny, Jefferson Barracks was a starting point for numerous military expeditions going west but had many uses during its long history. Initially an infantry training base, supply depot, and replacement center, it served as a hospital and place of recuperation during the Civil War. From 1871 to 1878 it was under the control of the Ordnance Department. From 1894 through World War II, it served as an induction center. Those who served at Jefferson Barracks include Zachary Taylor, Henry Atkinson, Jefferson Davis, Winfield Scott, Robert E. Lee, Ulysses S. Grant, William T. Sherman, Philip H. Sheridan, James Longstreet, Joseph E. Johnston, and John C. Fremont. Abandoned in 1946, it became home to various owners. The northern half is now Jefferson Barracks Historical Park. Three rock buildings remain from the famous post: the 1851 two-story laborer's house, the 1851 stable, and the 1857 powder magazine, now a museum that features life-size dioramas showing the garrison's history.

MUSEUMS

Jefferson National Expansion Memorial
National Historic Site Museum

Located at 11 North Fourth Street, St. Louis, the underground museum is open all year except Thanksgiving, Christmas Day, and New Year's Day; (314) 425-4465. The National Park Service created the museum to provide an introduction to the history of the American West, and a number of exhibits deal with Indian wars subjects. A bookstore offers a wide variety of items.

Oklahoma

HISTORIC SITES

Fort Gibson

The post is located one mile north of the town of Fort Gibson, off State Highway 80, east of Muskogee. The park and museum are open Monday through Saturday, 9 AM to 5 PM and Sunday 1 to 5 PM; (918) 478–2669.

The army established Fort Gibson in 1824 in the heart of Indian Territory. Originally a four-company post, the army expanded the fort in 1831 to house a regiment. In 1846, because it was subject to flooding, soldiers began work on a new post on a nearby hill but had completed only one building by 1857 when the fort was abandoned. Confederates occupied the fort at the beginning of the Civil War, but Union troops reclaimed the post and made it into a federal stronghold. The army stayed at Fort Gibson until 1890, completing the new post in the meantime. In 1936 the Works Progress Administration (WPA) reconstructed the original stockade and some of the outlying log buildings. Six rooms within the compound are open to the public. Remains of the fort's stone structures are found on the hill above the site. The property is maintained by the State Parks Division of the Oklahoma Department of Tourism and Recreation.

Fort Reno

Fort Reno is located about six miles northwest of El Reno. The army established Fort Reno in 1874 to guard the Cheyenne-Arapaho Indian Reservation, whose Darlington Agency had been established just across the North Canadian River in 1869. In September 1878 its troops unsuccessfully pursued the Northern Cheyennes who had left the agency. Soldiers from Fort Reno fired the shots on April 22, 1889, that started the Sooners land rush. In 1908 Fort Reno became a cavalry remount station, in 1938 a quartermaster depot, and during World War II a prisoner-of-war camp. In 1946 the U.S. Department of Agriculture acquired it for a livestock research station. Sixteen of the brick and stone buildings constructed between 1876 and 1890 remain, most remodeled and adapted to new uses. The post cemetery contains the grave of famous scout Ben Clark. Fort Reno now serves as an agricultural experiment station.

Fort Sill

Fort Sill is located four miles north of Lawton on U.S. Highways 277, 281, and 62. Facilities are open daily year-round from 9 AM to 4:30 PM; (405) 351-5123.

Established on January 8, 1869, Fort Sill played an important role in the subjugation of the Southern Plains tribes. Built by buffalo soldiers of the Ninth and Tenth Cavalry, it was the surrender point for many of those who participated in the Red River War of 1874–1875. Comanche chief Quanah Parker lived near there until his death. Fort Sill remains an active military post, serving as the U.S. Army Artillery and Guided Missile Center. A National Historic Landmark, it has a military museum housed in seven buildings dating from 1869–1875. Exhibits include field artillery equipment from all eras and cavalry, infantry, and Southern Plains Indian items of the frontier period. Buildings of special interest are the Old Guardhouse and the Old Post Chapel, built in 1875 with troop labor under Ranald Mackenzie. The Apache and Old Post Cemeteries contain the remains of Geronimo, Satanta, and Quannah Parker.

Fort Supply

On the campus of the William S. Key Correctional Center and Western State Hospital, historic Fort Supply is open Monday through Friday from 9 AM to 4 PM and on Saturday and Sunday by appointment. Fort Supply is administered by the Oklahoma Historical Society, maintained by the Department of Corrections, and supported by the Historic Fort Supply Foundation. Write Historic Fort Supply Foundation, William S. Key Correctional Center, Box 61, Ft. Supply OK 73841.

Established on November 18, 1868, to serve as a base for General Sheridan's campaign against the Plains Indians, Camp Supply was the debarkation point for George Custer's ride to the Battle of the Washita on November 27. Designated a fort in 1878, the post guarded the Cherokee Outlet and the nearby Western Cattle Trail (1874–1893), supervised land runs, and settled disputes among the Cheyennes and Arapahos and white cattlemen. Abandoned in 1894, it became Oklahoma's first state mental hospital in 1903. In 1988 it also became a minimum security facility. The Historic Fort Supply Foundation recently received funds to complete reconstruction of the 130-square-foot Camp Supply Stockade. The reconstruction will complement five remaining historic structures, including the commanding officers' quarters (1878), teamsters' cabin, the powder monkey's house, and the guardhouse (1892), which serves as a museum.

BATTLEFIELDS

Washita Battlefield

Located in Roger Mills County west of Altus on Highway 47A, this new National Park Service area covers a six-square-mile area in the Washita River Valley.

On November 27, 1868, Custer and the Seventh Cavalry attacked the fifty-one lodge village of Black Kettle's Southern Cheyennes. Only a week earlier Black Kettle and Little Robe had traveled to Fort Cobb to make peace overtures with General William Hazen. However, some of the young men had been out raiding, and it was their war trail that Custer had followed to the camp. Killing more than one hundred, Custer took fifty-three women and children prisoners. Lost in the battle were Major Joel Elliot and sixteen men, who were cut off and annihilated. Black Kettle and his wife also died in the encounter. The victory on the Washita made Custer the nation's most famous Indian fighter, and from then on he discarded his Civil War uniform and wore buckskins in the field. Very little has changed on the battlefield site, with farming activity now being the principal land use in the area. An overlook and interpretive signs explain the site.

MUSEUMS

Gilcrease Museum

The museum is located at 1400 Gilcrease Museum Road, Tulsa. It is open Monday through Saturday, from 9 AM to 5 PM and Sunday and holidays from 1 to 5 PM; (918) 582–3122.

The museum contains collections of American paintings, western art, and Native American artifacts. Galleries are devoted to the works of Frederick Remington, Charles Russell, George Catlin, and W. R. Leigh.

Kiowa Tribal Museum

Located west of Carnegie on Highway 9, the museum is open Monday through Friday from 8 AM to 4:30 PM; (405) 654–2300.

Featured are murals that explain Kiowa history, as well as exhibits that display the tribe's material culture.

Southern Plains Indians Museum

Located on the east edge of Anadarko, on Highway 62, the museum is open from 9 AM to 5 PM Monday through Saturday and 1 to 5 PM on Sunday, June through September. In the off-season it is closed on Monday.

Owned by the Department of the Interior's Arts and Crafts Board, the museum presents the material culture of the Southern Plains Indians. During the summer full-scale painted tipis are exhibited on the grounds.

The Northern Plains

The first major white penetration into the Northern Plains was the Oregon Trail. It eventually separated the great buffalo herds and divided such tribes as the Cheyennes and Arapahos into northern and southern branches. While fur traders blazed the trail in the mid-1830s, significant use did not occur until 1843, when a thousand home seekers traveled the route. In the next quarter-century, covered wagons were a familiar sight following the Great Platte River Road across Nebraska and Wyoming, eventually diverging onto trails to Oregon, Utah, and California. As migration increased, so did conflict. Travelers depleted the Indians' game, and soon hunting became difficult in regions near the trail, fueling resentment. In the late 1840s, the federal government ordered three military posts built to guard the Oregon-Mormon-California Trail: Fort Kearny in Nebraska, Fort Laramie in Wyoming, and Fort Hall in Idaho. As the pressure increased, whites sought to make some legal accommodation with the Plains Indians, a binding agreement concerning the use of this vast piece of property.

In September 1851, Indian Commissioners D. D. Mitchell and Thomas Fitzpatrick met with some ten thousand Sioux, Cheyennes, Arapahos, Shoshonis, and Crows at Fort Laramie to reach agreement concerning travel through the area. In return for an annual payment of $50,000 in trade goods, the Indians guaranteed whites safe passage and acknowledged the permanence of military posts in their homeland. But as migration began to occur in larger numbers—in 1852, nearly forty thousand persons traveled westward, at least ten thousand of whom were Mormons bound for Salt Lake City—dissatisfaction increased.

The Sioux

Serious trouble with the Sioux began in 1854, when a young hotspur at Fort Laramie upgraded a minor incident into a major happening. A recent graduate of West Point, Brevet Lieutenant John L. Grattan's best grades were in French and his worst in infantry tactics. On August 19 Grattan led twenty-nine infantrymen and a drunken interpreter in an attempt to arrest a Miniconjou brave who had killed and butchered a stray cow from a Mormon caravan. When the warrior refused to surrender, a fight ensued in which Grattan and his command perished; one man made it back to Fort Laramie before dying. Grattan's body, pincushioned with twenty-seven arrows, one of which passed entirely through his head, was finally identified by his pocket watch. General William S. Harney, known as the fastest foot-racer in the army and one of its most relentless pursuers, exacted revenge on September 3, 1855, when he caught Little Thunder's band of Brulés in camp on Blue Water Creek near Ash Hollow, Nebraska. He killed eighty-five and took seventy women and children prisoners. At Fort Pierre in March 1856, he dictated peace to the Sioux. On March 7 Inkapaduta and his band of Santees attacked settlers near Spirit Lake, Iowa, killing about forty men, women, and children and taking some captive, but this was an isolated incident, and the Sioux remained peaceful for the time being.

The Civil War, 1861–1865

The pace of westward expansion continued through the Civil War due to gold strikes in Idaho and Montana and the desire of many to find new lives on the frontier. Beginning in 1862 the army brought volunteer units west to guard telegraph and stage lines and routes of travel. Although usually less inclined to discipline, the volunteers often contained within their ranks men better educated and more physically fit than pre-war enlistees, as well as officers better versed in western ways and more aggressive in dealing with Indian problems.

As the Civil War got under way, a new challenge presented itself for troops stationed in the West: In the late fall of 1861 the transcontinental telegraph went into operation. The Pacific Telegraph Company, a subsidiary of Western Union, was the builder of the system through what is now Nebraska and Wyoming. The federal legislation passed on June 16, 1860, called for construction of a line roughly following the Oregon Trail from Omaha to Salt Lake City. Another line had been constructed east from Carson City, Nevada, the wires joining on October 24. Government officials believed that it was crucial to maintain close communication with the West Coast, and the telegraph made this possible. President Lincoln also recognized the importance of the gold and silver of the western territories in the war effort, and to retain political allegiance of frontier states he knew that it was crucial to keep sufficient troops in the region to protect migrant and freight routes, maintain communication systems, and secure the safety of new settlements.

Because of the technology of the time, telegraph relay stations had to be constructed every fifty to seventy-five miles. These housed a telegraph operator and one or more repairmen. To protect the stations, the army eventually sent troops to all these places, developing a compound of varying size at each. Some of these fixed outposts were tiny, with a force varying from four to twenty enlisted men, while others, especially after 1864, were enlarged to house a company or more. Most of the smaller garrisons had stockades built of logs, set in the ground close together and pinned, with portholes for defense. These little outposts became the target of Plains Indian animosity in the years that followed.

To protect communication and transportation lines on the central route, the army called Colonel Patrick E. Connor and his California Volunteers into action. Pressures began to lessen after the troops' arrival in the Salt Lake Valley in October 1862. On October 26 Connor officially established Fort Douglas, three miles east of Salt Lake City, as his base camp. Garrisoning Fort Bridger, his soldiers patrolled the emigrant road as far west as Pacific Springs. It took time, however, for Connor to do his work.

The Minnesota Uprising

While Connor and his men were marching to Utah, a major Indian war in Minnesota had ended. Restricted to reservations along the Minnesota River, the Santee Sioux had suffered from the corruption of Indian agents and contractors. With game scarce and starvation threatening, agent Thomas Galbraith refused to issue the large store of supplies just delivered until the system had given him his kickback. When the Santees appealed for assistance on August 15, trader Andrew Myrick told them that if they were hungry they could eat grass or their own excrement. Two days later four young warriors killed five white settlers. The next day Little Crow led a large force in an attack on the Lower Agency, killing twenty, taking a dozen women captive, and leaving Myrick dead with his mouth full of grass. A total of four hundred settlers died that day; before it was over, eight hundred civilians and over a hundred soldiers had lost their lives. After withstanding an assault on Fort Ridgley on August 20, troops rallied under the leadership of General Henry L. Sibley. His victory at Wood Lake on September 23 forced two thousand of the Sioux to surrender. On December 26, 1862, at Mankato, Minnesota, thirty-eight Santees convicted of murder and rape died on the gallows. Dr. William Mayo Sr., founder of the Mayo Clinic, stole one of the bodies and later used the skeleton in his medical practice.

This disturbance marked the beginning of a six-year war on the prairie and the plains. Moved to reservations at Crow Creek and into South Dakota, the Santees spread knowledge of their grievances to tribes farther west, contributing to their disaffection. In 1863 and 1864, Generals Henry Sibley and Alfred Sully campaigned against the Teton Sioux in North Dakota. Besides building Fort Sully on the Missouri and thoroughly arousing the tribes in the territory, Sully accomplished little during the first year. In 1864 his troops built Forts Rice and Berthold on the Missouri, and Sully defeated the Indians in the Battle of Killdeer Mountain. The Sioux retaliated by attacking Fort Berthold.

Post Civil War, 1865–1869

In early June 1865, Secretary of War Stanton decided that the surrendered Sioux camped near Fort Laramie should be transferred to Fort Kearny. On June 11 an escort consisting of 135 cavalrymen of the Seventh Iowa Cavalry, and Charles Elliston's uniformed Indian police, commanded by Captain William D. Fouts, left Fort Laramie with fifteen hundred to two thousand Sioux. All progressed smoothly until the morning of June 14, when a discontented warrior fired at Fouts, killing him instantly, and all of the Sioux, including the Indian police, left for the Platte. In the subsequent fighting Lieutenant John Wilcox reported a loss of four killed and four wounded besides Fouts and estimated that thirty Sioux were slain.

On July 25 the Sand Creek avengers, augmented by Northern Cheyenne and Sioux warriors, showed themselves on the bluffs to the north of Platte Bridge Station in central Wyoming. A detachment of Eleventh Kansas Cavalry drove the advance party off, killing two, including Chief High-Backed Wolf. The next day, at 7:30 AM, Major Martin Anderson sent Second Lieutenant Caspar Collins of the Eleventh Ohio Cavalry and a detachment of twenty-five men from Companies I and K of the Eleventh Kansas across the bridge to warn an approaching wagon train, commanded by First Sergeant Amos Custard, of the amassed Indian force. About one mile after crossing the bridge, overwhelming numbers of Cheyennes and Sioux surrounded Collins and his men. Wounded in the hip early in the fight, the young lieutenant took an arrow in the forehead and disappeared in a mass of warriors. The body found later was hardly recognizable. All but four others were able to make it back to Platte Bridge. Surrounded four miles from the Platte Bridge Station, only three of Sergeant Custard's little command of twenty-four men survived, being part of an advance group when attacked. After November 1865 the post was known as Fort Caspar to honor the young officer who had crossed his last bridge.

In late July General Patrick Connor's retaliatory Powder River expedition got under way. The expedition involved about two thousand men assembled at three points of departure. Connor's force was to march northwest from Fort Laramie along the eastern flanks of the Big Horn Mountains. Colonel Nelson Cole was to skirt the east and north sides of the Black Hills and then move west. Lieutenant Colonel Samuel Walker was to march directly north from Fort Laramie, joining Cole's force somewhere beyond the headwaters of the Cheyenne and then rendezvous with Connor's force on about September 1 in the vicinity of Tongue River. On August 29 Connor's main column struck a large Arapaho village on Tongue River. According to Connor, troops killed sixty-three Indians, burned two hundred fifty lodges, captured five hundred ponies, and burned tons of jerked buffalo meat, buffalo robes, and other camp equipment.

In the meantime Cole and Walker had joined forces on the Little Missouri and moved to the Powder River. On September 1, they had a skirmish, losing six men, and on September 8, they fought a desperate battle with an estimated three thousand warriors, perhaps the largest engagement ever fought by the army on the Northern Plains. The renowned Cheyenne warrior Roman Nose was with the attacking party. Mounted on a white warhorse, he rode three or four times across the soldier line within easy carbine shot but escaped unharmed, causing the battle to be known in Cheyenne history as "Roman Nose's Fight." After repelling repeated attacks with skillful use of artillery, the beleaguered force experienced a storm of freezing rain, which killed 414 animals during the night.

On September 13 Connor's Pawnee Scouts found the desperate command, and by September 20 the exhausted force reached Fort Connor. The general, who arrived at the post on September 24, planned to create another expeditionary force from Cole and Nelson's troops, but a courier soon arrived with a dispatch ordering him to assume command of the District of Utah in Salt Lake City. Thus, he had no choice but to disband the force and head west. The Powder River expedition was a failure in many respects. Instead of dealing a crippling blow to the hostiles, Connor's grand plan had been aborted by weather and terrain. However, the expedition focused public attention on the Bozeman Trail, and by establishing a military post on the road, it encouraged emigrant travel in 1866, which in turn would lead to further pressures to finish the job that Connor had begun. The conflict took a new turn as regular army troops returned to the frontier with the end of the Civil War.

The discovery of gold in Montana in 1862–1863 had generated new pressures. By 1866 at least ten thousand people lived in Bannock, Virginia City, and Helena, and hundreds lived in the surrounding camps. During the next decade miners extracted an average of ten million dollars per year in precious metals from this region. The safest way to reach the gold fields was to travel by steamboat on the Missouri River as far as it was navigable. An additional few days of stagecoach or wagon travel brought miners to their destination. The shortest route, blazed by John Bozeman, began north from the Oregon-California Trail near present-day Douglas, Wyoming, and ended in Virginia City, Montana, in the center of the gold fields. The so-called Bozeman Trail went through the prime hunting ground of the Sioux and Cheyenne, which brought swift retaliation.

On July 1 commissioners met with the Brulés and Oglalas at Fort Laramie to negotiate a treaty to sanction the new route. While the council was in session, Colonel Henry B. Carrington and his Eighteenth U.S. Infantry marched through on their way to garrison three posts along the trail—Fort Reno, Fort Phil Kearny, and Fort C. F. Smith. Oglala Chief Red Cloud left in disgust, declaring, "The Great Father sends us presents and wants a new road, but the white chief goes with soldiers to steal that road before the Indians say yes or no." The forts were kept almost under continuous siege by Red Cloud and his followers, which at times included not only other tribes of Sioux but significant numbers of Northern Cheyennes and some Arapahos. From July 26 to December 21, Indians made fifty-one hostile demonstrations in front of Fort Phil Kearny. In the same period ninety-six officers and soldiers and fifty-eight civilians were killed. Most of the deaths occurred on December 21, 1866, when Brevet Lieutenant Colonel William Judd Fetterman disobeyed orders and led eighty men across Lodge Trail Ridge into ambush, where fifteen hundred Sioux and their allies cut them down to the last man. On August 1 and 2, 1867, troops were successful in fights near Fort C. F. Smith (the Hayfield Fight) and Fort Phil Kearny (the Wagon Box Fight) when new weapons permitted small detachments of soldiers to inflict heavy casualties on Sioux and Cheyenne raiding parties.

On July 20, 1867, Congress passed legislation creating the Indian Peace Commission. When talks began at Fort Laramie late in the year, Red Cloud sent word that he would not make peace until the whites abandoned the forts on the Bozeman Trail. The army agreed to these terms, deciding to give priority to the protection of the Union Pacific Railroad across southern Wyoming. The railroad finally joined with its western counterpart, the Central Pacific, at Promontory Point, Utah, on May 10, 1869. Signed in the fall of 1868, the Fort Laramie Treaty formalized peace in the north. It provided for the abandonment of the Bozeman Trail forts and the creation of the Great Sioux Reservation encompassing the western half of what is now the state of South Dakota, including the Black Hills. The agreement also reserved the area between the Big Horn Mountains and the Black Hills as unceded Indian Territory, where whites were prohibited. Included in the treaty were promises to build residential and support structures and provide teachers and technicians of various kinds. The treaty stipulated that its land provisions could not be changed without the agreement of at least three-fourths of adult male Indians.

The Great Sioux War

The Fort Laramie Treaty of 1868 kept the nomadic Sioux and their allies north of the main transcontinental artery along the Platte, centering their activities in the Powder River country and along the Yellowstone. Although this worked for several years, white intrusion threatened the arrangement. First came proposals to build the Northern Pacific Railroad. When the Sioux rejected overtures for a right-of-way, surveyors went ahead anyway. The armed Indian response led in 1873 to a large military expedition under Colonel David S. Stanley, who fought several skirmishes with Sitting Bull. When the Panic of 1873 stopped plans for the railroad, attention turned to the Black Hills of Dakota Territory, rumored to contains vast riches in gold.

To investigate the rumors and to determine an appropriate site for a possible future military post, the army sent George Armstrong Custer on an expedition to the Black Hills in the summer of 1874. On July 30 Miner Horatio Ross discovered gold on French Creek near present-day Custer, South Dakota. Custer sent Charley Reynolds to Fort Laramie with the news, which produced a full-scale invasion of the Black Hills. At first the government attempted to purchase the land, meeting with five thousand Sioux in September 1875, near Red Cloud Agency. However, the Sioux were adamant. They called Custer's trail to the hills "The Thieves Road" and refused an offer of six million dollars to sell their land. The commission returned to Washington in failure. At the same time, complaints filed by white trespassers as well as by peaceful tribes along the Upper Missouri led the Indian Bureau to demand the return of free-roaming Sioux to their agencies in Dakota Territory and Nebraska.

On November 3, 1875, President Grant, Secretary of the Interior Zachary Chandler, Commissioner of Indian Affairs Edward P. Smith, Secretary of War William W. Belknap, and Generals Sheridan and Crook met at the White House to discuss the matter. The meeting resulted in two decisions: Orders to bar miners from the Black Hills would remain in effect, but the army would not enforce them; and steps would be taken to force Sitting Bull and his followers to leave unceded Indian Territory and return to their agencies. Runners soon carried the message that the Indians must return to the reservation in South Dakota by January 31, 1876, or be brought back by force. When they did not comply, General Sheridan took action, ordering what is probably the best-known and most-argued campaign in the Indian wars.

What evolved was a strategy of converging columns. General Alfred H. Terry, commander of the Department of the Dakota, moved west from Fort Abraham Lincoln, near present-day Bismarck, North Dakota. Under him were Lieutenant Colonel George Custer and the Seventh Cavalry. Terry ordered Colonel John Gibbon, commanding the District of Montana, to march east with troops from Fort Shaw and from Fort Ellis. Coming from the south was General George Crook, now commander of the Department of the Platte and Terry's equal. Crook's troops marched north from Fort Laramie and Fort Fetterman. Sheridan believed that each force was strong enough to meet and defeat any Indians encountered. There was no dictum to meet at a certain place at a certain time. Rather, the plan was to force the Indians into a pocket where they could be engaged by any of the columns.

First into the field was Crook's force of nine hundred men, which moved north from Fort Fetterman on March 1, 1876. The initial encounter of his advance column occurred on March 17 on Powder River near present-day Broadus, Montana. While Brevet Major General Joseph J. Reynolds destroyed the Cheyenne village, a counterattack forced a hasty withdrawal and recapture of the Indians' pony herd, leading eventually to the commander's court-martial. In late May Crook again took the field with about twenty companies of cavalry and infantry, some fourteen hundred men.

After an indecisive skirmish with the Sioux on June 9, he moved his command to the headwaters of Rosebud Creek, where on the morning of June 17, on the one-hundredth anniversary of the Battle of Bunker Hill, he met the combined Sioux and Cheyenne force under Crazy Horse, Two Moon, and other war chiefs, probably six hundred to one thousand warriors in all.

The battle lasted all day. In his official report, Crook declared: "My troops beat these Indians on a field of their own choosing, and drove them in utter rout from it, as far as the proper care of my wounded and prudence would justify." However, most historians have not been as positive in their judgments, pointing out that because the encounter prevented Crook from eventually uniting with Terry's column, the standoff was a strategic setback, and it precluded a successful outcome to the fight on the Little Bighorn. Crook officially reported ten dead and twenty-four wounded in the battle, while Crazy Horse later stated that Indian losses were thirty-six killed and sixty-three wounded. Crook's autobiography ends with a passage concerning the Battle of the Rosebud, suggesting that the event and those which followed were too painful for him to continue. It was the first time that he had not been clearly triumphant in an Indian fight.

Terry and Custer left Fort Abraham Lincoln on May 17. By June 9 they had united with Gibbon, and on June 21 they made their final plans aboard the steamer *Far West*. As Gibbon remembered, the purpose of the plan was not how to attack but more "to prevent the escape of the Indians, which was the idea pervading the minds of all of us." The strategy agreed to was this: Custer was to march up Rosebud Creek and move east and south of the Little Bighorn Valley, believed to hold the Indian village. He was then to turn and approach the camp riding north. Gibbon, with whom Terry traveled, was to ascend the Bighorn River with the slower infantry and enter the valley coming from the north, traveling south. If all worked out as planned, this convergence would occur on June 26, but Terry gave Custer the freedom to act with dispatch if conditions warranted it. Those who accuse Custer of disobeying orders forget that Terry once practiced law and chose his words carefully. Custer's was the premier striking force, and all expected him to initiate the battle.

Little Bighorn

After Terry reviewed the troops at noon, Custer and the Seventh Cavalry departed. After a long, hard march, Custer reached a point about twenty-five miles east of the Little Bighorn Valley late on the afternoon of June 24.

About 9 PM returning scouts informed their commander that the Indian trail led across the divide to the Little Bighorn. Custer called his officers together, telling them that after a few hours' rest he planned to follow the trail through the night, abandoning the plan outlined by Terry. At dawn the troops reached the Crow's Nest, a high promontory in the Little Wolf Mountains, where Custer's Indian scouts saw the Sioux camp and the large horse herd fifteen miles west. There Custer received reports that Indians had been seen observing them. Convinced that he had been discovered, he decided that he must attack.

The troops followed Reno Creek toward the Little Bighorn. At 12:07 Custer halted the column and divided the regiment into four parts. Custer retained Companies C, E, F, I, and L, giving Major Marcus A. Reno Companies A, G, and M and Captain Frederick L. Benteen Companies D, H, and K. Captain James McDougal with Company B was detailed to guard the pack train. Custer had split his command, because he feared that the Sioux and Cheyennes and their allies would break into small groups and disappear into the vast landscape. Every officer of that era knew that when accompanied by women and children, warriors did not stand and fight. Custer sent Benteen and his men off to the left to scout. He did not know exactly where the village was and feared that the Sioux and their allies might flee toward the Big Horn Mountains. Promising support, Custer instructed Reno and his three companies to ride down the valley and attack the village that lay before them, which was somewhat obscured by a bend in the river. Custer and his five companies kept to the high ground on the right, which were the bluffs rising above the Little Bighorn River. His intention was to find a place to ford the river somewhere in the rear of the encampment to cut off all retreat.

As he rode toward the village, Reno immediately encountered resistance in large numbers and dismounted his one hundred twelve men to fight on foot. He could now see the Indian village, sprawling for about three miles, filling the valley. In the camp were probably from twenty-five hundred to three thousand fighting men, although some have suggested as few as fifteen hundred and others as many as six thousand. When warriors began to circle his left, Reno ordered a retreat to the woods by the river. With numbers rapidly growing and no sign of support, Reno decided to mount, cross the river, and take position on the high bluffs, where Custer had last been seen on his march to the north. In a disorderly retreat, Reno lost about forty men but gained the bluffs. An officer and sixteen enlisted men remained behind, surviving by hiding in the brush. Shortly thereafter,

Benteen, who having found nothing on his scout and having received a cryptic message from Custer that read "Bring packs," arrived to reinforce Reno. Finally came McDougal with the pack train. Unable to discern what had happened to Custer, the troops dug in. On his own initiative, Captain Weir led his company in Custer's direction, but soon had to return in the face of overwhelming odds.

What did happen to Custer? The traditional story of Custer's demise is that he and his men were unsuccessful in trying to ford the river at Medicine Tail Coulee, withdrew to the high ground of Custer Ridge as Sioux and Cheyennes surged across the river, and fell in defending their position, the last few—including the flamboyant commander—dying on Custer Hill. To explain this ultimate defeat, historians have looked to suspicious origins, such as defective weapons, insufficient ammunition, or the megalomaniac personality of the Seventh's commander. More recent research, particularly that accomplished as a result of archaeological investigation at the battlefield in 1984 and 1986, has led to a different interpretation.

When he reached what is now Little Bighorn Battlefield proper, Custer had arranged his troops as follows: Cos. C, I, and L formed the right wing, while the left consisted of Companies E and F. The former occupied what are now called Calhoun Ridge and Custer Ridge, while the latter served as Custer's reconnoitering arm, seeking the best place to cross the Little Bighorn. The left wing eventually traveled far north of the present battlefield, where it discovered another ford that would allow the command to approach the village in the rear. It then returned to the rest of the command to wait for Benteen's battalion, which never came. The last trooper to leave Custer alive was a messenger to Benteen with the instruction to "Hurry up, Bring packs." Crucial to the defeat of Custer was the presence to the southeast of Captain Calhoun's Company L of a group of Sioux armed with Henry repeating rifles. When Company C made a foray against Indians creeping too close to the skirmish line established by Company L on Calhoun Hill, this group of Sioux surprised the attacking force and turned the offensive into a rout that spread through the rest of the command. It was Calhoun's troopers who took the brunt of the attack and fell back in disarray, carrying Keogh's company with them in the flight to Custer Hill. There the last group of officers died in what has been portrayed as "Custer's Last Stand." However, a group of from twenty to forty surviving enlisted men made a break for the river, where they finally succumbed in Deep Ravine, about two hundred yards southwest of Custer Hill.

On June 26, 1876, the Indians renewed the assault against Reno's forces. Twice the troops counterattacked to save themselves from being overrun. By early afternoon firing had subsided. That evening the Indians pushed off to the south, and the siege was over. On the morning of June 27 Gibbon's scouts, led by Lieutenant James H. Bradley, reached the valley and discovered the bodies of the Custer command, 218 men, mostly naked except for socks, and many mutilated. In joining with Reno's command, they found that Reno had 47 dead and many more wounded. Indian casualties were estimated at from 30 to 300 killed.

Ever since the Battle of the Little Bighorn, experts and buffs have speculated on the reasons for the outcome, fought over imagined troop movements, and assessed blame. Two of the most respected students of the battle, Robert Utley and John Gray, defend Custer. In *Cavalier in Buckskin*, Utley writes: "Given what he [Custer] knew at each decision point and what he had every reason to expect of his subordinates, one is hard pressed to say that he ought to have done differently." Gray supports the conclusion, and both fault Benteen for his inexplicable dawdling after receiving Custer's message to rush forward. The duo also criticize John Gibbon for not reporting the location of the Indian camp to Terry before the general sent Custer on his way. Utley ends his judgment with the statement that at the Little Bighorn "Custer's luck simply ran out."

The troops buried the Custer dead where they found them, digging shallow graves, making rock cairns, and putting up makeshift markers. The wounded were taken back to Bismarck on the *Far West*, and the nation, celebrating its one-hundredth anniversary, learned the shocking news. Terry and Crook remained in the field without success. On September 5, low on supplies, Crook gave up and headed for the Black Hills, an eight days' march to the south. On September 9 his advance party under Captain Anson Mills discovered and attacked a sizable village at Slim Buttes, the ensuing two-day battle resulting in a few casualties on both sides. Dead was an Oglala chief, American Horse. In his tipi, Private William McClinton recovered Custer's flag.

After replenishing themselves on captured dried meat and the flesh of Indian ponies, Crook pushed on to the Black Hills, camping in the vicinity of Crook City and enjoying regular rations once more. Some soldiers were so famished that they mixed their newly issued flour and sugar into a batter and ate it raw. Crook's command moved on to Camp Robinson, Nebraska, before departing for Wyoming on November 3. The general's displeasure with the whole summer heightened when he learned that his wife had broken her arm in an accident while riding an Arkansas railroad.

Crook somewhat bolstered a sagging reputation by leading a fall expedition into Wyoming, which broke the Northern Cheyennes' will to resist. The telling blow was the destruction of Dull Knife's village on the Red Fork of Powder River, engineered by subordinate Ranald Mackenzie. On November 25 Mackenzie's force of six hundred men of the Fourth Cavalry and about four hundred Indian scouts surprised Dull Knife's camp of one hundred eighty-three lodges. The Cheyennes lost about forty in the battle and became refugees in the winter cold, as Mackenzie had destroyed the village and its contents. For all intents and purposes, this ended the free life of the Northern Cheyennes.

Nelson A. Miles and the Fifth Infantry delivered the next telling blow. Attacking Crazy Horse's village on Tongue River in the Wolf Mountains on January 8, Miles routed about five hundred Sioux and Northern Cheyennes. At the same time, Sitting Bull and his followers crossed the line into Canada, remaining there, more or less, until 1881. On April 22, 1877, Two Moon led about three hundred Cheyennes and Oglalas into Miles's camp at the mouth of Tongue River to make peace, while the majority of his tribesman under Dull Knife, Little Wolf, and Old Bear surrendered at Red Cloud Agency in Nebraska. Two Moon and thirty of his band became army scouts for Miles, participating in the battle against Lame Deer and his Sioux in May and in action against the Nez Percés at Bear Paw in late September. Miles repaid the assistance of Two Moon and his warriors by letting the band remain in the vicinity.

Miles's constant pressure led to the surrender of Crazy Horse and his band of 898 men, women, and children on May 6, 1877, at Fort Robinson. Crazy Horse died at this post on September 5 from a bayonet wound incurred when trying to escape from the guardhouse where he had been ordered imprisoned by General Crook. In early September government representatives met with cowed Sioux leaders, who two months later signed a treaty ceding the Black Hills. The commission ignored the 1868 treaty stipulation that required ratification by three fourths of all adult males living on the reservation.

The Cheyenne Outbreak

At Fort Robinson, Dull Knife and Little Wolf learned that the government had decreed that all Northern Cheyennes would be sent to Indian Territory. The chiefs urged their tribesmen to abide by the wishes of the government. There seems to have been a belief on the part of the Northern Cheyennes that they could come back in a year if they did not like it in the South. On May 28, 1877, the journey to Indian Territory began. In the group were 937 men, women, and children. Seventy days later, on August 5, they arrived at the Cheyenne and Arapaho Agency, selecting a campsite about eight miles north. Within a year the newcomers were ready to return to their homeland. Starved, ravaged by disease, preyed on by white gangs of horse thieves, unwilling to farm, critical of the civilized ways of their southern brethren, rankled by the fact that the Northern Arapahos had been allowed to remain in the North, and with fifty of their children dead, they had had enough. At 10:10 PM on September 9, 353 Cheyennes—92 men, 120 women, 69 boys, and 72 girls—quietly left the foreign place, leaving fires burning and lodge poles standing to fool distant military pickets. After discovery of their departure the next morning at 3 AM, the pursuit of the army began, eventually involving 1300 men in three military departments.

Essentially following the Western Cattle Trail from Oklahoma through Kansas, Dull Knife and Little Wolf and their followers skirmished with army units on September 13 at Turkey Springs, September 14 at Red Hill, September 17 and 21–22 at Sand Creek, and September 27 at Punished Woman Creek, each time eluding troops to continue north. When the fleeing Cheyennes reached Northeast Kansas, warriors roamed the countryside, killing forty male white settlers, some said in revenge for a mass killing of their kinsmen by whites in the area in 1875. When in Nebraska, Dull Knife and Little Wolf separated, the former heading for Fort Robinson and Red Cloud Agency, the latter to the traditional homeland in Montana. Dull Knife had 149 people and Little Wolf 126.

On October 23 two companies of the Third Cavalry ascended Chadron Creek to discover Dull Knife and his followers. Taken to Fort Robinson, they learned on January 3 that the Great Father had decided they must be sent back to Indian Territory. Refusal to return eventually led Post Commander Henry Wessells to imprison the Cheyennes in a cavalry barracks, cutting off heat, food, and finally water. Barricading doors and covering windows with cloth to conceal their movements, the captives tore up the floor and constructed rifle-pits to command the windows. At 10:10 PM on January 9, the Cheyennes began firing. The men moved forward through the windows with children under their arms, while the women followed, and once again Dull Knife and his band dashed for freedom. However, this time they were not so fortunate. Soldiers sent volley after volley into the fleeing band. Twenty-two men, eight women, and two children died in the initial exodus. The retreat continued for four miles into the darkness until the fugitives reached neighboring hills where pursuit was impracticable.

Twelve days later four companies of soldiers caught the largest number of remaining Cheyennes, pinning them down in an oblong depression about forty miles north of Fort Robinson. When the smoke cleared, the pit presented a singular and horrible appearance. Huddled together in piles were twenty-three bodies of the slain. Among the nine still surviving were two young girls, aged fourteen and fifteen, discovered under the bodies of young men who had fallen lifeless on them. The dead Indians were buried in the pit where they had died. In the meantime, after eighteen days of wandering, Dull Knife and what was left of his family reached Pine Ridge, where they were hidden by Sioux relatives. The Sioux erected a lodge under a little bluff on Wounded Knee Creek.

After wintering in a sheltered valley near the forks of the Niobrara River, Little Wolf and his followers headed north. On March 25 they surrendered to Lieutenant W. P. Clark on the Yellowstone and were sent to Fort Keogh. In November Indian Bureau officials permitted the Northern Cheyennes at Pine Ridge to transfer to Montana to join the rest. At General Nelson A. Miles's request, Dull Knife was allowed to return to the valley of the Rosebud. An executive order of November 26, 1884, established a permanent home for the Northern Cheyennes in south central Montana east of the Crow Reservation.

The only fight between the Crows and the U.S. government occurred in 1887. When taunted in a speech by Sitting Bull and inspired by a vision of indestructibility received while participating in the Cheyenne sun dance, Sword Bearer and sixty followers shot up several buildings at Crow Agency. This led to a skirmish with U.S. troops and the death of the leader at the hands of a tribal policeman.

The last trouble in Montana occurred in 1890, when Head Chief and Heart Mule, two young Cheyennes who had killed a settler several months before, decided to confront the U.S. Army troops sent to find them. One troop of First Cavalry answered the challenge to meet them at Lame Deer, the agency headquarters. An eyewitness described what followed in the *Army and Navy Journal* of September 27, 1890:

> [Dressed in their finery], the warriors rode out from a timbered butte across the valley and gaining the highest point of an adjacent hill circled their ponies and sang their death songs. This over they opened fire on the troopers below. In a few minutes they were flanked and driven from the rocks at the crest of this hill and then, although with

plenty of room for escape in other directions, they charged down the steep incline, one mounted and the other—whose horse had been shot—on foot. Across the valley they went, under a hail of bullets from 50 carbines, towards the line of a fresh troop which had just occupied the opposite crest. . . . One of them deliberately rode through Lieut. Pitcher's line, shooting three horses as he came, but doing no other damage. He was pierced by seven bullets and died almost at the feet of the Cheyenne spectators who occupied the ridge. The second . . . wounded and his clothes torn by the storm of lead, was driven to a cut in the bed of the valley, where he fought desperately until killed.[5]

The Ghost Dance

The last trouble between U.S. troops and the Sioux occurred in 1890 as the result of the Ghost Dance movement. When one civilization is hard pressed by another, one tendency is to seek comfort in ritual designed to bend time backward or to accelerate it forward, desiring either an earlier Garden of Eden or the coming of the millennium. The late nineteenth-century Sioux looked both ways in their search for means to drastically change the present. The central figure in the ghost dance movement was the Paiute medicine man Wavoka, known to whites as Jack Wilson. On November 30, 1890, the *New York Times* published a letter by John S. Mayhugh in which the recent special census agent of Indians for Nevada described Wavoka and his visions:

He is an intelligent, fine looking Indian of about thirty-five years of age, who goes into trances, or seemingly so, for twelve to fourteen hours in presence of large numbers of Indians, who come upon invitation of the prophet. Upon his recovery he relates to them what he has seen. He tells them he has been to heaven and that the Messiah is coming to the earth again, and will put the Indians in possession of this country; that he has seen in heaven a heap of Indians, some of whom were dressed in white man's clothes. He counsels the Indians not to disturb the white folks, saying that the blanket or rabbit skin that was put over the moon by the Indians long ago will soon fall off and then the moon, which is a-fire will destroy the whites.[6]

A century later, it is easy to understand the appeal of the new religion. Life on the reservation had been difficult for nomadic peoples. First, on

April 10, 1883, came the prohibition of the sun dance and other "barbarous" customs. Next, on March 2, 1889, Congress passed an act reducing Sioux holdings from the western half of South Dakota to six small reservations. About the same time, the federal government decreased the beef allotment, creating widespread hunger and further discontent. In view of these setbacks, it is no wonder that the Miniconjous were receptive to a new religion promising the return of their ancestors and buffalo and the disappearance of whites from the earth. The one thing that changed the ghost dance from a spiritual revival into a potentially life-threatening movement was the ancillary view that those who wore the ghost dance shirt were immune from harm by bullets. This suggested violent confrontation would be part of the return of the old ways.

Crisis occurred on December 15 when the Standing Rock Reservation police killed Sitting Bull while trying to arrest him. Sitting Bull had been participating in the dances, and, fearing his influence, agent James McLaughlin wanted him under control. Previously, the Miniconjou chief Big Foot, long known as a peace maker, had received a request from Oglala chiefs to journey to Pine Ridge Agency and settle differences between factions. Sitting Bull's death precipitated the decision to go south, and on December 23 Big Foot's band left the Cheyenne River Reservation, departing without permission. On December 28 companies of the Seventh Cavalry caught up with the travelers, making camp at Wounded Knee Creek, South Dakota.

Wounded Knee

The next morning when Colonel James W. Forsyth ordered the Indians to give up their arms, a fight erupted in which Big Foot and 152 Sioux men, women, and children died, along with 25 soldiers. Suffering from pneumonia, Big Foot had not been able to flee but feigned death for a time before being dispatched in a hail of flying bullets. Ironically, the Henry Clay of his people died in irreconcilable conflict. Photographed before the mass burial trench, his distorted, frozen body is a haunting picture of the failure of U.S. Indian policy in the nineteenth century.

Before it was over probably another hundred of the refugees died from wounds or exposure in the freezing night. During the past several decades, the story of Wounded Knee has been used for political purposes, becoming a symbol of the treatment of all Indian peoples by the white majority. Dee Brown's *Bury My Heart at Wounded Knee* (1971), while methodologically flawed, created new awareness of what is essentially a sad chapter in American history, the loss of freedom and the near loss of identity by a proud people whose skills were not suited for life in an emerging industrial society and whose numbers were not large enough to make an impact in a democratic society.

For another fifteen years, occasional flare-ups occurred. General unrest over the disposition of fallen timber on the Chippewa Reservation at Leech Lake, Minnesota, led to widespread armed conflict in October 1898. When authorities sent troops to recapture two Chippewa men who had escaped arrest over a whiskey-selling incident, disgruntled tribesmen rallied, and a two-day battle ensued in which Captain Melville C. Wilkinson of the Third Infantry, five enlisted men, and two tribal policemen died. Negotiations were able to settle the matter, with Chippewa snipers receiving short prison terms and fines. On June 3, 1899, the men received full pardons. The last major twentieth-century incident occurred in September 1906, when about four hundred unhappy Utes from Utah left their reservation and headed for Pine Ridge. Near Gillette, Wyoming, they killed two cowboys, and troops of the Sixth Cavalry left in pursuit. Discussions resulted in permission for the Utes to settle on the Cheyenne River Reservation in South Dakota, but in 1908 the Indians decided to return to their previous home.

As the years passed, trouble between Indians and whites became civil matters, handled by tribal police and law enforcement agencies. Symbolic of the loss of power of the once indomitable Plains tribes was the arrest of Red Cloud in July 1894 for poaching. Caught by the sheriff of Natrona County, Wyoming, Red Cloud, the man who once ruled the Powder River Country and forced the U.S. Government to back down on the Bozeman Trail, spent time in the Casper jail. To pay his fine of sixty-six dollars he forfeited two horses.

In looking back one can say that the U.S. Army eventually accomplished its mission. It responded after each setback, and there were many, to keep trails open and communications functioning. It finally subdued the tribes of the West and permitted white settlement to continue. As an agent of the U.S. Government, it went about its task with less self-interest than most. Led by men and composed of men, it exhibited human defects and shortcomings and occasionally lost control under stress, performing acts of cruelty and barbarism. The Indians of the American West were the losers in the war, not only in terms of land and possessions, but in terms of self-destiny and self-worth. They made a valiant fight, but they were doomed from the beginning, outnumbered and unequipped to sustain conflict against Euro-American society with all its resources and technological might. Theirs was the loser share, cultural confusion, containment, and despair.

Minnesota

HISTORIC SITES

Fort Ridgely State Park

The fort is located about seven miles south of Fairfax on Highway 4; (612) 726–1171.

The army established Fort Ridgely in 1853 to defend the frontier and watch over the Sioux living in the Minnesota Valley. In 1862 it became a center of resistance in the Minnesota Uprising. In the beginning it provided refuge for settlers attacked by Little Crow and his followers. On August 20 and 22, first about 400 and then 800 Sioux attacked the post, but 180 troops and a number of civilian refugees repulsed repeated charges, using artillery to good effect. Now a Minnesota state park, Fort Ridgley features a restored stone commissary that contains a museum, a reconstructed powder magazine, and exposed building foundations. The prairie and woodland setting remains essentially unimpaired.

Fort Snelling

The fort is reached by the Fort Snelling exits on Minnesota Highways 5 and 55. It is located south of Minneapolis between the Mississippi River and the Twin Cities International Airport; (612) 726–9430.

Established in 1819, Fort Snelling for many years was the northern outpost on the Indian frontier. Built on a one-hundred-foot-high bluff overlooking the confluence of the Minnesota and Mississippi Rivers, the diamond-shaped fort had towers commanding its four corners. A quarter-mile east was the Indian agency. When the frontier advanced to the Great Plains, the post lost its importance, and the army abandoned it in 1857. Reactivated in 1861, it served as a training center for Civil War troops and played a role in putting down the 1862 Minnesota Uprising. In 1881 the post became the headquarters of the Department of the Dakota. Later serving as a training center, it was finally deactivated in 1946. In 1969 the Minnesota Historical Society acquired the old fort property from the Veterans Administration for inclusion in Fort Snelling State Park. It has reconstructed the guard complex, 560 feet of the original wall, a pentagonal tower, powder magazine, and other structures. Living history is an important part of the interpretive program.

BATTLEFIELDS

Birch Coulee State Memorial Park

The battlefield is located in Renville County, just off U.S. 71, about one mile north of Morton.

On September 2 Chief Little Crow's Santee Sioux surrounded a command of 180 volunteer troops at Fort Ridgely under Captain Hiram P. Grant. For thirty-one hours, the Sioux kept the force pinned down, killing 22 and wounding 60 before a relief column under Colonel Henry Sibley reached the scene. This battle marked the high point of Sioux dominance. The relatively unchanged battleground is now preserved in the thirty-two-acre Birch Coulee State Memorial Park.

Wood Lake Battlefield State Park

The battlefield is located in Yellow Medicine County, just off Minnesota 274, about seven miles south of Granite Falls.

On September 23, about one thousand four hundred troops under Colonel Henry Sibley met seven hundred warriors under Chief Little Crow in a battle that resulted in the death of thirty Sioux and the loss of seven soldiers. The battle ended the campaign against the Sioux in southern Minnesota. A state park preserves an acre of the battlefield, the rest being farmed in private ownership.

INDIAN HERITAGE SITES

Pipestone National Monument

The monument is adjacent to the city of Pipestone and can be reached by Highways 75, 23, and 30. It is open daily from 8 AM to 5 PM; (507) 825–5463.

Since the seventeenth century Indians have been mining red clay sandstone from the pipestone quarry in southwestern Minnesota to carve their calumets and ceremonial pipes. When it became a national monument in 1937, the authorizing legislation made the quarry open to all Native Americans. Now a unit in the National Park System, the monument covers 283 acres and includes a visitor center and museum.

Montana

HISTORIC SITES

Fort Assiniboine

The post is located about one-half mile south of the intersection of Highways 2 and 87, about seven miles southwest of Havre.

The army established Fort Assiniboine (1879–1911) to prevent Sitting Bull and his followers from coming back across the Canadian border, some thirty-eight miles north. It became an Agricultural Experiment Station in 1913, when most of its buildings were torn down. Remaining are a guardhouse and a multiplex officers' quarters.

Fort C. F. Smith

The site is located forty miles southwest of Crow Agency on Highway 313 on the Crow Indian Reservation.

Built in 1866 as the northern-most fort to protect the Bozeman Trail, Fort C. F. Smith lasted until the summer of 1868, when the army abandoned it as part of the agreement that resulted in the Fort Laramie Treaty signed by Red Cloud that fall. On August 1, 1867, troops from Fort C. F. Smith held off large numbers of Northern Cheyennes and Sioux in the Hayfield Fight. All that remains today are mounds of earth that indicate the location of buildings.

Fort Missoula

The post is located just off Highway 93 at the southwestern edge of Missoula. The museum is open during the summer from 10 AM to 5 PM, Tuesday to Saturday, and on Sunday from noon to 5 PM Winter hours are noon to 5 PM, Tuesday through Saturday; (406) 728–3476.

Founded in 1877 to protect settlers in the Bitterroot Valley, Fort Missoula served as the holding place for Nez Percés captured in the Battle of the Big Hole, in which its troops participated. The army abandoned Fort Missoula in 1915 but activated it in 1921. It remained in service until 1947 and since that time has had many uses. Today the National Guard and the Forest Service utilize most of the grounds. Of the frontier fort, two buildings remain, a stone powder magazine (1878) and the noncommissioned officers' (NCO) quarters. A former quartermaster's storehouse serves as the Fort Missoula Historical Museum. The post cemetery contains burials from Fort Ellis.

BATTLEFIELDS

Big Hole Battlefield National Monument

The battlefield is located in Beaverhead County on State 43, about twelve miles west of Wisdom. The visitor center is open from 8 AM to 8 PM in summer and from 8 AM to 5 PM the rest of the year; (406) 689–3155.

Early in the morning of August 8, Colonel John Gibbon led a force of 162 officers and men of the Seventh Infantry and a group of civilian volunteers in an attack on the Nez Percé village on the Big Hole River. Surprised in their beds, the Nez Percés rallied, forcing the troops into a wooded area on the opposite side of the river. Fighting continued until the next morning, when a small group of warriors covered the band's retreat. Gibbon suffered heavy losses, 29 dead and 40 wounded, while killing 89 Nez Percés, about 50 of whom were women and children. This National Park Service battlefield remains unchanged in a beautiful natural setting. A museum and self-guiding trails are on site, which includes the Indian camp and battle lines.

Bear Paw Battlefield

The battlefield is reached sixteen miles south of Highway 2 at Chinook by way of county road 240.

Here on September 28 troops under Colonel Nelson A. Miles caught Chief Joseph and the Nez Percés about forty miles from the Canadian border, ending for most of them their twelve hundred-mile flight to freedom. After six days of fighting, 414 men, women, and children surrendered, while a few under Chief White Bird escaped into Canada. The Nez Percés went into exile into Indian Territory in Oklahoma before returning to the Northwest in 1884. The state of Montana recently donated its one hundred sixty acres to the National Park Service. Included in the park are the Nez Percé village and battle sites. Two monuments and a self-guiding trail with markers interpret this unimpaired site.

Canyon Creek

To reach the battlefield, leave I-90 at Laurel and travel 8.3 miles north on Highway 532.

On September 13, 1877, Colonel Samuel Sturgis and three hundred fifty men of the Seventh Cavalry caught the Nez Percés who had escaped the army's trap near Yellowstone National Park at Canyon Creek. In a pitched battle the Nez Percés were able to find shelter in the narrow canyon and hold off Sturgis's troops. That night they slipped out the north end of the canyon and continued on their way to Canada. Killed in the fight were three men of the Seventh Cavalry. The Nez Percés did not lose a man but lost hundreds of horses. The battlefield is now used for agricultural purposes by private ownership. A monument gives information at the site.

Hayfield Fight Site

Located in Big Horn County, the site is located on a private ranch within the boundaries of Big Horn Canyon National Recreation Area.

On August 1, 1867, about five hundred to one thousand Northern Cheyennes and Sioux attacked nineteen soldiers and six civilians carrying on a haying operation outside Fort C. F. Smith on the Bozeman Trail. After Lieutenant Sigismund Sternberg died in the early fighting, Al Colvin, a civilian who had been an officer during the Civil War, assumed command. Armed with new breech-loading Springfield rifles, the little force held off their attackers, inflicting heavy losses.

Lame Deer Battlefield

The site is located in Rosebud County, on the Northern Cheyenne Indian Reservation, within the city limits of Lame Deer.

On May 7 troops under Colonel Nelson A. Miles defeated a band of Miniconjou Sioux under Chief Lame Deer. Killed in the engagement were Lame Deer, his son, and twelve warriors. After the rest of the Miniconjous reported to the reservation, only Sitting Bull and his immediate followers roamed free on the Northern Plains. The site has been heavily impacted by the town of Lame Deer. The local chamber of commerce provides a guide to visit the place where Chief Lame Deer died, and a monument marks the spot.

Little Bighorn Battlefield National Monument

The battlefield is located in Big Horn County just off I-90, about one mile southeast of its junction with U.S. 212, two miles from Crow Agency. The National Park Service area is open from 8 AM to 8 PM Memorial Day through Labor Day, from 8 AM to 6 PM during spring and fall, and from 8 AM to 4:30 PM during winter; (406) 638–2621.

The most famous battle between the U.S. Army and the Plains Indians occurred in the valley of the Little Bighorn on June 25, 1876. According to one of the Sioux participants, the fight lasted as long as it takes a hungry man to eat his dinner, and when it was over Lieutenant Colonel George Armstrong Custer, his brother Tom, a captain and two-time Congressional Medal of Honor recipient, his youngest brother Boston, his nephew Autie Reed, his brother-in-law Captain James Calhoun, and 215 men of the Seventh Cavalry were dead. On a dusty hill four miles away, the rest of Custer's regiment, under the leadership of Major Marcus A. Reno and Captain Frederick Benteen, continued to fight for two days before the Sioux, Northern Cheyennes, and Northern Arapahos left the valley. Losing perhaps as many as 100 warriors, the Indian coalition had won its greatest victory.

Included at the Little Bighorn National Monument is the site of "Custer's Last Stand" and the hill where Reno and Benteen fought on June 25 and 26. On site are a visitor center, museum exhibits, battlefield and road markers, self-guiding trails, and uniformed interpreters. Near the visitor center is Custer Battlefield National Cemetery, which includes the dead from many of the region's Indian wars.

Reynolds' Fight on the Powder River

Located in Powder River County, the battlefield is accessible by an unimproved road about four miles northeast of Moorhead.

On St. Patrick's Day, 1876, an advance force of General Crook's column, under Colonel Joseph J. Reynolds, surprised a Northern Cheyenne village on Powder River. The initial charge allowed the troops to capture the village, which Reynolds burned. In the meantime the Cheyennes regrouped and were able to recapture their pony herd from the retreating cavalry. Reynolds was later court-martialed for failure to press his advantage, but West Point classmate President Grant suspended the sentence. Used as ranch land, the battlefield remains relatively unchanged, except for some silting on the village site. On the northern edge of Moorhead is an interpretive marker.

Rosebud Battlefield State Park

The battlefield is located in Big Horn County just off Highway 314, about nine miles southwest of Kirby.

On June 17 as many as one thousand warriors under Crazy Horse met a similar number of cavalry and mounted infantry under General George Crook and a contingent of Crow and Shoshoni scouts in an all-day battle that ended with the military in possession of the field. However, Crook returned to his base camp near present-day Sheridan, Wyoming, to receive reinforcements, leaving Custer and Gibbon to continue the search for the Indians. Among the Northern Cheyennes, the engagement is known as "the battle in which the sister saved her brother." When dismounted in battle, a young warrior was about to be killed when his sister raced to his rescue and carried him away to safety. Now a Montana State Park, the battlefield retains it integrity. Three large metal signs provide interpretation.

Wolf Mountains Battlefield

The battlefield is located eight miles southeast of Birney. An unimproved road divides the site.

On January 8, 1877, Colonel Nelson A. Miles fought Crazy Horse and eight hundred warriors on the banks of Tongue River in the Wolf Mountains. The group included not only Oglalas but many of the Northern Cheyennes who had survived Mackenzie's attack on their village at the Red Fork of Powder River five weeks earlier. Using his howitzers to repulse the Sioux and Northern Cheyennes, Miles moved up the bluff to force the warriors to withdraw under cover of a snowstorm. Kept on the move, most of these warriors surrendered at Fort Robinson in the spring. Today the battlefield lies on private ranch land, which can be viewed from a gravel road that bisects the site.

MUSEUMS

Montana Historical Society

Located at 225 North Roberts in Helena, the museum is open Memorial Day to Labor Day from 8 AM to 8 PM. From Labor Day to Memorial Day, Monday through Friday, the museum is open from 8 AM to 5 PM and on Saturday from 9 AM to 5 PM; (406) 449–2694.

The museum includes exhibits on military and Indian history. Of special interest is the collection of art by Charles M. Russell.

Museum of the Plains Indians

The museum is located at the junction of Highways 2 and 89 at the western edge of Browning. It is open daily from 10 AM to 4:30 PM, June through September, and Monday through Friday during the rest of the year.

Browning is the administrative headquarters for the Blackfeet Reservation. Run by the Department of the Interior's Indian Arts and Crafts Board, the museum displays material culture and art and sells Native American goods. The museum hosts North American Indian Days during the second weekend in June.

INDIAN HERITAGE SITES

Dull Knife and Little Wolf Grave Sites

The grave sites are located just off Highway 212 in Lame Deer in the cemetery east of Dull Knife Community College.

Two of the old man chiefs of the Northern Cheyennes, Dull Knife (1810–1883) and Little Wolf (1821–1904), led their people from Oklahoma in an attempt to return to their Montana homeland in 1878–1879. Both remains had been buried in the mountains, but George Bird Grinnell had them exhumed and put in the Lame Deer cemetery in 1917 so that they might be honored.

Chief Plenty Coups State Park

The park is thirty-five miles south of Billings and one mile west of Pryor off Highway 416. It is open daily from 8 AM to 8 PM. The museum hours are from 10 AM to 5 PM May 1 to September 30 and at other times by appointment; (406) 252–1289.

Situated on the Crow Reservation in south central Montana, Chief Plenty Coups State Park includes the home of Chief Plenty Coups, his burial site, and a medicine springs. One can learn the story of Plenty Coups and the Crow people in a museum on site.

Nebraska

HISTORIC SITES

Fort Atkinson State Historical Park

The fort is located one mile east of Fort Calhoun, nine miles north of Omaha, on Highway 75. The park is open daily from Memorial Day through Labor Day and weekends in September and October from 9 AM to 5 PM; (402) 468–5611.

Garrisoned from 1819 to 1827, Fort Atkinson consisted of a 450-foot-square barracks quadrangle with two bastions. The first post built west of the Missouri River, it protected fur trade and frontier interests. The Nebraska Game and Parks Commission has restored most of the fort and operates an interpretive center on site, where one can view films and exhibits on Lewis and Clark and the fur trade.

Fort Hartsuff State Historical Park

Reach Fort Hartsuff by traveling seventy miles north of Grand Island, Nebraska, on Highway 218 and then turn west on Highway 91. Grounds are open daily from 8 AM to 8 PM year-round. Visitor facilities are open daily from Memorial Day through Labor Day and on weekends in May, September, and October.

The army established Fort Hartsuff in 1874 to protect settlers in the North Loup Valley and the Pawnee Indian Reservation. Workers built the grout structures for one company of infantry. Abandoned in 1881 Fort

Hartsuff is now administered by the Nebraska Game and Parks Commission. Restored and reconstructed buildings include the post adjutant's office, guardhouse, commanding officer's quarters, officers' quarters, enlisted men's barracks, laundresses' quarters and bakery, post hospital, quartermaster's storehouse, and stables. Costumed personnel provide interpretation. Fort Hartsuff remains one of the most complete forts in the West.

Fort Kearny State Historical Park

To reach the military post go three miles south of Kearney on Highway 44, then four miles east on Highway L540A. The grounds are open year-round from 8 AM to 8 PM. The visitor center is open daily from 9 AM to 5 PM Memorial Day through Labor Day; (308) 234-9513.

Established in 1848 to protect the Oregon, California, and Mormon Trails, Fort Kearny continued in operation until 1871. Guarding the Pony Express and the Pacific Telegraph, the post served as an outfitting post for a number of expeditions against the Plains Indians. JEB Stuart and Alfred Sully were two of the young officers to serve here who became Civil War generals. Administered by the Nebraska Game and Parks Commission, the state park contains the original parade ground, a reconstructed Civil War era stockade, a few other buildings, and a modern visitor center.

Fort Robinson State Park

Fort Robinson is located a few miles east of Crawford. It is open daily from 8 AM to 5 PM Monday through Saturday and Sunday from 9 AM to 5 PM Memorial Day through Labor Day. Hours vary during the off-season; (308) 665-2852.

Established in 1874 to guard nearby Red Cloud Agency, Fort Robinson remained an active military post until 1948. In 1919 it became a quartermaster's remount station for U.S. Army horses. From 1942-1945 it guarded a nearby prisoner-of-war camp. Transferred to the U.S. Department of Agriculture in 1948 for use as a beef cattle research station, it became a state property in 1971. Forty-nine buildings remain from the 1875-1912 period.

Fort Robinson was the scene of Crazy Horse's death on September 5, 1877. Several buildings relating to the story have been reconstructed. It was also at Fort Robinson that Dull Knife and his Northern Cheyenne followers were imprisoned and escaped on January 7, 1879. Stationed at Fort Robinson in the early 1890s were buffalo soldiers of the Ninth Cavalry. The Nebraska Historical Society and the University of Nebraska operate museums and interpretive programs on site. Sleeping accommodations are available in 1870s officers' quarters and a company barracks.

Fort Sidney

The commandant's home is at 1108 Sixth Avenue, Sidney, Nebraska. Facilities are open daily from 9 to 11 AM and from 1 to 3 PM May 15 through September 15. In the winter the hours are 1 to 4 PM daily and by appointment; (308) 254–2150.

Established to protect Union Pacific railroad crews in the summer of 1867, Sidney Barracks moved to a new site in 1869, where it developed into a full-fledged military post. Named Fort Sidney in 1874, it served until 1894. Scattered in the present town of Sidney are the former commanding officer's quarters (1871), an officers' duplex (1884), and the powder magazine (1872). The Cheyenne County Historical Association operates museums in the commanding officer's quarters and the officers' duplex.

BATTLEFIELDS

Blue Water Battlefield

Located in Garden County, the battlefield extends about eight miles north up Blue Water Creek Valley from the U.S. 26 bridge across Blue Water Creek, about two miles northwest of Lewellen.

Colonel William S. Harney and six hundred men from Fort Leavenworth took the field in the summer of 1855 to punish the Sioux for the Grattan Fight. Just above the junction of Blue Water Creek with the North Platte, Harney discovered a Brulé Sioux village under Little Thunder. On September 3 Harney sent his dragoons downstream, while he and his infantry marched up the valley from the Platte, catching the Brulés in a pincer movement. In the fight troops killed eighty warriors and captured seventy women and children. The defeat kept the Sioux subdued for almost a decade. Except for farming activities, the site is undisturbed. Although the site is privately owned, the traveler may view it from the forty-acre Ash Hollow State Historical Park that overlooks the battlefield.

Mud Springs Battlefield

The battlefield is located about twenty-five miles north of Sidney and about eight miles northwest of Dalton on a county road from Highway 385.

In the late summer of 1864 the army stationed volunteer troops at Mud Springs to protect the emigrant trail and the telegraph lines from possible Indian attack. On February 4 a thousand Southern Cheyenne and Sioux who had laid waste to Julesburg in revenge for Sand Creek reached the site. Reinforced by troops from Fort Mitchell and Fort Laramie under Colonel William O. Collins, the little outpost held out for three days; the most fighting occurred on February 6, after which the war party moved north. The army suffered seven wounded, three seriously. On February 8 Collins's command of about one hundred sixty men followed the raiders ten miles north, engaging about two thousand warriors at Rush Creek, on the south bank of the North Platte River. There the command narrowly escaped disaster, saved in part by supporting artillery fire. A plot 150 feet square preserves the ground once occupied by Mud Springs Station and is marked by a stone monument. The remainder of the battle site is on private farmland.

War Bonnet Battlefield

This battlefield is located in Sioux County, Nebraska, on a secondary road, about seventeen miles northwest of Harrison.

Here on July 17 the Fifth Cavalry under Colonel Wesley Merritt attacked one thousand Sioux encamped on Warbonnet (Hat) Creek. In the battle Buffalo Bill Cody killed Chief Yellow Hand, taking "the First Scalp for Custer," an episode re-enacted for hundreds of thousands in Cody's Wild West Show and in a movie starring Joel McCrae. Merritt's action sent these fugitives from Spotted and Red Cloud agencies back to their reservations. Used for grazing, this property remains relatively unchanged. Two monuments provide information.

INDIAN HERITAGE SITES

Horse Creek Treaty Site

The site is located about six miles south of Henry, Nebraska, on private land, but can be viewed from U.S. Highway 26, where the Nebraska Historical Society has a turnout and interpretive sign. About ten thousand Plains Indians gathered here to sign the Fort Laramie Treaty of 1851. The agreement provided yearly annuities in compensation for the use of the Oregon Trail and generally assigned tribes to certain areas in the Northern Plains region.

Massacre Canyon Site

Located eighteen miles west of McCook adjacent to Highway 34 is a monument marking the site. On August 5, 1873, about one thousand Brulé and Oglala warriors surprised seven hundred Pawnees while engaged in a buffalo hunt. The better-armed and more numerous Sioux killed or wounded from seventy to one hundred of their traditional enemies. This was the last communal buffalo hunt for the Pawnees, who three years later were sent to a reservation in Oklahoma. The thirty-five-foot granite monument that marks the site has engraved faces of Sioux leader John Grass and the Pawnee chief Ruling-His-Sun.

North Dakota

HISTORIC SITES

Fort Abercrombie State Historic Site

Take exit 37 from I-29 to approach Fort Abercrombie on Highway 81. The museum is open from 8 AM to 5 PM daily from May 16 through September 15; (701) 553–8513.

Established on August 10, 1858, on the banks of the Red River to help protect wagon trains traveling from St. Paul to the Montana gold fields, Fort Abercrombie suffered constant pressure from the Sioux during the Minnesota Uprising of 1862. On September 3–6 several hundred warriors besieged the post unsuccessfully. On September 29 reinforcements from Fort Snelling helped the garrison withstand another attack. Troops left the site on October 23, 1877. The state of North Dakota has reconstructed the palisade and a blockhouse and maintains a small museum; one original building remains.

Fort Abraham Lincoln State Park

The park is located five miles south of Mandan on Highway 1806. The Custer Home is open for tours daily from 9 AM to 8:30 PM Memorial Day through Labor Day and by appointment the rest of the year; (701) 258–0203.

George Armstrong Custer commanded this post from 1873 to 1876. Custer and the Seventh Cavalry left here in 1874 to explore the Black Hills and in 1876 to battle the Sioux and Northern Cheyennes. The headquarters of the Seventh Cavalry moved to Fort Meade, South Dakota, in 1882. In 1891, after the completion of the railroad and the confinement of the Sioux on reservations, the army abandoned Fort Abraham Lincoln, and settlers dismantled the post. The state of North Dakota has reconstructed and refurnished the Custer Home as well as a cavalry barracks. Nearby are the carefully reconstructed earth lodges of the Mandan Indians. On the bluff to the north is the site of the infantry post, Fort McKeen (1872), with reconstructed blockhouses. In June the park hosts Frontier Army Days to recreate life at the post in the mid-1870s.

Fort Buford State Historic Site

Located one mile southwest of Buford off Highway 1804, the site is open daily from 8 AM to 5 PM May 16 through September 15 and the rest of the year by appointment; (701) 572–9034.

Begun in June 1866, and expanded with the remains of Fort Union in 1867, the post housed six companies of infantry and cavalry at its height. Critically located at the confluence of the Missouri and Yellowstone Rivers, Fort Buford figured prominently in the campaigns against the Sioux and Northern Cheyennes in the 1870s and 1880s, serving as an important logistical base. It was the scene of the surrender of Sitting Bull in 1881. Also held here for a short time were Chief Joseph and the Nez Percés and Unkpapa leaders Gall and Crow King. Units that served here included the buffalo soldiers of the Tenth Cavalry and Twenty-fifth Infantry. Two buildings remain, one of which, an officers' quarters, houses a museum.

Fort Union Trading Post National Historic Site

Take Highway 2 west from Williston. The park is open Memorial Day through Labor Day from 8 AM to 8 PM, and from 9 AM to 5:30 PM the rest of the year; (701) 572–9803.

Built near the confluence of the Missouri and Yellowstone Rivers in 1829 by the American Fur Company, Fort Union was the fur trade center for the Upper Missouri Valley. Its clients were Crows, Assiniboine, Blackfeet, and trappers, and it became a place of rendezvous for entrepreneurs, explorers, surveyors, artists, naturalists, and other travelers and adventurers. When the fur trade declined, its owners left. In 1864–1865 Alfred Sully's troops used it temporarily but soon built Fort Buford nearby, cannibalizing the post.

In 1966 Congress accepted the site of Fort Union, eventually funding replication of the post. Today the reconstructed Bourgeois House is the visitor center and administrative office for the park. Also reconstructed, the Indian trade house has been refurnished to the period of the 1850s. The Fort Union Trading Post Rendezvous occurs in mid-June.

Fort Totten State Historic Site

Near Devils Lake, Fort Totten State Historic Site is approached from State Route 57. The post is accessible year-round. The Interpretive Center is open daily from May 16 to September 15 from 8 AM to 5 PM; (701) 224–2666.

Established as a military post in 1867, Fort Totten became an Indian boarding school in 1891. The state of North Dakota acquired the remarkably preserved site in 1960. Seventeen structures form a walled compound, most of them built from 1868 to 1871. In the restored commissary store-house is the interpretive center, featuring exhibits and a bookstore.

BATTLEFIELDS

Big Mound Battlefield

The battlefield is located in Kidder County about ten miles north of Tappen from the I-94 exit.

On July 24 General Henry Sibley encountered about three thousand Sioux, a mixed group of peaceful Sissetons and renegades under Inkapaduta who were hunting buffalo. After a parley in which warriors shot and killed military surgeon Joseph Weiser, Sibley fought them in a running battle, killing thirteen. A small state-owned tract contains a marker and cairn of rocks that marks the spot of the killing of Dr. Weiser and the beginning of the battle. Now used for ranching, the battlefield is privately owned.

Killdeer Mountain Battlefield

The battlefield is located in Dunn County about eleven miles northwest of Killdeer.

On July 28 a force of two thousand two hundred men under Brigadier General Alfred Sully attacked sixteen hundred Santees and Tetons at the base of Killdeer Mountain, killing about one hundred warriors and destroying their village. This ended Sully's campaign against the Sioux who had participated in the 1862 Minnesota Uprising. A large rock marker and the gravestones of two soldiers killed in the battle are preserved on a one-acre tract owned by the state. Ranch buildings, an artificial lake, and some cultivated land occupy some of the battlefield, which is privately owned.

Whitestone Hill Battlefield State Park

Located in Dickey County on an unimproved road about five miles southwest of Merricourt, Whitestone Hill Battlefield State Park preserves the relatively undisturbed site. The park is open May 16 to September 15 from 8 AM to 5 PM Thursday through Monday. It is closed on Tuesday and Wednesday; (701) 224–2666.

Sent west in 1863 to punish the Sioux in the aftermath of the Minnesota Uprising, General Alfred Sully with Nebraska and Iowa Volunteer Cavalry attacked 4000 Yanktonai and Unkpapa Sioux at Whitestone Hill. Fighting battles on September 3 and 5, Sully's troops soundly defeated the Sioux, killing 150 warriors and capturing 300 women and children. The destruction of the Indian camp led to the eventual return of many of the survivors to the reservation. On the hill in the center of the park are markers for the 22 army dead. Also within the park is a twenty-foot-high statue of a bugler mounted on a parapet, blowing taps.

INDIAN HERITAGE SITES

Knife River Villages National Historic Site
Located three miles north of Stanton by county road, the park is open daily from 9 AM to 6 PM, June through Labor Day. In the off-season, it closes at 4:30 PM; (701) 745-3309.

This National Park Service area preserves the remains of Mandan and Hidatsa earth lodge settlements on the Knife and Missouri Rivers. Evidence indicates occupation as early as 1300. Exhibits in an interpretive center recreate the daily life, and visitors may take walking tours to the site of the villages.

South Dakota

HISTORIC SITES

Fort Meade
The fort is located one mile east of Sturgis on Highway 234. The museum is open from 9 AM to 5 PM May 1 to Memorial Day, from 8 AM to 7 PM Memorial Day through Labor Day, and from 9 AM to 5 PM Labor Day to September 30; (605) 347-9822.

The army originally established the post in 1878 to maintain peace between settlers and travelers to the newly opened Black Hills and the Sioux tribes recently dispossessed. In early years Fort Meade was the headquarters of the Seventh Cavalry. Here in 1880 Major Marcus A. Reno was found guilty of window peeping and dismissed from the service. Fort Meade sent troops to Wounded Knee, monitored the wanderings of the Utes from Utah to South Dakota and their return to Utah in 1906–1908, and served as a training center in later years. It became a Veterans Administration facility in 1944. Most of the original buildings have disappeared, but some officers' quarters remain from the 1880s. The Old Fort Meade Museum and Historical Association operates a museum on site.

Fort Sisseton State Park
The fort is located six miles northwest of Eden. The visitor center is open from 11 AM to 7 PM daily from Memorial Day through Labor Day. The

grounds are open all year-round. For more information contact Park Manager, Roy Lake State Park, RR2, Lake City SD 567247; (605) 448–5701.

Established in 1864 as Fort Wadsworth to control the Sioux in the area following the Minnesota Uprising, the post guarded transportation routes and early settlement in the region. Renamed Fort Sisseton in 1876, the post continued until 1889. Its principal duty in its later years was to watch over the nearby Sisseton Indian Reservation. During the 1930s the WPA used the site and restored fourteen of the fort's stone and brick buildings. The recent recipient of a million dollar grant from funds made available through the Intermodal Surface Transportation Efficiency Act, the South Dakota Department of Game, Fish, and Parks will be able to accelerate its present restoration program. Historic structures surround the parade grounds, making it one of the most architecturally complete frontier forts. The museum is located in the barracks, which is partially refurnished. Fort Sisseton Days are held during the first week in June.

BATTLEFIELDS

Slim Buttes Battlefield

Located in Harding County on State 20, the battlefield is located about two miles west of Reva.

On September 9, 1876, an advance party of General Crook's command, led by Captain Anson Mills, discovered a Sioux camp on Rabbit Creek. Charging the village, Mills took possession and held his ground with an outnumbered force until the main column arrived. When fully engaged, the army's thirty-six companies overwhelmed the three hundred warriors who opposed them. The Indian's resistance prompted General Wesley Merritt to remark, "The world has not a light cavalry to match them." Capturing the mortally wounded American Horse and a few others, Crook's troops burned the village of thirty-seven lodges. The army's casualties were three killed and twelve wounded. This was the army's first victory over those who had fought Custer. Unimpaired, the battlefield consists of pine dotted hills and unbroken prairie. On a hill near the road are a monument and several markers.

Wounded Knee

The site of the Wounded Knee Tragedy is located in Shannon County on a secondary road, about sixteen miles northeast of the town of Pine Ridge.

On December 29 when troops of the Seventh Cavalry under Major James Forsyth attempted to disarm three hundred fifty Miniconjous under

Chief Big Foot, a shot fired by Black Cloud precipitated a melee in which troops opened up with two Hotchkiss guns. Killed in a fight that need not have happened were women and children and some young boys on vacation from school. Found on the field were over 150 bodies, buried in a mass grave on a hill overlooking Wounded Knee Creek. Many others died later in the freezing cold. Army casualties were twenty-five dead and thirty-nine wounded. The tragedy has become a symbol of Indian grievances. In 1973 AIM members engaged in a gun battle on site with FBI agents, during which two men were killed. Today, the scene remains in private and tribal ownership, and a number of markers interpret the site. Souvenir stands are usually present, where visitors may purchase tribal goods of various kinds. On the hill above the battleground is the mass burial site, marked by a memorial shaft, now in the middle of the Wounded Knee Cemetery.

MUSEUMS

Akta Lakota Museum and Cultural Center
Located on the campus of the St. Joseph Indian School north of Chamberlain, the museum is open year-round; (605) 734–3452.

Exhibits promote Sioux heritage, past and present. High-quality crafts are offered for sale.

Sioux Indian Museum
Located in downtown Rapid City, the Sioux Indian Museum is open all year-round; (605) 358–0057.

Permanent exhibits present the rich diversity of historic Sioux arts, and two changing exhibition galleries feature the works of contemporary artists. The museum is administered by the Department of the Interior's Arts and Crafts Board.

INDIAN HERITAGE SITES

Bear Butte State Park
Bear Butte is located about eight miles northeast of Sturgis, off Highway 34. According to Cheyenne oral tradition, it was here that Sweet Medicine received the Sacred Arrows. Today Cheyennes use the area for vision quests and spiritual renewal. A park visitor center traces the meaning of Bear Butte in Cheyenne history, and a foot trail leads to the top of the butte, affording a panoramic view of the surrounding area.

Red Cloud's Grave

This site is located on Cemetery Hill near the Red Cloud Heritage Center, just west of the town of Pine Ridge, on U.S. Highway 18.

The leader of the Oglala Sioux died in 1909, having lived in peace for forty-one years following the signing of the Fort Laramie Treaty of 1868. A warrior who counted eighty coups, he became an elder statesman on the Pine Ridge Reservation, often resisting attempts by agency officials to enforce white ways on the Sioux. The nearby Red Cloud Heritage Center contains a permanent art collection and museum shop.

Sitting Bull Burial Site

The site is located across the Missouri River bridge from Mobridge. Take Highway 12 and then proceed south on Highway 1806.

Initially planned in the creation of the Missouri River dams was the inundation of Fort Yates and the original Sitting Bull burial site. Therefore, in April 1953 Sioux activists reclaimed the bones in the dark of night and reburied them on a site overlooking the Missouri near the mouth of Grand River, ensuring that others would not disturb the body by filling the grave with twenty tons of steel rails and concrete. A bust sculpted by Korezack Ziokowskie marks the grave site.

Wyoming

HISTORIC SITES

Fort Bridger State Historic Site

Fort Bridger is near Lyman in southwestern Wyoming, just off I-80. The site is open daily from April 15 to October 15 and on weekends during the rest of the year; (307) 782–3842.

Fort Bridger was established in 1858 and survived as a busy but relatively peaceful garrison until 1890. After the army left, it became a community center and the home of its post trader, Judge W. A. Carter. A number of buildings have been restored and refurnished. Nearby, the state of Wyoming has reconstructed the Jim Bridger trading post (1843–1858). During Labor Day weekend, some five hundred re-enactors gather for the Fort Bridger Rendezvous.

Fort Caspar

In Casper, Wyoming, take the Poplar Street exit from I-25. Fort Caspar is located near the junction of West Thirteenth Street and Fort Caspar Road.

In the summer, it is open Monday through Saturday from 9 AM to 5 PM and on Sunday from noon to 5 PM. Otherwise, it is open Monday through Friday from 9 AM to 5 PM and Sunday from 1 to 4 PM; (307) 235–8462.

Established in May 1862 to protect the Oregon Trail, the Platte Bridge, and the Pacific Telegraph, Fort Caspar (first called Platte Bridge Station) lasted until 1867. It was from here on July 26, 1865, that Lieutenant Caspar Collins and a detachment left the post to relieve Sergeant Amos Custard's wagon train. Collins and four others died in an ambush, the rest of the twenty-six making it back to the fort. Custard and twenty-one of his men succumbed a few hours later when the Cheyenne and Sioux overran their corralled wagons.

During the mid-1930s the WPA reconstructed the original fort that includes administrative offices, living quarters, a telegraph station, and the sutler's store. Fort Caspar buildings are refurnished, and during summer months uniformed guides are in residence. The sutler's store contains one of the best bookstores on western history in the region, and an excellent museum is on the grounds. On the river bank is a replica of the ferry used by Mormons beginning in 1847.

The site of the first engagement on July 26, known as the Battle of Platte Bridge, is one mile north of Fort Caspar on private land used for commercial purposes. The site of the Battle of Red Buttes, where Sergeant Custard and his men died, remains in dispute, some locating it as much as five miles north, while others favor sites much closer to the fort.

Fort Fetterman State Historic Site

Six miles northwest of Douglas, Wyoming, on Highway 93 is Fort Fetterman. The museum is open daily during the summer from 9 AM to 5 PM; (307) 358–2864.

Established to guard the Bozeman Trail in 1867, it became a base of operations for General Crook in the Sioux Campaign of 1876–1877. It was abandoned in 1884, and two original buildings remain. Foundations are identified by interpretive markers. A museum, housed in the officers' quarters, has exhibits that tell the history of the post.

Fort Fred Steele State Historic Site

The fort is located two miles north of I-80 fifteen miles east of Rawlins.

Established in the summer of 1868 to protect workers constructing the Union Pacific Railroad, Fort Fred Steele figured prominently in the Ute Uprising of 1879. Major Thomas T. Thornburg's troops left the post to punish the Utes for an attack on their agency in nearby Colorado but met disaster at the Battle of Milk River. Here the Utes ambushed and killed Thornburg, thirteen others, and wounded forty-three. After its abandonment in 1886, local residents occupied the buildings. Today only a powder magazine, foundations, and ruins remain. Nearby is a self-guiding interpretive center. The Wyoming State Parks and Historic Sites administers the property.

Fort Laramie National Historic Site
Located off U.S. Highway 26, three miles from the town of Fort Laramie, the National Historic Site is open daily year-round from 8 AM to 4:30 PM and to 8 PM in summer; (307) 837–2221.

In 1834 Sublette and Campbell built the first Fort Laramie (Fort William) at the confluence of the Laramie and North Platte Rivers. The fort was later replaced by an adobe post (Fort John) in 1841. The U.S. Army purchased the fur trading post in 1849 to guard the Oregon Trail and officially named it Fort Laramie. The garrison later protected the Pony Express and the Pacific Telegraph, emigrants on the Mormon Trail, gold seekers on the way to California, and miners headed for the Montana gold fields. In 1876–1877 it was an important post in campaigns against the Sioux and Cheyennes. Abandoned in 1890 it became a National Park Service area in 1938.

A listing of its inhabitants and visitors is a recounting of the great names in Western History: fur traders William Sublette, Robert Campbell, Jim Bridger, Thomas Fitzpatrick, James Bordeaux, and John Richard Sr.; military leaders William S. Harney, William Tecumseh Sherman, Philip Sheridan, George Crook, Eugene Carr, Ranald Mackenzie, and Wesley Merritt; junior officers John Grattan, Caspar Collins, John G. Bourke, Charles King, and Anson Mills; flamboyant western characters Buffalo Bill, Wild Bill Hickok, Calamity Jane, and Captain Jack Crawford; Indian leaders Conquering Bear, Man-Afraid-of-His-Horses, Red Cloud, Crazy Horse, and Spotted Tail; and scouts Big Bat Pourier, Little Bat Garnier, Frank Grouard, and Frank North.

Twenty-one buildings and ruins remain. Completely refurnished are Old Bedlam (the post headquarters and bachelor officers' quarters), the sutler's store, the powder magazine, three sets of officers' quarters, the post bakery, and the cavalry barracks. The post commissary serves as the visitor center.

Fort Phil Kearny State Historic Site
Ten miles north of Buffalo take exit 44 from I-90. The visitor center is open Memorial Day to Labor Day from 8 to 5 PM; (307) 684–7629.

Today Fort Phil Kearny State Historic Site preserves the setting and subsurface remains of what one U.S. Army inspector reported in 1867 as the best stockaded post he had ever seen. Built by Colonel Henry Beebe Carrington in 1866 to protect the Bozeman Trail, Fort Phil Kearny was practically under siege by Red Cloud and his warriors until abandoned in 1868, when it was burned to the ground. From here on December 21, 1866, Captain William Fetterman and his command of eighty men left to follow a decoy into ambush and death at the hands of fifteen hundred Sioux and Northern Cheyennes. On site are a small museum and outdoor exhibits. The state has marked the corners of the fort and the foundations of many buildings.

Fort D. A. Russell

Located in Cheyenne, the post is reached from a well-marked exit from I-25.

The army established Fort D. A. Russell in 1867 to protect Union Pacific railroad workers. It remains an active military post, under the name of Francis E. Warren Air Force Base. Although none of the original frame buildings survive, many nineteenth-century brick structures remain, including barracks, officers' quarters, the post hospital (1887), and the headquarters building (1894–1905).

Fort Washakie

The fort is located in Fremont County in the town of Fort Washakie.

From 1871 to 1909 Fort Washakie was the protector of the Wind River Reservation, created for the friendly Shoshonis in 1868 and named for their famous warrior chief. For the first few years it also guarded mining settlements in the South Pass area and later served as an outfitting point for expeditions into the Big Horn Basin and Yellowstone National Park. In 1909 it became the agency headquarters for the reservation, a role it continues today. A few of the military structures remain, most having been adapted for new uses. Nearby is a cemetery containing the grave of Chief Washakie.

BATTLEFIELDS

Connor Battlefield State Historic Site

The site is adjacent to Ranchester from exit 9 off I-90.

In mid-July district commander Patrick E. Connor led five hundred troops into north central Wyoming in search of Plains Indians who had been raiding since spring along the Oregon Trail and elsewhere. On August 29 his command surprised an Arapaho village on Tongue River, killing sixty-three, capturing five hundred ponies, and burning two hundred fifty lodges, while suffering only seven wounded, one of whom later died. This was the only success in Connor's Powder River expedition, which saw other units under Colonel Nelson Cole and Lieutenant Colonel Samuel Walker fail to accomplish their missions and return to Connor's supply base in destitute condition. The site has been developed by the state of Wyoming into a picnic and campground. A commemorative stone monument stands in the center of the park.

Dull Knife Battlefield

The battlefield is located on private land twenty-three miles west of Kaycee on an unimproved road. A small fee is charged to visit the site.

Eleven hundred men under Ranald Mackenzie attacked the Northern Cheyenne village on the Red Fork of Powder River on November 25, 1876. Taking the tribesmen under Dull Knife and Little Wolf by surprise, the troops destroyed the village and its winter supply of food, forcing the Cheyennes to seek shelter many miles away with Crazy Horse's band. The Cheyennes lost forty men, while Mackenzie's casualties were First Lieutenant John A. McKinney and five men killed and twenty-six wounded. The defeat broke the power of the Northern Cheyennes, causing them to surrender at Fort Robinson, Nebraska, in the spring. The battlefield remains untouched in a beautiful valley on a privately owned ranch.

Grattan Fight

The battlefield is located on private land near the banks of the North Platte River, about three miles west of Lingle on Highway 26.

The first real trouble between the U.S. Army and the Plains Indians occurred on August 19, 1854, eight miles southeast of Fort Laramie when Lieutenant John L. Grattan, twenty-nine enlisted men, and a drunken interpreter attempted to arrest a Miniconjou brave who had killed and butchered a stray cow from a Mormon caravan. When the warrior refused to give himself up, a fight ensued in which Grattan and his command perished. The enlisted men killed in this engagement are buried in Fort McPherson National Cemetery, Nebraska. A state monument at the side of Highway 26 designates the site.

Fetterman Battlefield State Historic Site

The battlefield is located five miles north of Fort Phil Kearny on Highway 87.

Disaster came for the military at Fort Phil Kearny on December 21,

1866, when Brevet Lieutenant Colonel William Judd Fetterman disobeyed orders and led eighty men across Lodge Trail Ridge into ambush, where fifteen hundred Sioux and their allies cut them down to the last man. A self-guiding trail with interpretive markers permits the visitor to traverse the mile-long site. A rock monument marks the location of the demise of the last of those killed in the fight, including Fetterman and Captain Frederick Brown.

Wagon Box State Historic Site

Located in Johnson County, the site can be reached about two miles south of Story by Highways 194 and 195.

On August 2 about fifteen hundred Sioux attacked a detachment of twenty-eight infantrymen guarding a woodcutters' camp about six miles from Fort Phil Kearny. Protected by the wagon boxes formed in a corral, the defenders had recently been armed with new breech-loading Springfields that gave them rapid fire power. The surprised Sioux lost as many as one hundred warriors in several frontal assaults. A one-acre site owned by the state of Wyoming contains a stone monument with interpretive plaque. The Fort Phil Kearny/Bozeman Trail association owns another twenty-six acres. The vista to the west of the Big Horn Mountains remains unchanged.

MUSEUMS

Buffalo Bill Historical Center

Located on the northeast edge of Cody, the museum complex is open daily from 8 AM to 5 PM May to October; from 7 AM to 10 PM June through August; from 8 AM to 8 PM in September and October; and from 10 AM to 3 PM Tuesday through Sunday, March through November. The center is closed December through February.

The Buffalo Bill Historical Center is composed of four museums: the Buffalo Bill Museum, the Cody Firearms museum, the Whitney Gallery of Western Art, and the Plains Indian Museum. The latter covers the culture of the Sioux, Cheyenne, Shoshoni, Crow, Arapaho, and Blackfeet tribes. In the Whitney Gallery of Art, the visitor will find Frederick Remington's studio replicated and Paxson's "Custer's Last Stand."

Notes

Abbreviations

ANJ   *Army and Navy Journal*
ANR   *Army and Navy Register*
CDL   *Cheyenne Daily Leader*
NT   *National Tribune*
SDH   *South Dakota History*

Introduction

1. Richard F. Burton, *The City of the Saints* (Niwot: University Press of Colorado, 1990), p. 44.
2. "A Look Behind," ANR, January 1, 1882, p. 4.
3. NT, January 1, 1891, p. 2.
4. "A Look Behind," ANR, January 1, 1882, p. 4.
5. Allen R. Millet and Peter Maslowski, *For the Common Defense* (New York: The Free Press, 1984), p. 237.
6. CDL, April 3, 1868, p. 1.
7. Richard G. Hardorff, *Lakota Recollections* (Spokane WA: Arthur H. Clark Company, 1991), p. 132.
8. Stanley Vestal, *New Sources of Indian History, 1850–1891* (Norman: Oklahoma University Press, 1934), pp. 131, 140; Wesley Merritt, "Arms and Equipment," ANJ, May 4, 1878, p. 628.

Part 1

Chapter 1: Causes and Limiting Factors

1. For differing ideas of land use see D'Arcy McNickle, "Indian and European," in *The Rape of Indian Lands*, ed. Paul W. Gates (New York: Arno Press, 1979), p. 5; J. P. Kinney, *A Continent Lost—A Civilization Won* (Baltimore: Johns Hopkins Press, 1937), pp. 1–5; and Julius W. Pratt, "The Ideology of American Expansion," in *Essays in Honor of William E. Dood*, ed. Avery Craven (Chicago: University of Chicago Press, 1935), pp. 333–48. Works concerning ideas about Indian capabilities include Antonello Gerbi, *The Dispute of the New World* (Pittsburgh: University of Pittsburgh Press, 1973), pp. 250 ff.; Bernard W. Sheehan, *Seeds of Extinction* (Chapel Hill: University of North Carolina Press, 1973), especially pp.

66–116; and Sherry L. Smith, *The View from Officers' Row* (Tucson: University of Arizona Press, 1990). Studies chronicling the dealings of the Indian Ring include George H. Phillips, "The Indian Ring in Dakota," SDH 2 (fall 1972); and Elsie M. Rushmore, *The Indian Policy During Grant's Administration* (Jamaica NY: Marion Press, 1914), pp. 19, 25–28.

For explication of military limitations see Maurice Matloff, ed., *American Military History* (Washington DC: Office of Chief of Military History, 1969), p. 282; "Army" in *Index Rerum* (n.p., 1883); and Robert Wooster, *The Military and United States Indian Policy* (New Haven CT: Yale University Press, 1988), pp. 144, 170–71. Stressing the importance of immigration and the railroads are Steve Ambrose, "Custer Had It Coming," *Harvard Magazine* 78 (June 1976); Frederick Merk, *Manifest Destiny* (New York: Vintage Books, 1963), pp. 24, 33, 53–55, 265; and Walter Prescott Webb, *The Great Plains* (New York: Grosset & Dunlap, 1931), pp. 273–80.

2. Raymond DeMallie, "Touching the Pen," in *Ethnicity on the Great Plains*, ed. Frederick C. Luebke (Lincoln: University of Nebraska Press, 1980), p. 47.
3. Quoted in Charles F. Bates, "The Red Man and the Black Hills," *The Outlook* 146 (July 27, 1927), 411.
4. Frances Carrington, *My Army Life and the Fort Phil Kearny Massacre* (Denver: Pruett Press, 1990), p. 314.
5. James D. Richardson, ed., *A Compilation of the Messages and Papers of the Presidents, 1789–1897*, 10 vols. (Washington DC: Government Printing Office, 1896–1899), vol. 2: 415–16.
6. Minutes of a Conference with Spotted Tail, April 16, 1867, Records of the Special Commission to Investigate the Fetterman Massacre, Indian Bureau Records, Record Group 75, National Archives. Hereafter cited as "Special Commission."
7. ANJ, October 26, 1867, p. 155.
8. "Official Exposure," ANJ, February 9, 1867, p. 391.
9. Todd Randall, April 16, 1867, Special Commission.
10. Letter from Commissioner Lewis V. Bogy, Washington DC, January 23, 1867, to Interior Secretary O. H. Browning, in *House Executive Document* No. 171, 39th Congress, 2 sess., Vol. 11, 1866, p. 13
11. Henry B. Carrington, *The Indian Question* (Boston: DeWolfe & Fiske Company, 1909), p. 12.
12. George Forsyth, *Thrilling Days in Army Life* (New York: Harper & Brothers, 1900), p. 7.
13. Crane Brinton, *A History of Western Morals* (New York: Harcourt, Brace & World, Inc., 1959), pp. 330, 339.
14. Eugene F. Ware, *The Indian War of 1864* (Lincoln: University of Nebraska Press, 1994), p. 28.
15. *The Miners Journal*, November 19, 1867, p. 1
16. Edward Howland, "Our Indian Brothers," *Harper's* 56 (April 1878), 773.

17. Walter Mills, *A Study of American Military History* (New York: G. P. Putnam's Sons, 1956), pp. 37, 41–43.
18. Report of the Secretary of War, 1:36.
19. "Indian Affairs," *Inter-Ocean*, June 24, 1876, p. 9.
20. "Little Big Horn," *Chicago Tribune*, August 7, 1876, p. 5.
21. Allen R. Millet and Peter Maslowski, *For the Common Defense* (New York: The Free Press, 1984), p. 237.

Chapter 2: Opponents

1. For helpful general works on Indians in the West and cultural areas see Alvin M. Josephy, *The Indian Heritage of America* (New York: Alfred A. Knopf, 1968), chaps. 9, 10, 13–16; Arrell M. Gibson, *The American Indian* (Lexington MA: D.C. Heath and Company, 1980), chaps. 14–16; Alice B. Kehoe, *North American Indians* (Englewood Cliffs NJ: Prentice-Hall, Inc., 1981), chaps. 3, 6–8; William Brandon, *The American Heritage Book of Indians* (New York: American Heritage Publishing, Co., 1961), chaps. 13–15; and Frederick W. Hodge, *Handbook of American Indians North of Mexico*, 2 vols. (New York: Patent Books, Inc., 1960). The definitive work on Indian tribes is the Smithsonian Institution's new *Handbook of North American Indians* (1976 to present), being published in twenty volumes.

   For a look at populations in the late twentieth century see Douglas R. Parks, et al. "Peoples of the Plains," in *Anthropology on the Great Plains*, eds. W. Raymond Wood and Margot Liberty (Lincoln: University of Nebraska Press, 1980), pp. 284–95. For other culture areas, I have used Russell Thornton, *American Indian Holocaust and Survival: A Population History since 1492* (Norman: University of Oklahoma Press, 1987); and John U. Terrell, *American Indian Almanac* (New York: Thomas Y. Crowell Company, 1974), pp. 27, 359, 389. Terrell presents in convenient form compilations made by early anthropologists James Mooney, John R. Swanson, and A. L. Kroeber.
2. The best short discussion of army organization is Don Russell, "The Army of the Frontier, 1865–1891," in *"No Pride in the Little Big Horn"* ed. Francis B. Taunton (London: The English Westerners' Society, 1987), pp. 71–80, originally published in *Chicago Westerners' Brand Book* (January 1960). See also Robert M. Utley, *Frontier Regulars* (New York: Macmillan Publishing Co., Inc., 1973), chapt. 2; Edward M. Coffman, *The Old Army* (New York: Oxford University Press, 1986), chaps. 5–7; and George Patten, *Patten's Army Manual* (New York: J. Fortune, 1894).
3. "A Word for Non-Coms," ANR, April 19, 1887, p. 228.
4. William F. Hynes, *Frontier Soldiers* (n.p.: Grand Council Fire of American Indians, 1943), p. 54.

Chapter 3: Material Culture

1. General works on Indian clothing and accouterments are Robert H. Lowie,

Indians of the Plains (New York: McGraw-Hill, 1954); Hodge, *Handbook of American Indians North of Mexico*; and Jon M. White, *Everyday Life of the North American Indians* (New York: Indian Head Books, 1979). For information on Indian weapons see J. H. Bill, "Notes on Arrow Wounds," *American Journal of Medical Science* 64 (October 1862), 369; John Gibbon in ANJ, June 15, 1877, p. 730; and Richard A. Fox, *Archaeology, History, and Custer's Last Battle* (Norman: University of Oklahoma Press, 1993), pp. 7–79.

2. E. G. Latta, "Winning of the West," NT, December 22, 1921, p. 5.

3. "F." in ANJ, April 2, 1882, p. 573.

4. Excellent studies of army uniforms are M. T. Ludington, *Uniforms of the Army of the United States* (Washington DC: Quartermaster General's Department, 1889); Gordon S. Chappell, *The Search for the Well-Dressed Soldier* (Tucson: Arizona Historical Society, 1972); and Douglas C. McChristian, *The U. S. Army in the West* (Norman: University of Oklahoma Press, 1995). For women's clothing see Janet Burgess, *Clothing Guidelines for the Civil War Era* (Davenport IA: Amazon Drygoods, 1985), pp. 3–20; and Charles Hecklinger, *Dress and Cloak Cutter: Women's Costumes 1877–1882* (Mendocino CA: R. L. Shep, 1987).

5. ANJ, August 31, 1872, p. 42.

6. Eugene Bandel, *Frontier Life in the Army, 1854–1861* (Glendale CA: Arthur H. Clark, Company, 1932), p. 124.

7. Alfred A. Woodhull, *Medical Report upon the Uniform and Clothing of the Soldier of the U.S. Army* (Washington DC: Surgeon General's Office, April 15, 1868), p. 4.

8. A. G. Brackett, "Our Cavalry," *Journal of the Military Service Institution of the United States* 4, no. 16 (1883), p. 384.

9. Private Taleteller, "A Tale of Tail," ANR, November 3, 1883.

10. George H. Holliday, *On the Plains in '65* (n.p., 1883), p. 73.

11. Useful studies of army weapons are Arcadi Gluckman, *United States Martial Pistols and Revolvers* (Buffalo NY: Ken Worthy Press, 1939); and *United States Muskets, Rifles, and Carbines* (Buffalo NY: Otto Ulbrich Co., 1948); McChristian, *The U.S. Army in the West*, pp. 105–43; Eugene Carr, "The Question of Arms," ANJ, April 27, 1878, p. 610; Wesley Merritt, "Arms and Equipment," ANJ, May 4, 1878, p. 628. To identify incidents in which the army used the howitzer in the Indian wars see William A. Kupke, *The Indian and the Thunderwagon* (Silver City NM: William A. Kupke, 1992).

12. Excellent works on horse equipment include Randy Steffen, *United States Military Saddles, 1812–1943* (Norman: University of Oklahoma Press, 1973); *The Horse Soldier*, 4 vols. (Norman: University of Oklahoma Press, 1979); and *Ordnance Memoranda No. 29*: Horse Equipment and Cavalry Accoutrements (Tucson: Westernlore Press, 1984), pp. 26–31.

13. Margaret Carrington, *Absaraka* (Lincoln: University of Nebraska Press, 1983), p. 74.

14. ANJ, December 5, 1868, p. 245.

Chapter 4: Warfare

1. For information on Indian war customs see James Mooney, "Military Societies," *Handbook of North American Indians* 1 (1960), 861–63; Marian W. Smith, "The War Complex," *Proceedings of the American Philosophical Society* 78 (1938), 425–64; A. F. Chamberlain, "War and War Discipline," in *Handbook of American Indians*, vol. 2: 914–15; Richard Burton, *The Look of the West* (Lincoln: University of Nebraska Press, n.d.), pp. 177–78; An Army Officer, "How the Apache Fights," *The Illustrated American*, January 4, 1896, p. 13; and James Cook, "The Art of Fighting Indians," *American Mercury* 23 (June 1931).

2. Charles W. King, "Arms and Tactics," ANJ, March 27, 1880, p. 685.

3. "Custer Tragedy," *Inter-Ocean*, July 9, 1876, p. 1.

4. Philip Katcher, *The American Indian Wars 1860–1890* (London: Osprey Publishing Company, 1977), p. 12.

5. Lucullus McWhorter, *Hear Me My Chiefs* (Caldwell ID: Caxton Printers, 1962), p. 249.

6. Dixon, *Hero of Beecher Island* (Lincoln: University of Nebraska Press, 1994), p. 92.

7. Vestal, *New Sources of Indian*, p. 138.

8. Ware, *The Indian War of 1864*, p. 254.

9. Memorials, Records, Lincoln Post No. 1, Department of Kansas, G.A.R. (Topeka KS: n.d.), p. 50.

10. Margaret Carrington, *Absaraka*, pp. 83, 183.

11. Veritas, "Plan of a Campaign Against the Indians," ANJ, April, 20, 1867, p. 553.

12. A. G. Brackett, "The Question of Equipment," ANJ, July 6, 1878, p. 718.

13. W. J. Hoffman, "Poisoned Weapons," MS No. 599, Dakota, National Anthropological Archives, Smithsonian Institution, Washington DC, pp. 2–3.

14. "Custer Tragedy," *Inter-Ocean*, July 9, 1876, p. 1.

15. "Equipment," ANJ, June 29, 1878, p. 762.

16. For military tactics and strategy see Thomas W. Dunlay, "Fire and Sword," in *The American Indian Experience*, ed. Philip Weeks (Arlington Heights IL: Forum Press, 1988), pp. 133–52; Don Rickey Jr., *War in the West* (Crow Agency MT: Custer Battlefield Historical and Museum Association, 1956), pp. 8–11; Horace Porter, "Philosophy of Courage," *Century Magazine* 36 (June 1888); Charles K. Mills, *Harvest of Barren Regrets* (Glendale CA: Arthur H. Clark Company, 1985), p. 298; "Cavalry Against Indians," ANJ, May 11, 1878, p. 647; Randolph B. Marcy, *The Prairie Traveler* (West Virginia Pulp and Paper Company, 1961), pp. 164–88; Edward S. Farrow, *Camping on the Trail* (Philadelphia: American Arms Publishing, 1902); and "How Frontiersmen Fight Indians, CDL, August 10, 1876, p. 1.

17. Studies concerning army training include James S. Hutchins, "Mounted Riflemen," in *Probing the American West*, ed. K. Ross Toole, et al. (Santa Fe: University of New Mexico), p. 83; Douglas C. McChristian, *An Army of Marksmen* (Fort Collins CO: Old Army Press, 1981), pp. 33–34, 48–49, 51–52, 81; Edward S. Farrow, "Mountain Scouting," ANJ, May 28, 1881, p. 6; and "Hints to Campaigners," ANJ, September 2, 1863, p. 39.

18. Correspondent, ANJ, August 30, 1879, p. 63.

19. "A Late Captain of Infantry," *Hints Bearing on the United States Army, with an Aim at the Adaptation, Availability, Efficiency and Economy Thereof* (Philadelphia: Henry B. Ashmead, Book and Job Printer, 1858), p. 26.

20. *Winners of the West* (November 30, 1935), p. 1.

21. C. W. King, "Arms," ANJ, March 27, 1880, p. 685.

22. "Indian Trailers," ANJ, July 3, 1869, p. 727.

23. Charles F. Lummis, *General Crook and the Apache Wars* (Flagstaff AZ: 1966), p. 17.

24. John D. McDermott, "We Had a Terribly Hard Time Letting Them Go," *Nebraska History* 77 (summer 1996), 81–82.

25. John Gibbon, "Arms to Fight Indians," *United Service* 1 (April 1879), 240.

26. Captain Henry Romeyn, "How It Feels to Be Shot," ANJ, March 9, 1878, p. 484.

27. "Scalped," ANJ, July 26, 1869, p. 716.

Chapter 5: Indian and Army Life

1. For information on Indian domestic life see R. Douglas Hurt, *Indian Agriculture* (Lawrence: University Press of Kansas, 1987), pp. 42–64; Alice C. Fletcher, *Indian Games and Dances* (Lincoln: University of Nebraska Press, 1994); Reginald and Gladys Laubin, *The Indian Tipi* (Norman: University of Oklahoma Press, 1960); and Tom McHugh, *The Time of the Buffalo* (New York: Alfred A. Knopf, 1972), pp. 83–109.

2. Marion P. Maus, "The New Indian Messiah," *Harper's Weekly* (December 6, 1890), 944; John D. McDermott, "Centennial Voices," SDH 22 (winter 1990), 250–57.

3. For a discussion of religious beliefs see Ake Hultkrantz, *Native Religions* (New York: Harper Collins, 1987), pp. 26, 128–32; George B. Grinnell, *The Story of the Indian* (New York: D. Appleton and Company, 1924), pp. 195–201; Leslie Spier, "The Sun Dance of the Plains Indians," *Anthropological Papers of the American Museum of Natural History* 16 (1921), 451–527; Margot P. Liberty, "Priest and Shaman on the Plains," *Plains Anthropologist* 15 (May 1970), 74–75; and H. C. Yarrow, *Introduction to the Study of the Mortuary Customs* (Washington DC: Government Printing Office, 1880), pp. 66–76.

4. *Omaha Daily Herald*, June 22, 1878, p. 5.

5. "Religion," ANJ, July 6, 1878, p. 718.

6. Carrington, *The Indian Question*, p. 17.

7. Carrington, *The Indian Question*, pp. 16–17.

8. Works treating army society and customs are Don Rickey, *Forty Miles a Day on Beans and Hay* (Norman: University of Oklahoma Press, 1963); Edward M. Coffman, *The Old Army* (New York: Oxford University Press, 1986); Oliver Knight, *Life and Manners in the Frontier Army* (Norman: University of Oklahoma Press, 1978); Patricia Y. Stallard, *Glittering* (Fort Collins CO: Old Army Press, 1978), pp. 53–73; John D. McDermott, "Crime and Punishment in the United States Army," *Journal of the West* 7 (April 1968), 246–55; Duane M. Greene, *Ladies and Officers of the United States Army* (Chicago: Central Publishing Company, 1880); David Michael Delo, *Peddlers and Post Traders* (Salt Lake City: University of Utah Press, 1992); and W. N. Davis Jr., "Post Canteens for the Army," *The Public Service Review* 4 (July 1889), 262–65.

9. G. Jones in *Winners of the West* (December 1930), p. 8.

10. Mark Hersey, ANJ, August 16, 1890, p. 527.

11. J. Ross Brown, ANJ, January 23, 1869, p. 359.

12. "Wind," ANR, November 28, 1885, p. 764.

13. Charles Brown, "Diary," July 1861, Special Collections, Creighton University Library, Omaha, Nebraska.

14. G. A. July 23, 1867, ANJ, August 10, 1867, p. 810.

15. William Bisbee, *Through Four American Wars* (Boston: Meadow Publishing Company, 1931), p. 168.

16. Elizabeth Custer, *Following the Guidon* (New York: Harper & Brothers, 1890), p. 300.

17. "On Mount Ararat," ANJ, July 17, 1869, p. 758.

18. "Army Life," ANJ, February 17, 1867, p. 415.

19. Glendolin Danon Wagner, *Old Neutriment* (Lincoln: University of Nebraska Press, 1989), pp. 115–16.

20. "Army Life," ANJ, February 17, 1867, p. 415.

21. "Attack," ANR, May 25, 1878, p. 678.

22. "The Malingers," ANJ, August 31, 1878, p. 58.

23. Axel Dahlgren, NT, October 7, 1920, p. 8.

24. John D. McDermott, "The Frontier Scout," *North Dakota History* 61 (fall 1994), 31.

25. Colorado, ANJ, February 29, 1868, p. 441.

26. James Tucker, "Eventful Years," NT, November 24, 1921, p. 7.

27. Axel Dahlgren, NT, October 7, 1920.

28. Squibon, "Scraps," ANJ, March 6, 1867, p. 455.

29. Letter from Charles Lester to his sister, April 1867, FOLA-MP-73, Fort Laramie National Historic Site, Wyoming.

30. Frances Carrington, *My Army Life*, p. 200.

31. "Fort Whipple Barracks," ANJ, July 5, 1879, p. 814.

32. George A. Forsyth, *The Story of the Soldier* (New York: D. Appleton-Century, 1900), pp. 132–33.

Chapter 6: The Indian Wars in Literature and the Arts

1. For Custer's and Cooper's comments, see Custer, *My Life on the Plains* (New York: Sheldon & Co., 1874), pp. 11–17, 183; *The Deerslayer* (New York: Dodd, Mead, 1952), pp. 6, 35, 37, 46, 157, 394, 452, 454, 457; *The Last of the Mohicans* (New York: Dodd, Mead, 1951), pp. 30, 345, 114, 120; *The Pathfinder* (New York: The Modern Library, 1952), pp. 19, 22, 49, 87, 191; *The Prairie* (New York: Dodd, Mead, 1954), pp. 14, 41, 61, 363, 368; and *The Pioneers* (Philadelphia: Macrea, Smith Company, 1927), pp. 457, 496.

2. For the ideas of King, Garland, and Jackson and their interpreters see Don Russell, *Campaigning with King*, ed. Paul L. Hedren (Lincoln: University of Nebraska Press, 1990), pp. xv, 96–97, 137; Hamlin Garland, *The Captain of the Gray-Horse Troop* (New York: Harper, 1902), pp. 100–101, 333; Jackson, *A Century of Dishonor*, p. 431; and Valerie Sherer Mathes, *Helen Hunt Jackson and Her Indian Reform Legacy* (Norman: University of Oklahoma Press, 1997).

3. For works on the western see John R. Milton, *The Novel of the American West* (Lincoln: University of Nebraska Press, 1980), pp. 28 ff.; Richard W. Etulain, "The Historical Western, 1937–43," *South Dakota Review* 5 (spring 1967); and John Tuska, ed., *The American West in Fiction* (Lincoln: University of Nebraska Press, 1982), pp. 244–45. For Indian writers see A. Lavonne Brown Ruoff, *Literature of the American Indian* (New York: Chelsea House, 1991), pp. 89–101.

4. Studies of western films include George N. Fein and W. K. Evasion's *The Westerns: From Silent to Cinerama* (1973); and Brian W. Dippie, *Custer's Last Stand: The Anatomy of an American Myth* (Lincoln: University of Nebraska Press, 1994), pp. 35–36, 96–107, 109–10.

5. Works on western art include Don Russell, *Custer's Last* (Fort Worth TX: Amon Carter Museum, 1968), and *Custer's List* (Fort Worth TX: Amon Carter Museum, 1969), pp. 28–46; Harold McCracken, *Great Painters and Illustrators of the Old West* (New York: Dover, 1988), pp. 64, 168–78, 187–94, 209–16; and Gustav Kobbe, "Schreyvogel's American Soldier Pictures," *Uncle Sam's Magazine* 15 (June 1901), 13–22. For American Indian art, see Garrick Mallery, *Picture-Writing of the American Indians*, 2 vols. (New York: Dover, 1972), vol. 2: 563–66; John C. Ewers, *Plains Indian Painting* (Stanford CA: Stanford University Press, 1939), pp. 3–36; and Joyce M. Szabo, *Howling Wolf and the History of Ledger Art* (Albuquerque: University of New Mexico Press), pp. 91–96, 118–21, 143.

Chapter 7: Conclusions

1. For information regarding engagements and casualties see Russell, "The Army

of the Frontier," p. 80, and "How Many Indians Were Killed?" *The American West* 10 (July 1973), 42–47, 61–63; Chronological List of Actions, Office Memoranda, Adjutant's General Office, pp. 20–56; "Indian War Veterans," NT, September 22, 1927, p. 2.

2. For military strengths and weaknesses see "Reforms," ANR, December 19, 1891, p. 807; Millet and Maslowski, *For the Common Defense*, p. 241; Utley, "The Contribution of the Frontier," in *The Harmon Memorial Lectures in Military History*, ed. Harry R. Borowski (Washington DC: Office of Air Force History, 1988), pp. 528–33; Quincy Write, "The Study of War," in David L. Siles, ed., *International Encyclopedia of the Social Sciences*, vol. 16 (New York: Macmillan Company & The Free Press, 1968), p. 465; Lidell Hart, *Thoughts on War* (London: Faber and Faber, 1944), p. 16; Luther L. Bernard, *War and Its Causes* (New York: Henry Holt, 1944), p. 232.

3. "General Crook Address," ANJ, June 21, 1884, p. 11.

4. William Bisbee, "What Has the Army Done?," ANJ, May 30, 1885, p. 341.

5. Josiah Hubbard, "A Little Taste of Indian Warfare," *The Army and Navy Club of Connecticut, Report of the Twenty-Ninth Annual Meeting, Pequot House, June 21, 1907* (Case Lackwood & Brainard Company, 1907), p. 48.

6. Eugene F. Ware, *Indian War of 1864*, p. 308.

7. Henry B. Carrington, *The Indian Question*, p. 11.

8. For impacts on Indian lands and culture see Thornton, *American Indian*, pp. 31, 133; *The American Indian Digest* (Phoenix: Thunderbird Enterprises, 1993), p. 19; Norman A. Ross, comp., *Index to the Expert Testimony Before the Indian Claims Commission* (New York: Clearwater Publishing Company, 1973); James B. Fry, *Army Sacrifices, or Briefs from Official Pigeon-Holes* (New York: D. Van Nostrand, 1879), p. 4.

9. 105 *Stat.* 1631.

10. For a discussion of the phenomenon see John D. McDermott, "Why Cultural Heritage Tourism?" *Trail Talk*, February 1994, p. 3; "Spreading the Word," *Association of Montana Newsletter*, winter 1994, p. 9; "The Challenge of History," *Great Plains Tourism Connection* 2 (spring 1993), p. 3; and "Never Underestimate the Power of History," *Tourismreader* 2 (April 1991), 12–13.

11. McDermott, "Custer and the Little Bighorn Story," p. 104.

12. Arthur Schlesinger Jr., *The Disuniting of America: Reflections on a Multicultural Society* (New York: W. W. Norton & Company, 1992); Kent Blaser, "Something Old, Something New," *Nebraska History* 77 (summer 1966), 67–77.

13. Chief Joseph, "An American Indian's View of Indian Affairs," *North American Review* 128 (April 1897), 421–33.

Part 2: Places to Visit

1. Two excellent guides are Robert G. Ferris, ed., *Soldier and Brave: Historical*

Places Associated with . . . the Indian Wars (Washington DC: Department of the Interior, 1971); and Paul L. Hedren, *Traveler's Guide to the Great Sioux War* (Helena: Montana Historical Society Press, 1996). Indispensable are the many volumes by Herbert M. Hart, including *Old Forts of the Northwest* (Seattle: Superior Publishing Company, 1963); *Old Forts of the Southwest* (New York: Bonanza Books, 1964), *Tour Guide to Old Western Forts* (Fort Collins CO: Old Army Press, 1980), and *Tour Guide to Old Forts of Montana, Wyoming, North and South Dakota* (Boulder CO: Pruett Publishing, 1980). Native American sites are ably chronicled in George Cantor, *North American Indian Landmarks* (Detroit: Visible Ink Press, 1993); and Arnold Marquis, *A Guide to America's Indians* (Norman: University of Oklahoma Press, 1974).

2. A good place to start for those interested in following the Indian wars in detail are the two volumes by Robert M. Utley, *Frontiersmen in Blue* (New York: Macmillan, 1967) and *Frontier Regulars*. Overview studies include Coffman, *The Old Army*; Robert G. Athearn, *William Tecumseh Sherman* (Norman: University of Oklahoma Press, 1956); Paul A. Hutton, *Phil Sheridan and His Army* (Lincoln: University of Nebraska Press, 1985); and Wooster, *The Military and United States Indian Policy*, p. 89.

Useful regional studies include Robert H. Jones, *The Civil War in the Northwest* (Norman: University of Oklahoma Press, 1960); Odie B. Faulk, *Crimson Desert* (New York: Oxford University Press, 1974); William Leckie, *The Military Conquest of the Southern Plains* (Norman: University of Oklahoma Press, 1963); Jerome A. Greene, *Yellowstone Command* (Lincoln: University of Nebraska Press, 1991); Charles M. Robinson III, *A Good Year to Die* (New York: Random House, 1995); Ray H. Glassley, *Pacific Northwest Indian Wars* (Portland OR: Binfords and Mort, 1953); E. A. Schwartz, *The Rogue River Indian* (Norman: University of Oklahoma Press, 1996); and Robert M. Utley, *Last Days of the Sioux Nation* (New Haven CT: Yale University Press, 1963).

Those interested in the Battle of the Little Bighorn should read Edgar I. Stewart, *Custer's Luck* (Norman: University of Oklahoma Press, 1955); Robert M. Utley, *Cavalier in Buckskin* (Norman: University of Oklahoma Press, 1988); John S. Gray, *Custer's Last Campaign* (Lincoln: University of Nebraska Press, 1991); and *Centennial Campaign* (Fort Collins CO: Old Army Press, 1976); and Fox, *Archaeology, History, and Custer's Last Battle*.

3. Charles King, "George Crook," in *War Papers Read Before the Commandery of the State of Wisconsin, Military Order of the Loyal Legion of the United States* (Milwaukee: Burdick, Armitage & Allen, 1891), vol. 1: 261.

4. ANR, April 10, 1886, p. 23.

5. ANJ, September 27, 1890. See also Margot Liberty, "I Will Play with the Soldiers," *Montana Magazine*, autumn 1964.

6. John S. Mayhugh, "The Messiah and His Prophet," *New York Times*, November, 30, 1890, p. 2.

Fifty Basic Books

Many good books have been written about the Indian wars in the West. If my library were destroyed in a fire, these are the fifty books that I would replace first.

Athearn, Robert G. *William Tecumseh Sherman and the Settlement of the West.* Norman: University of Oklahoma Press, 1956.

Brandon, William. *The American Heritage Book of Indians.* New York: American Heritage Publishing, Co., Inc., 1961.

Brown, Dee. *Fetterman Massacre.* Lincoln: University of Nebraska Press, 1962.

Carrington, Margaret. *Absaraka: Home of the Crows, Being the Experience of an Officer's Wife on the Plains.* Lincoln: University of Nebraska Press, 1983.

Coffman, Edward M. *The Old Army: A Portrait of the American Army in Peacetime, 1784–1898.* New York: Oxford University Press, 1986.

Custer, Elizabeth. *Boots and Saddles.* Norman: University of Oklahoma Press, 1962.

Custer, George Armstrong. *My Life on the Plains.* Norman: University of Oklahoma Press, 1968.

Faulk, Odie B. *Crimson Desert: Indian Wars of the American Southwest.* New York: Oxford University Press, 1974.

Finerty, John F. *War-path and Bivouac, or The Conquest of the Sioux.* Chicago: M. A. Donohue & Company, 1890. Reprint, Norman: University of Oklahoma Press, 1961.

Forsyth, George. *The Story of the Soldier.* New York: D. Appleton-Century, 1900.

Fox, Richard A. *Archaeology, History, and Custer's Last Battle.* Norman: University of Oklahoma Press, 1993.

Gray, John S. *Centennial Campaign: The Sioux War of 1876.* Fort Collins CO: Old Army Press, 1976.

———. *Custer's Last Campaign: Mitch Boyer and the Little Bighorn Reconstructed.* Lincoln: University of Nebraska Press, 1991.

Greene, Jerome A. *Yellowstone Command: Colonel Nelson A. Miles and the Great Sioux War of 1876–1877.* Lincoln: University of Nebraska Press, 1991.

Grinnell, George B. *The Fighting Cheyennes.* New York: Scribners, 1915. 2d. ed. by the University of Oklahoma Press, 1956.

Hedren, Paul. *Fort Laramie in 1876: Chronicle of a Frontier Post at War*. Lincoln: University of Nebraska Press, 1988.

Heizer, Robert E., ed. *Handbook of North American Indians*. Washington DC: Smithsonian Institution, 1976 to present. Being published in twenty volumes. See especially vol. 4, *History of Indian-White Relations*, ed. by Wilcomb E. Washburn (1988).

Hodge, Frederick Webb, ed. *Handbook of American Indians North of Mexico*, 2 vols. New York: Patent Books, Inc., 1960.

Hutton, Paul Andrew. *Phil Sheridan and His Army*. Lincoln: University of Nebraska Press, 1985.

Hyde, George E. *Life of George Bent*. Norman: University of Oklahoma Press, 1968.

———. *Red Cloud's Folk: A History of the Oglala Sioux Indians*, rev. ed. Norman: University of Oklahoma Press, 1957.

Josephy, Alvin M. Jr. *The Nez Perce Indians and the Opening of the Northwest*. New Haven CT: Yale University Press, 1965.

King, Charles. *Campaigning with Crook and Stories of Army Life*. New York: Harper & Brothers, 1890.

Knight, Oliver. *Following the Indian Wars: The Story of the Newspaper Correspondents among the Indian Campaigners*. Norman: University of Oklahoma Press, 1960.

———. *Life and Manners in the Frontier Army*. Norman: University of Oklahoma Press, 1978.

Leckie, William H. *Buffalo Soldiers: A Narrative of the Negro Cavalry in the West*. Norman: University of Oklahoma Press, 1967.

Mangum, Neil C. *Battle of the Rosebud: Prelude to the Little Bighorn*. El Segundo CA: Upton & Sons, 1987.

McChristian, Douglas C. *The U. S. Army in the West, 1870–1880: Uniforms, Weapons, and Equipment*. Norman: University of Oklahoma Press, 1995.

McDermott, John D. *Forlorn Hope: A Study of the Battle of White Bird Canyon and the Beginning of the Nez Perce Indian War*. Boise ID: Idaho Historical Society, 1978.

———. *Frontier Crossroads: The History of Fort Caspar and the Upper Platte Crossing*. Casper WY: Fort Caspar Museum, 1997.

Miles, Nelson A. *Personal Recollections and Observations*. New York: The Werner Company, 1896.

Mills, Anson. *My Story*. Washington DC: Press of Byron H. Adams, 1918.

Nye, Wilbur S. *Carbine and Lance: The Story of Old Fort Sill*. Norman: University of Oklahoma Press, 1943.

Olson, James C. *Red Cloud and the Sioux Problem*. Lincoln: University of Nebraska Press, 1965.

Rankin, Charles, ed. *Legacy: New Perspectives on the Battle of the Little Bighorn*. Helena: Montana Historical Society, 1996.

Rickey, Don. *Forty Miles a Day on Beans and Hay.* Norman: University of Oklahoma Press, 1963.

Russell, Don. *The Lives and Legends of Buffalo Bill.* Norman: University of Oklahoma Press, 1960.

Stands in Timber, John, and Margot Liberty. *Cheyenne Memories.* New Haven CT: Yale University Press, 1967. Reprint, Lincoln: University of Nebraska Press, 1972.

Stewart, Edgar I. *Custer's Luck.* Norman: University of Oklahoma Press, 1955.

Utley, Robert M. *Cavalier in Buckskin: George Armstrong Custer and the Western Military Frontier.* Norman: University of Oklahoma Press, 1988.

———. *Frontier Regulars: The United States Army and the Indian, 1866–1890.* New York: Macmillan Publishing Company, 1973.

———. *Frontiersmen in Blue: The United States Army and the Indian, 1848–1865.* New York: Macmillan Publishing Company, 1967.

———. *The Lance and the Shield: A Life and Times of Sitting Bull.* New York: Henry Holt and Company, 1993.

———. *Last Days of the Sioux Nation.* New Haven CT: Yale University Press, 1963.

Vaughn, J. W. *Indian Fights: New Facts on Seven Encounters.* Norman: University of Oklahoma Press, 1966.

———. *Reynold's Campaign on the Powder River.* Norman: University of Oklahoma Press, 1961.

———. *With Crook on the Rosebud.* Harrisburg PA: Stackpole, 1956.

Vestal, Stanley. *New Sources of Indian History, 1850–1891.* Norman: University of Oklahoma Press, 1934.

Ware, Eugene F. *The Indian War of 1864,* intro. by John D. McDermott. Lincoln: University of Nebraska Press, 1994.

Wooster, Robert. *The Military and United States Indian Policy, 1865–1903.* New Haven CT: Yale University Press, 1988.